CHEAT CODE EXPLOSION

FOR CONSOLES

DANGER

COMBUSTIBLE

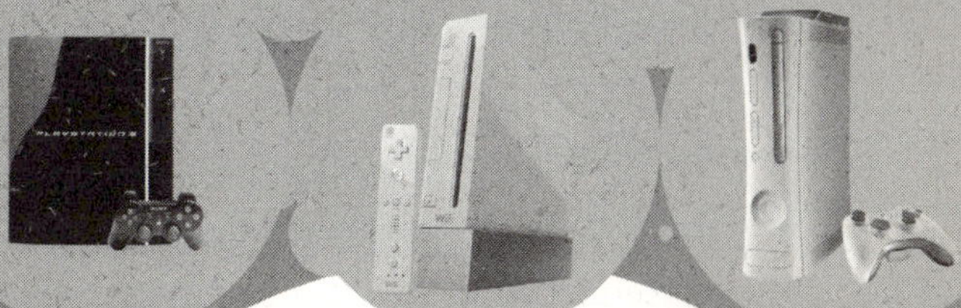

FLIP THIS BOOK OVER FOR HANDHELD SYSTEMS
Nintendo DS™
PlayStation® Portable
Game Boy® Advance

LOOK FOR CODEY
When you see Codey's face, you've found the newest and coolest codes!

SPECIAL SECTION: GUITAR HERO & ROCK BAND

GAMES LIST

GUITAR HERO

UNLOCK ALL

At the Main menu, press Yellow, Orange, Blue, Blue, Orange, Yellow, Yellow.

GUITAR HERO GUITAR CHEAT

At the Main menu, press Blue, Orange, Yellow, Blue, Blue.

CROWD METER CHEAT

At the Main menu, press Yellow, Blue, Orange, Orange, Blue, Blue, Yellow, Orange.

MONKEY HEAD CROWD CHEAT

At the Main menu, press Blue, Orange, Yellow, Yellow, Yellow, Blue, Orange.

SKULL HEAD CROWD CHEAT

At the Main menu, press Orange, Yellow, Blue, Blue, Orange, Yellow, Blue, Blue.

AIR GUITAR CHEAT

At the Main menu, press Orange, Orange, Blue, Yellow, Orange.

NO VENUE CHEAT

At the Main menu, press Blue, Yellow, Orange, Blue, Yellow, Orange.

GUITAR HERO II

AIR GUITAR

At the Main menu, press Yellow, Yellow, Blue, Orange, Yellow, Blue.

EYEBALL HEAD CROWD

At the Main menu, press Blue, Orange, Yellow, Orange, Yellow, Orange, Blue.

MONKEY HEAD CROWD

At the Main menu, press Orange, Blue, Yellow, Yellow, Orange, Blue, Yellow, Yellow.

FLAMING HEAD

At the Main menu, press Orange, Yellow, Orange, Orange, Yellow, Orange, Yellow, Yellow.

HORSE HEAD

At the Main menu, press Blue, Orange, Orange, Blue, Orange, Orange, Blue, Orange, Orange, Blue.

HYPER SPEED

At the Main menu, press Orange, Blue, Orange, Yellow, Orange, Blue, Orange, Yellow.

PERFORMANCE MODE

At the Main menu, press Yellow, Yellow, Blue, Yellow, Yellow, Orange, Yellow, Yellow.

GUITAR HERO III: LEGENDS OF ROCK

To enter the following cheats, strum the guitar while holding the listed buttons. For example, if the code lists Yellow + Orange, hold the Yellow and Orange buttons as you strum. Air Guitar, Precision Mode and Performance Mode can be toggled on and off from the Cheats menu. You can also change between five different levels of Hyperspeed at this menu.

UNLOCK EVERYTHING

Select Cheats from the Options. Choose Enter Cheat and enter the following (no sounds play while this code is entered):

Green + Red + Blue + Orange
Green + Red + Yellow + Blue
Green + Red + Yellow + Orange
Green + Yellow + Blue + Orange
Green + Red + Yellow + Blue
Red + Yellow + Blue + Orange
Green + Red + Yellow + Blue
Green + Yellow + Blue + Orange
Green + Red + Yellow + Blue
Green + Red + Yellow + Orange
Green + Red + Yellow + Orange
Green + Red + Yellow + Blue
Green + Red + Yellow + Orange

An easier way to illustrate this code is to represent Green as 1, progressing down the guitar neck to Orange as 5. For example, if you have 1345, you would hold Green + Yellow + Blue + Orange while strumming: 1245 + 1234 + 1235 + 1345 + 1234 + 2345 + 1234 + 1345 + 1234 + 1235 + 1235 + 1234 + 1235.

ALL SONGS

Select Cheats from the Options. Choose Enter Cheat and enter:

Yellow + Orange
Red + Blue
Red + Orange
Green + Blue
Red + Yellow
Yellow + Orange
Red + Yellow
Red + Blue
Green + Yellow
Green + Yellow
Yellow + Blue
Yellow + Blue
Yellow + Orange
Yellow + Orange
Yellow + Blue
Yellow
Red
Red + Yellow
Red
Yellow
Orange

NO FAIL

Select Cheats from the Options. Choose Enter Cheat and enter:

Green + Red
Blue
Green + Red
Green + Yellow
Blue
Green + Yellow
Red + Yellow
Orange
Red + Yellow
Green + Yellow
Yellow
Green + Yellow
Green + Red

AIR GUITAR

Select Cheats from the Options. Choose Enter Cheat and enter:

Blue + Yellow
Green + Yellow
Green + Yellow
Red + Blue
Red + Blue
Red + Yellow
Red + Yellow
Blue + Yellow
Green + Yellow
Green + Yellow
Red + Blue
Red + Blue
Red + Yellow
Red + Yellow
Green + Yellow
Green + Yellow
Red + Yellow
Red + Yellow

HYPERSPEED

Select Cheats from the Options. Choose Enter Cheat and enter:

Orange
Blue
Orange
Yellow
Orange
Blue
Orange
Yellow

PERFORMANCE MODE

Select Cheats from the Options. Choose Enter Cheat and enter:

Red + Yellow
Red + Blue
Red + Orange
Red + Blue
Red + Yellow
Green + Blue
Red + Yellow
Red + Blue

EASY EXPERT

Select Cheats from the Options. Choose Enter Cheat and enter:

Green + Red
Green + Yellow
Yellow + Blue
Red + Blue
Blue + Orange
Yellow + Orange
Red + Yellow
Red + Blue

PRECISION MODE

Select Cheats from the Options. Choose Enter Cheat and enter:

Green + Red
Green + Red
Green + Red
Red + Yellow
Red + Yellow
Red + Blue
Red + Blue
Yellow + Blue
Yellow + Orange
Yellow + Orange
Green + Red
Green + Red
Green + Red
Red + Yellow
Red + Yellow
Red + Blue
Red + Blue
Yellow + Blue
Yellow + Orange
Yellow + Orange

BRET MICHAELS SINGER

Select Cheats from the Options. Choose Enter Cheat and enter:

Green + Red
Green + Red
Green + Red
Green + Blue
Green + Blue
Green + Blue
Red + Blue
Red
Red
Red
Red + Blue
Red
Red
Red
Red + Blue
Red
Red
Red

GUITAR HERO ENCORE: ROCKS THE 80S

UNLOCK EVERYTHING

At the Main menu, press Blue, Orange, Yellow, Red, Orange, Yellow, Blue, Yellow, Red, Yellow, Blue, Yellow, Red, Yellow, Blue, Yellow.

HYPERSPEED

At the Main menu, press Yellow, Blue, Orange, Orange, Blue, Yellow, Yellow, Orange.

PERFORMANCE MODE

At the Main menu, press Blue, Blue, Orange, Yellow, Yellow, Blue, Orange, Blue.

AIR GUITAR

At the Main menu, press Yellow, Blue, Yellow, Orange, Blue, Blue.

EYEBALL HEAD CROWD

At the Main menu, press Yellow, Blue, Orange, Orange, Orange, Blue, Yellow.

MONKEY HEAD CROWD

At the Main menu, press Blue, Blue, Orange, Yellow, Blue, Blue, Orange, Yellow.

FLAME HEAD

At the Main menu, press Yellow, Orange, Yellow, Orange, Yellow, Orange, Blue, Orange.

HORSE HEAD

At the Main menu, press Blue, Orange, Orange, Blue, Yellow, Blue, Orange, Orange, Blue, Yellow.

GUITAR HERO: AEROSMITH

To enter the following cheats, strum the guitar while holding the listed buttons. For example, if the codes lists Yellow + Orange, hold Yellow and Orange as you strum. Air Guitar, Precision Mode, and Performance Mode can be toggled on and off from the Cheats menu. You can also change between five different levels of Hyperspeed at this menu.

ALL SONGS

Red + Yellow
Green + Red
Green + Red
Red + Yellow
Red + Yellow
Green + Red
Red + Yellow
Red + Yellow
Green + Red
Green + Red
Red + Yellow
Red + Yellow
Green + Red
Red + Yellow
Red + Blue

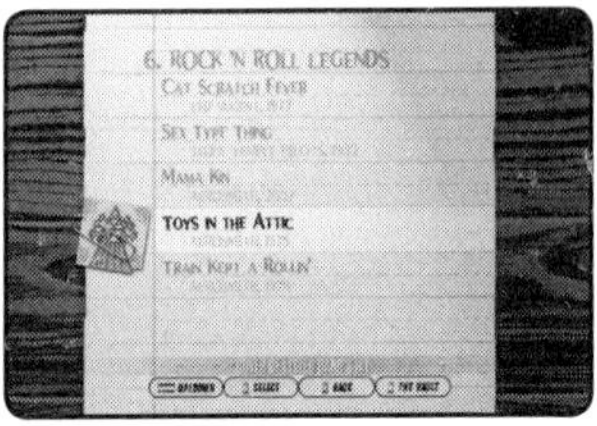

AIR GUITAR

Red + Yellow
Green + Red
Red + Yellow
Red + Yellow
Red + Blue
Red + Blue
Red + Blue
Red + Blue
Red + Blue
Yellow + Blue
Yellow + Blue
Yellow + Orange

HYPERSPEED

Yellow + Orange
Yellow + Orange
Yellow + Orange
Yellow + Orange
Yellow + Orange
Red + Yellow
Red + Yellow
Red + Yellow
Red + Yellow
Red + Blue
Red + Blue
Red + Blue
Red + Blue
Red + Blue
Yellow + Blue
Yellow + Orange
Yellow + Orange

NO FAIL

Green + Red
Blue
Green + Red
Green + Yellow
Blue
Green + Yellow
Red + Yellow
Orange
Red + Yellow
Green + Yellow
Yellow
Green + Yellow
Green + Red

PERFORMANCE MODE

Green + Red
Green + Red
Red + Orange
Red + Blue
Green + Red
Green + Red
Red + Orange
Red + Blue

PRECISION MODE

Red + Yellow
Red + Blue
Red + Blue
Red + Yellow
Red + Yellow
Yellow + Blue
Yellow + Blue
Yellow + Blue
Red + Blue
Red + Yellow
Red + Blue
Red + Blue
Red + Yellow
Red + Yellow
Yellow + Blue
Yellow + Blue
Yellow + Blue
Red + Blue

GUITAR HERO WORLD TOUR

The following cheats can be toggled on and off at the Cheats menu.

QUICKPLAY SONGS

Select Cheats from the Options menu, choose Enter New Cheat and press Blue, Blue, Red, Green, Green, Blue, Blue, Yellow.

ALWAYS SLIDE

Select Cheats from the Options menu, choose Enter New Cheat and press Green, Green, Red, Red, Yellow, Red, Yellow, Blue.

AT&T BALLPARK

Select Cheats from the Options menu, choose Enter New Cheat and press Yellow, Green, Red, Red, Green, Blue, Red, Yellow.

AUTO KICK

Select Cheats from the Options menu, choose Enter New Cheat and press Yellow, Green, Red, Blue (x4), Red.

EXTRA LINE 6 TONES

Select Cheats from the Options menu, choose Enter New Cheat and press Green, Red, Yellow, Blue, Red, Yellow, Blue, Green.

FLAME COLOR

Select Cheats from the Options menu, choose Enter New Cheat and press Green, Red, Green, Blue, Red, Red, Yellow, Blue.

GEM COLOR

Select Cheats from the Options menu, choose Enter New Cheat and press Blue, Red, Red, Green, Red, Green, Red, Yellow.

STAR COLOR

Select Cheats from the Options menu, choose Enter New Cheat and press Red, Red, Yellow, Red, Blue, Red, Red, Blue.

AIR INSTRUMENTS

Select Cheats from the Options menu, choose Enter New Cheat and press Red, Red, Blue, Yellow, Green (x3), Yellow.

HYPERSPEED

Select Cheats from the Options menu, choose Enter New Cheat and press Green, Blue, Red, Yellow, Yellow, Red, Green, Green. These show up in the menu as HyperGuitar, HyperBass, and HyperDrums.

PERFORMANCE MODE

Select Cheats from the Options menu, choose Enter New Cheat and press Yellow, Yellow, Blue, Red, Blue, Green, Red, Red.

INVISIBLE ROCKER

Select Cheats from the Options menu, choose Enter New Cheat and press Green, Red, Yellow (x3), Blue, Blue, Green.

VOCAL FIREBALL

Select Cheats from the Options menu, choose Enter New Cheat and press Red, Green, Green, Yellow, Blue, Green, Yellow, Green.

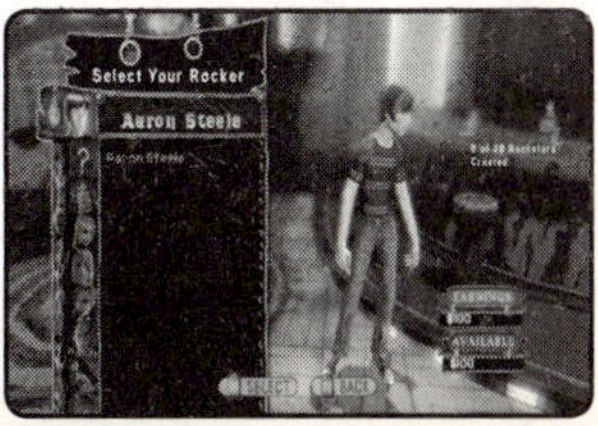

AARON STEELE!

Select Cheats from the Options menu, choose Enter New Cheat and press Blue, Red, Yellow (x5), Green.

JONNY VIPER

Select Cheats from the Options menu, choose Enter New Cheat and press Blue, Red, Blue, Blue, Yellow (x3), Green.

NICK

Select Cheats from the Options menu, choose Enter New Cheat and press Green, Red, Blue, Green, Red, Blue, Blue, Green.

RINA

Select Cheats from the Options menu, choose Enter New Cheat and press Blue, Red, Green, Green, Yellow (x3), Green.

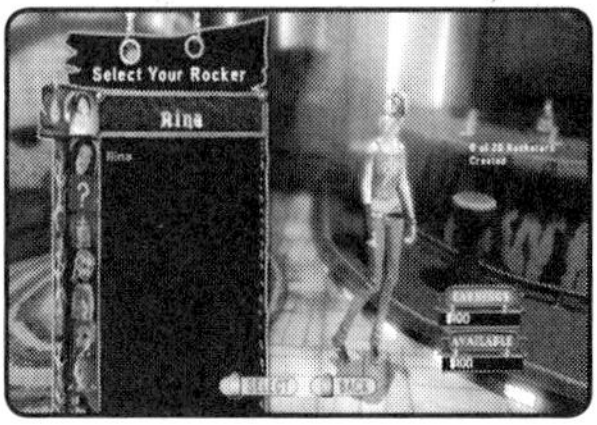

ROCK BAND

ALL SONGS

At the title screen, press Red, Yellow, Blue, Red, Red, Blue, Blue, Red, Yellow, Blue. Saving and all network features are disabled with this code.

TRANSPARENT INSTRUMENTS

Complete the hall of fame concert with that instrument.

GOLD INSTRUMENT

Complete the solo tour with that instrument.

SILVER INSTRUMENT

Complete the bonus tour with that instrument.

ROCK BAND 2

Most of these codes disable saving, achievements, and Xbox LIVE play.

UNLOCK ALL SONGS

Select Modify Game from the Extras menu, choose Enter Unlock Code and press Red, Yellow, Blue, Red, Red, Blue, Blue, Red, Yellow, Blue or Y, B, X, Y, Y, X, X, Y, B, X. Toggle this cheat on or off from the Modify Game menu.

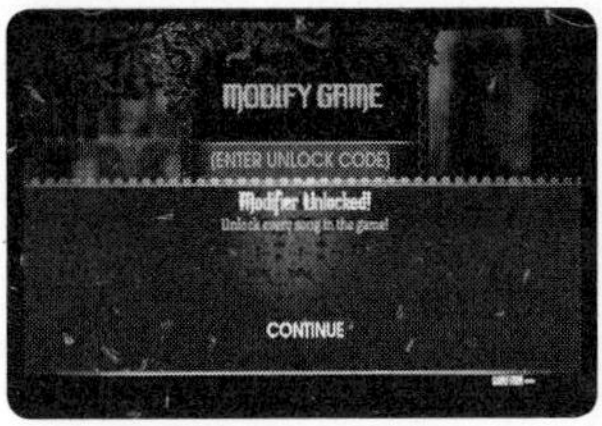

SELECT VENUE SCREEN

Select Modify Game from the Extras menu, choose Enter Unlock Code and press Blue, Orange, Orange, Blue, Yellow, Blue, Orange, Orange, Blue, Yellow or (for Xbox 360) X, Left Bumper, Left Bumper, X, B, X, Left Bumper, Left Bumper, X, B. Toggle this cheat on or off from the Modify Game menu.

NEW VENUES ONLY

Select Modify Game from the Extras menu, choose Enter Unlock Code and press Red, Red, Red, Red, Yellow, Yellow, Yellow, Yellow or (for Xbox 360) Y (x4), B (x4). Toggle this cheat on or off from the Modify Game menu.

PLAY THE GAME WITHOUT A TRACK

Select Modify Game from the Extras menu, choose Enter Unlock Code and press Blue, Blue, Red, Red, Yellow, Yellow, Blue, Blue or (for Xbox 360) X, X, Y, Y, B, B, X, X. Toggle this cheat on or off from the Modify Game menu.

AWESOMENESS DETECTION

Select Modify Game from the Extras menu, choose Enter Unlock Code and press Yellow, Blue, Orange, Yellow, Blue, Orange, Yellow, Blue, Orange or (for Xbox 360) B, X, Left Bumper, B, X, Left Bumper, B, X, Left Bumper. Toggle this cheat on or off from the Modify Game menu.

STAGE MODE

Select Modify Game from the Extras menu, choose Enter Unlock Code and press Blue, Yellow, Red, Blue, Yellow, Red, Blue, Yellow, Red or (for Xbox 360) X, B, Y, X, B, Y, X, B, Y. Toggle this cheat on or off from the Modify Game menu.

PLAYSTATION® 3

CONTENTS

BAJA: EDGE OF CONTROL

CAREER COMPLETE 100%

Select Cheat Codes from the Options menu and enter SHOWTIME.

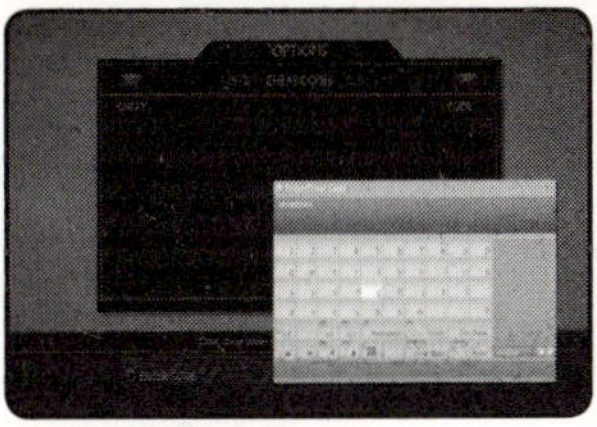

INSTALL ALL PARTS

Select Cheat Codes from the Options menu and enter SUPERMAX.

THE BIGS

START A ROOKIE WITH HIGHER STATS

When you create a rookie, name him HOT DOG. His stats will be higher than when you normally start.

BLAZING ANGELS 2: SECRET MISSIONS OF WWII

ALL MISSIONS AND PLANES UNLOCKED

At the main menu, hold L2 + R2, and press □, L1, R1, △, △, R1, L1, □.

GOD MODE

Pause the game, hold L2, and press □, △, △, □. Release L2, hold R2 and press △, □, □, △. Re-enter the code to disable it.

INCREASED DAMAGE WITH ALL WEAPONS

Pause the game, hold L2, and press L1, L1, R1. Release L2, hold R2, and press R1, R1, L1. Re-enter the code to disable it.

BLAZING ANGELS: SQUADRONS OF WWII

ALL MISSIONS, MEDALS & PLANES

At the Main menu, hold **L2** + **R2** and press □, **L1**, **R1**, △, △, **R1**, **L1**, □.

GOD MODE

Pause the game, hold **L2** and press □, △, △, □. Release **L2**, hold **R2** and press △, □, □, △. Re-enter the code to disable it.

INCREASED DAMAGE

Pause the game, hold **L2** and press **L1**, **L1**, **R1**. Release **L2**, hold **R2** and press **R1**, **R1**, **L1**. Re-enter the code to disable it.

BURNOUT PARADISE

BEST BUY CAR

Pause the game and select Sponsor Product Code from the Under the Hood menu. Enter Bestbuy. Need A License to use this car offline.

CIRCUIT CITY CAR

Pause the game and select Sponsor Product Code from the Under the Hood menu. Enter Circuitcity. Need Burnout Paradise License to use this car offline.

GAMESTOP CAR

Pause the game and select Sponsor Product Code from the Under the Hood menu. Enter Gamestop. Need A License to use this car offline.

WALMART CAR

Pause the game and select Sponsor Product Code from the Under the Hood menu.. Enter Walmart. Need Burnout Paradise License to use this car offline.

"STEEL WHEELS" GT

Pause the game and select Sponsor Product Code from the Under the Hood menu. Enter G23X 5K8Q GX2V 04B1 or E60J 8Z7T MS8L 51U6.

LICENSES

LICENSE	NUMBER OF WINS NEEDED
D	2
C	7
B	16
A	26
Burnout Paradise	45
Elite License	All events

CARS MATER-NATIONAL

ALL ARCADE RACES, MINI-GAMES, AND WORLDS

Select Codes/Cheats from the options and enter PLAYALL.

ALL CARS

Select Codes/Cheats from the options and enter MATTEL07.

ALTERNATE LIGHTNING MCQUEEN COLORS

Select Codes/Cheats from the options and enter NCEDUDZ.

ALL COLORS FOR OTHERS

Select Codes/Cheats from the options and enter PAINTIT.

UNLIMITED TURBO

Select Codes/Cheats from the options and enter ZZOOOOM.

EXTREME ACCELERATION

Select Codes/Cheats from the options and enter 0TO200X.

EXPERT MODE

Select Codes/Cheats from the options and enter VRYFAST.

ALL BONUS ART

Select Codes/Cheats from the options and enter BUYTALL.

FULL AUTO 2: BATTLELINES

ALL CARS

Select Cheat Codes from Extras and enter 47GIV3MECARS.

ALL MISSIONS

Select Cheat Codes from Extras and enter IMFEDUPWITHTHIS.

SCEPTRE AND MINI-ROCKETS

Select Cheat Codes from Extras and enter 10E6CUSTOMER. This vehicle and weapon become available in Arcade Mode and Head to Head.

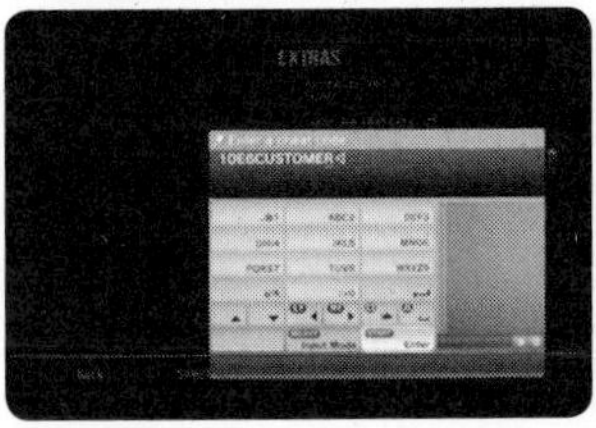

VULCAN AND FLAMETHROWER

Select Cheat Codes from Extras and enter 5FINGERDISCOUNT. This vehicle and weapon become available in Arcade Mode and Head to Head.

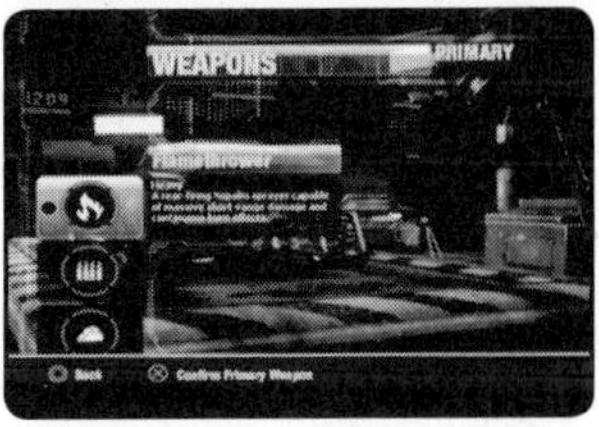

GRID

ALL DRIFT CARS

Select Bonus Codes from the Options. Then choose Enter Code and enter TUN58396.

ALL MUSCLE CARS

Select Bonus Codes from the Options. Then choose Enter Code and enter MUS59279.

BUCHBINDER EMOTIONAL ENGINEERING BMW 320SI

Select Bonus Codes from the Options. Then choose Enter Code and enter F93857372. You can use this in Race Day or in GRID World once you've started your own team.

EBAY MOTORS MUSTANG

Select Bonus Codes from the Options. Then choose Enter Code and enter DAFJ55E01473MO. You can use this in Race Day or in GRID World once you've started your own team.

GAMESTATION BMW 320SI

Select Bonus Codes from the Options. Then choose Enter Code and enter G29782655. You can use this in Race Day or in GRID World once you've started your own team.

MICROMANIA PAGANI ZONDA R

Select Bonus Codes from the Options. Then choose Enter Code and enter M38572343. You can use this in Race Day or in GRID World once you've started your own team.

PLAY.COM ASTON MARTIN DBR9

Select Bonus Codes from the Options. Then choose Enter Code and enter P47203845. You can use this in Race Day or in GRID World once you've started your own team.

IRON MAN

CLASSIC ARMOR
Clear One Man Army vs. Mercs.

EXTREMIS ARMOR
Clear One Man Army vs. Maggia.

MARK II ARMOR
Clear One Man Army vs. Ten Rings.

HULKBUSTER ARMOR
Clear One Man Army vs. AIM-X. Can also be unlocked when clear game save data from Incredible Hulk is stored on the same console.

CLASSIC MARK I ARMOR
Clear One Man Army vs. AIM.

ULTIMATE ARMOR
Clear Mission 13: Showdown.

JUICED 2: HOT IMPORT NIGHTS

ASCARI KZ1
Select Cheats and Codes from the DNA Lab menu and enter KNOX. Defeat the challenge to earn the car.

AUDI TT 1.8L QUATTRO
Select Cheats and Codes from the DNA Lab menu and enter YTHZ. Defeat the challenge to earn the car.

BMW Z4 ROADSTER
Select Cheats and Codes from the DNA Lab menu and enter GVDL. Defeat the challenge to earn the car.

FRITO-LAY INFINITI G35
Select Cheats and Codes from the DNA Lab menu and enter MNCH. Defeat the challenge to earn the car.

HOLDEN MONARO
Select Cheats and Codes from the DNA Lab menu and enter RBSG. Defeat the challenge to earn the car.

HYUNDAI COUPE 2.7L V6
Select Cheats and Codes from the DNA Lab menu and enter BSLU. Defeat the challenge to earn the car.

INFINITI G35
Select Cheats and Codes from the DNA Lab menu and enter MRHC. Defeat the challenge to earn the car.

KOENIGSEGG CCX
Select Cheats and Codes from the DNA Lab menu and enter KDTR. Defeat the challenge to earn the car.

MITSUBISHI PROTOTYPE X
Select Cheats and Codes from the DNA Lab menu and enter DOPX. Defeat the challenge to earn the car.

NISSAN 350Z
Select Cheats and Codes from the DNA Lab menu and enter PRGN. Defeat the challenge to earn the car.

NISSAN SKYLINE R34 GT-R
Select Cheats and Codes from the DNA Lab menu and enter JWRS. Defeat the challenge to earn the car.

SALEEN S7
Select Cheats and Codes from the DNA Lab menu and enter WIKF. Defeat the challenge to earn the car.

SEAT LEON CUPRA R
Select Cheats and Codes from the DNA Lab menu and enter FAMQ. Defeat the challenge to earn the car.

KUNG FU PANDA

UNLIMITED CHI

Select Cheats from the Extra menu and enter Down, Right, Left, Up, Down.

INVULNERABILITY

Select Cheats from the Extra menu and enter Down, Down, Right, Up, Left.

FULL UPGRADES

Select Cheats from the Extra menu and enter Left, Right, Down, Left, Up.

FULL AWESOME METER

Select Cheats from the Extra menu and enter Up, Down, Up, Right, Left. This gives Po 4X damage.

MULTIPLAYER CHARACTERS

Select Cheats from the Extra menu and enter Left, Down, Left, Right, Down.

OUTFITS

Select Cheats from the Extra menu and enter Right, Left, Down, Up, Right.

LAIR

CHICKEN VIDEO

At the cheat menu, enter chicken.

COFFEE VIDEO

At the cheat menu, enter 686F7420636F66666565.

UNLOCKS STABLE OPTION FOR ALL LEVELS

At the cheat menu, enter koelsch. Saving is disabled with this code.

THE LEGEND OF SPYRO: DAWN OF THE DRAGON

UNLIMITED LIFE

Pause the game, hold L1 and press Right, Right, Down, Down, Left with the Left Analog Stick.

UNLIMITED MANA

Pause the game, hold R1 and press Up, Right, Up, Left, Down with the Left Analog Stick.

MAXIMUM XP

Pause the game, hold R1 and press Left, Right, Right, Up, Up with the Left Analog Stick.

ALL ELEMENTAL UPGRADES

Pause the game, hold L1 and press Left, Up, Down, Up, Right with the Left Analog Stick.

LEGO BATMAN

BATCAVE CODES

Using the computer in the Batcave, select Enter Code and enter the following codes.

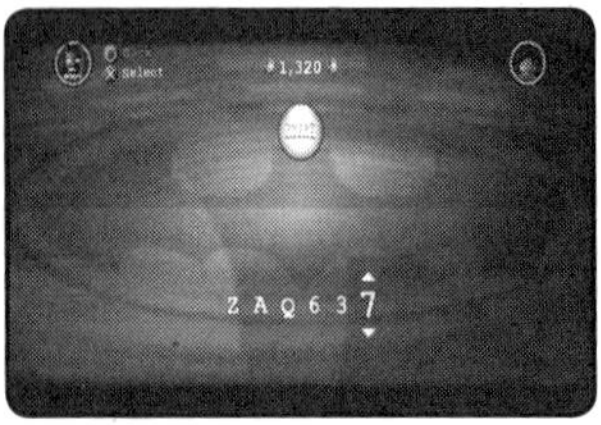

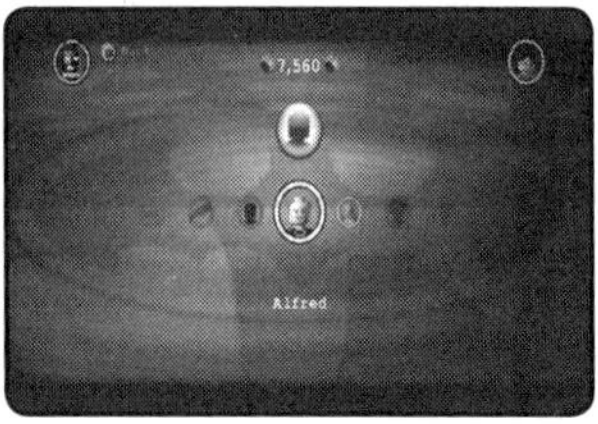

CHARACTERS

CHARACTER	CODE
Alfred	ZAQ637
Batgirl	JKR331
Bruce Wayne	BDJ327
Catwoman (Classic)	M1AAWW
Clown Goon	HJK327
Commissioner Gordon	DDP967
Fishmonger	HGY748
Freeze Girl	XVK541
Joker Goon	UTF782
Joker Henchman	YUN924
Mad Hatter	JCA283
Man-Bat	NYU942
Military Policeman	MKL382
Nightwing	MVY759
Penguin Goon	NKA238

CHARACTER	CODE
Penguin Henchman	BJH782
Penguin Minion	KJP748
Poison Ivy Goon	GTB899
Police Marksman	HKG984
Police Officer	JRY983
Riddler Goon	CRY928
Riddler Henchman	XEU824
S.W.A.T.	HTF114
Sailor	NAV592
Scientist	JFL786
Security Guard	PLB946
The Joker (Tropical)	CCB199
Yeti	NJL412
Zoo Sweeper	DWR243

VEHICLES

VEHICLE	CODE
Bat-Tank	KNTT4B
Bruce Wayne's Private Jet	LEA664
Catwoman's Motorcycle	HPL826
Garbage Truck	DUS483
Goon Helicopter	GCH328
Harbor Helicopter	CHP735
Harley Quinn's Hammer Truck	RDT637
Mad Hatter's Glider	HS000W
Mad Hatter's Steamboat	M4DM4N
Mr. Freeze's Iceberg	ICYICE
The Joker's Van	JUK657

VEHICLE	CODE
Mr. Freeze's Kart	BCT229
Penguin Goon Submarine	BTN248
Police Bike	LJP234
Police Boat	PLC999
Police Car	KJL832
Police Helicopter	CWR732
Police Van	MAC788
Police Watercraft	VJD328
Riddler's Jet	HAHAHA
Robin's Submarine	TTF453
Two-Face's Armored Truck	EFE933

CHEATS

CHEAT	CODE
Always Score Multiply	9LRGNB
Fast Batarangs	JRBDCB
Fast Walk	ZOLM6N
Flame Batarang	D8NYWH
Freeze Batarang	XPN4NG
Extra Hearts	ML3KHP
Fast Build	EVG26J
Immune to Freeze	JXUDY6
Invincibility	WYD5CP
Minikit Detector	ZXGH9J

CHEAT	CODE
More Batarang Targets	XWP645
Piece Detector	KHJ554
Power Brick Detector	MMN786
Regenerate Hearts	HJH7HJ
Score x2	N4NR3E
Score x4	CX9MAT
Score x6	MLVNF2
Score x8	WCCDB9
Score x10	18HW07

LEGO INDIANA JONES: THE ORIGINAL ADVENTURES

CHARACTERS

Approach the blackboard in the Classsroom and enter the following codes.

CHARACTER	CODE
Bandit	12N68W
Bandit Swordsman	1MK4RT
Barranca	04EM94
Bazooka Trooper (Crusade)	MK83R7
Bazooka Trooper (Raiders)	S93Y5R
Belloq	CHN3YU
Belloq (Jungle)	TDR197
Belloq (Robes)	VEO29L
British Commander	B73EUA
British Officer	VJ5TI9
British Soldier	DJ5I2W
Captain Katanga	VJ3TT3
Chatter Lal	ENW936
Chatter Lal (Thuggee)	CNH4RY
Chen	3NK48T
Colonel Dietrich	2K9RKS
Colonel Vogel	8EAL4H
Dancing Girl	C7EJ21
Donovan	3NFTU8
Elsa (Desert)	JSNRT9
Elsa (Officer)	VMJ5US
Enemy Boxer	8246RB
Enemy Butler	VJ48W3
Enemy Guard	VJ7R51
Enemy Guard (Mountains)	YR47WM
Enemy Officer	572E61
Enemy Officer (Desert	2MK450
Enemy Pilot	B84ELP
Enemy Radio Operator	1MF94R
Enemy Soldier (Desert)	4NSU7Q

CHARACTER	CODE
Fedora	V75YSP
First Mate	0GIN24
Grail Knight	NE6THI
Hovitos Tribesman	HOV1SS
Indiana Jones (Desert Disguise)	4J8S4M
Indiana Jones (Officer)	VJ850S
Jungle Guide	24PF34
Kao Kan	WM046L
Kazim	NRH23J
Kazim (Desert)	3M29TJ
Lao Che	2NK479
Maharajah	NFK5N2
Major Toht	13NS01
Masked Bandit	N48SF0
Mola Ram	FJUR31
Monkey Man	3RF6YJ
Pankot Assassin	2NKT72
Pankot Guard	VN28RH
Sherpa Brawler	VJ37WJ
Sherpa Gunner	ND762W
Slave Child	0E3ENW
Thuggee	VM683E
Thuggee Acolyte	T2R3F9
Thuggee Slave Driver	VBS7GW
Village Dignitary	KD48TN
Village Elder	4682E1
Willie (Dinner Suit)	VK93R7
Willie (Pajamas)	MEN4IP
Wu Han	3NSLT8

EXTRAS

Approach the blackboard in the Classsroom and enter the following codes. Some cheats need to be enabled by selecting Extras from the pause menu.

CHEAT	CODE
Artifact Detector	VIKED7
Beep Beep	VNF59Q
Character Treasure	VIES2R
Disarm Enemies	VKRNS9
Disguises	4ID1N6
Fast Build	V83SL0
Fast Dig	378RS6
Fast Fix	FJ59WS
Fertilizer	B1GW1F
Ice Rink	33GM7J
Parcel Detector	VUT673
Poo Treasure	WWQ1SA
Regenerate Hearts	MDLP69
Secret Characters	3X44AA
Silhouettes	3HE85H
Super Scream	VN3R7S
Super Slap	0P1TA5
Treasure Magnet	H86LA2
Treasure x10	VI3PS8
Treasure x2	VM4TS9
Treasure x4	VLWEN3
Treasure x6	V84RYS
Treasure x8	A72E1M

LEGO STAR WARS: THE COMPLETE SAGA

The following still need to be purchase after entering the codes.

CHARACTERS

ADMIRAL ACKBAR

At the bar in Mos Eisley Cantina, select Enter Code and enter ACK646.

BATTLE DROID (COMMANDER)

At the bar in Mos Eisley Cantina, select Enter Code and enter KPF958.

BOBA FETT (BOY)

At the bar in Mos Eisley Cantina, select Enter Code and enter GGF539.

BOSS NASS

At the bar in Mos Eisley Cantina, select Enter Code and enter HHY697.

CAPTAIN TARPALS

At the bar in Mos Eisley Cantina, select Enter Code and enter QRN714.

COUNT DOOKU

At the bar in Mos Eisley Cantina, select Enter Code and enter DDD748.

DARTH MAUL

At the bar in Mos Eisley Cantina, select Enter Code and enter EUK421.

EWOK

At the bar in Mos Eisley Cantina, select Enter Code and enter EWK785.

GENERAL GRIEVOUS

At the bar in Mos Eisley Cantina, select Enter Code and enter PMN576.

GREEDO

At the bar in Mos Eisley Cantina, select Enter Code and enter ZZR636.

IG-88

At the bar in Mos Eisley Cantina, select Enter Code and enter GIJ989.

IMPERIAL GUARD

At the bar in Mos Eisley Cantina, select Enter Code and enter GUA850.

JANGO FETT
At the bar in Mos Eisley Cantina, select Enter Code and enter KLJ897.

KI-ADI MUNDI
At the bar in Mos Eisley Cantina, select Enter Code and enter MUN486.

LUMINARA
At the bar in Mos Eisley Cantina, select Enter Code and enter LUM521.

PADMÉ
At the bar in Mos Eisley Cantina, select Enter Code and enter VBJ322.

R2-Q5
At the bar in Mos Eisley Cantina, select Enter Code and enter EVILR2.

STORMTROOPER
At the bar in Mos Eisley Cantina, select Enter Code and enter NBN431.

TAUN WE
At the bar in Mos Eisley Cantina, select Enter Code and enter PRX482.

VULTURE DROID
At the bar in Mos Eisley Cantina, select Enter Code and enter BDC866.

WATTO
At the bar in Mos Eisley Cantina, select Enter Code and enter PLL967.

ZAM WESELL
At the bar in Mos Eisley Cantina, select Enter Code and enter 584HJF.

SKILLS

DISGUISE
At the bar in Mos Eisley Cantina, select Enter Code and enter BRJ437.

FORCE GRAPPLE LEAP
At the bar in Mos Eisley Cantina, select Enter Code and enter CLZ738.

VEHICLES

DROID TRIFIGHTER
At the bar in Mos Eisley Cantina, select Enter Code and enter AAB123.

IMPERIAL SHUTTLE
At the bar in Mos Eisley Cantina, select Enter Code and enter HUT845.

TIE INTERCEPTOR
At the bar in Mos Eisley Cantina, select Enter Code and enter INT729.

TIE FIGHTER
At the bar in Mos Eisley Cantina, select Enter Code and enter DBH897.

ZAM'S AIRSPEEDER
At the bar in Mos Eisley Cantina, select Enter Code and enter UUU875.

MADDEN NFL 07

MADDEN CARDS

Select Madden Cards from My Madden. Then select Madden Codes and enter the following:

CARD	PASSWORD
#199 Gold Lame Duck Cheat	5LAWOO
#200 Gold Mistake Free Cheat	XL7SP1
#210 Gold QB on Target Cheat	WROAOR
#220 Super Bowl XLI Gold	RLA9R7
#221 Super Bowl XLII Gold	WRLUF8
#222 Super Bowl XLIII Gold	NIEV4A
#223 Super Bowl XLIV Gold	M5AB7L
#224 Aloha Stadium Gold	YI8P8U
#225 1958 Colts Gold	B57QLU
#226 1966 Packers Gold	1PL1FL
#227 1968 Jets Gold	MIE6WO
#228 1970 Browns Gold	CL2TOE
#229 1972 Dolphins Gold	NOEB7U
#230 1974 Steelers Gold	YOOFLA
#231 1976 Raiders Gold	MOA11I
#232 1977 Broncos Gold	C8UM7U
#233 1978 Dolphins Gold	VIU007
#234 1980 Raiders Gold	NLAPH3
#235 1981 Chargers Gold	COAGI4
#236 1982 Redskins Gold	WL8BRI
#237 1983 Raiders Gold	HOEW71
#238 1984 Dolphins Gold	M1AM1E
#239 1985 Bears Gold	QOETO8
#240 1986 Giants Gold	ZI8S2L
#241 1988 49ers Gold	SP2A8H
#242 1990 Eagles Gold	2L4TRO
#243 1991 Lions Gold	J1ETRI
#244 1992 Cowboys Gold	W9UVI9

CARD	PASSWORD
#245 1993 Bills Gold	DLA3I7
#246 1994 49ers Gold	DR7EST
#247 1996 Packers Gold	F8LUST
#248 1998 Broncos Gold	FIES95
#249 1999 Rams Gold	S9OUSW
#250 Bears Pump Up the Crowd	B1OUPH
#251 Bengals Cheerleader	DRL2SW
#252 Bills Cheerleader	1PLUYO
#253 Broncos Cheerleader	3ROUJO
#254 Browns Pump Up the Crowd	T1UTOA
#255 Buccaneers Cheerleader	S9EWRI
#256 Cardinals Cheerleader	57IEPI
#257 Chargers Cheerleader	F7UHL8
#258 Chiefs Cheerleader	PRI5SL
#259 Colts Cheerleader	1R5AMI
#260 Cowboys Cheerleader	Z2ACHL
#261 Dolphins Cheerleader	C5AHLE
#262 Eagles Cheerleader	PO7DRO
#263 Falcons Cheerleader	37USPO
#264 49ers Cheerleader	KLOCRL
#265 Giants Pump Up the Crowd	C4USPI
#266 Jaguars Cheerleader	MIEH7E
#267 Jets Pump Up the Crowd	COLUXI
#268 Lions Pump Up the Crowd	3LABLU
#269 Packers Pump Up the Crowd	4HO7VO
#270 Panthers Cheerleader	F2IASP
#282 All AFC Team Gold	PRO9PH
#283 All NFC Team Gold	RLATH7

MAJOR LEAGUE BASEBALL 2K7

MICKEY MANTLE ON THE FREE AGENTS LIST

Select Enter Cheat Code from the My 2K7 menu and enter themick.

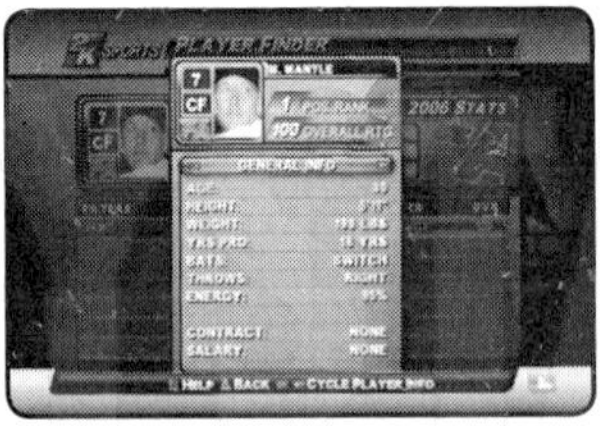

ALL CHEATS

Select Enter Cheat Code from the My 2K7 menu and enter Black Sox.

ALL EXTRAS

Select Enter Cheat Code from the My 2K7 menu and enter Game On.

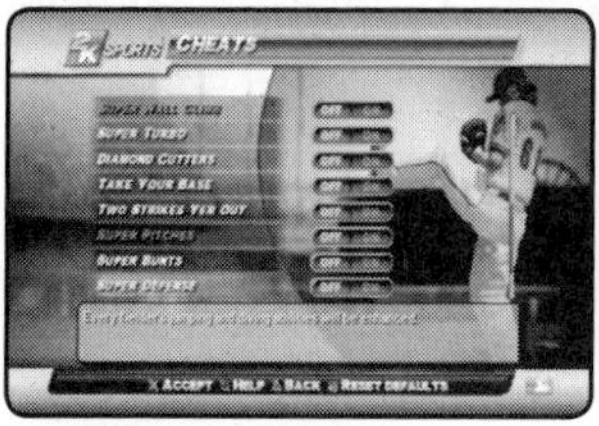

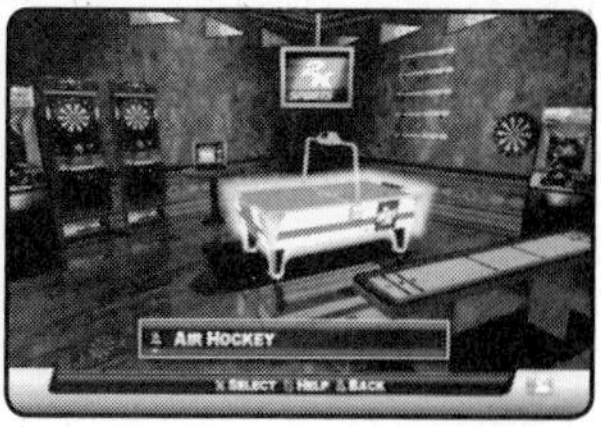

UNLOCK EVERYTHING

Select Enter Cheat Code from the My 2K7 menu and enter Derek Jeter. This does not unlock the Topps cheats.

MIGHTY MICK CHEAT

Select Enter Cheat Code from the My 2K7 menu and enter mightymick.

TRIPLE CROWN CHEAT

Select Enter Cheat Code from the My 2K7 menu and enter triplecrown.

BIG BLAST CHEAT

Select Enter Cheat Code from the My 2K7 menu and enter m4murder.

MARVEL ULTIMATE ALLIANCE

UNLOCK ALL SKINS

At the Team Menu, press Up, Down, Left, Right, Left, Right, Start.

UNLOCKS ALL HERO POWERS

At the Team Menu, press Left, Right, Up, Down, Up, Down, Start.

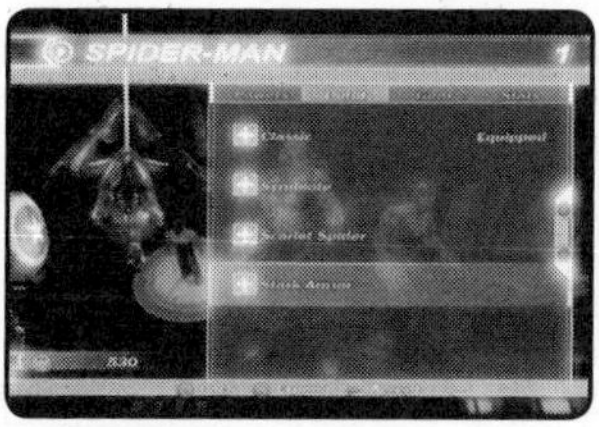

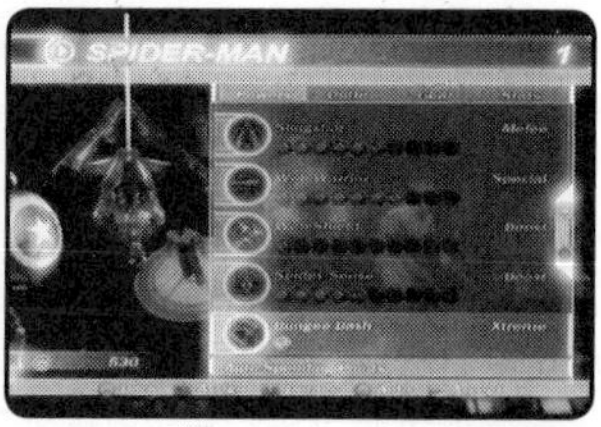

ALL HEROES TO LEVEL 99

At the Team Menu, press Up, Left, Up, Left, Down, Right, Down, Right, Start.

UNLOCK ALL HEROES

At the Team Menu, press Up, Up, Down, Down, Left, Left, Left, Start.

UNLOCK DAREDEVIL

At the Team Menu, press Left, Left, Right, Right, Up, Down, Up, Down, Start.

UNLOCK SILVER SURFER

At the Team Menu, press Down, Left, Left, Up, Right, Up, Down, Left, Start.

GOD MODE

During gameplay, press Up, Down, Up, Down, Up, Left, Down, Right, Start.

TOUCH OF DEATH

During gameplay, press Left, Right, Down, Down, Right, Left, Start.

SUPER SPEED

During gameplay, press Up, Left, Up, Right, Down, Right, Start.

FILL MOMENTUM

During gameplay, press Left, Right, Right, Left, Up, Down, Down, Up, Start.

UNLOCK ALL COMICS

At the Review menu, press Left, Right, Right, Left, Up, Up, Right, Start.

UNLOCK ALL CONCEPT ART

At the Review menu, press Down, Down, Down, Right, Right, Left, Down, Start.

UNLOCK ALL CINEMATICS

At the Review menu, press Up, Left, Left, Up, Right, Right, Up, Start.

UNLOCK ALL LOAD SCREENS

At the Review menu, press Up, Down, Right, Left, Up, Up Down, Start.

UNLOCK ALL COURSES

At the Comic Missions menu, press Up, Right, Left, Down, Up, Right, Left, Down, Start.

MLB 08: THE SHOW

ALL CLASSIC STADIUMS

At the main menu, press Down, Right, Circle, Square, Left, Triangle, Up, L1. The controller will vibrate if entered correctly.

MLB 07: THE SHOW

CLASSIC STADIUMS

At the Main Menu, press Down, Up, Right, Down, Up, Left, Down, Up.

GOLDEN/SLIVER ERA PLAYERS

At the Main Menu, press Left, Up, Right, Down, Down, Left, Up, Down.

MOTORSTORM

UNLOCK EVERYTHING

At the Main menu, hold **L1** + **L2** + **R1** + **R2** + **R3** (while pressed Up) + **L3** (while pressed Down).

BIG HEADS ON ATVS AND BIKES

Pause the game and hold **L1** + **L2** + **R1** + **R2** + **R3** (while pressed Right), + **L3** (while pressed Left).

MX VS. ATV UNTAMED

ALL RIDING GEAR

Select Cheat Codes from the Options and enter crazylikea.

ALL HANDLEBARS

Select Cheat Codes from the Options and enter nohands.

NASCAR 09

ALL FANTASY DRIVERS

Select EA Extras from My Nascar, choose Cheat Codes and enter CHECKERED FLAG.

WALMART TRACK AND THE WALMART CAR

Select EA Extras from My Nascar, choose Cheat Codes and enter Walmart Everyday.

NASCAR 08

ALL CHASE MODE CARS

Select cheat codes from the options menu and enter checkered flag.

EA SPORTS CAR

Select cheat codes from the options menu and enter ea sports car.

FANTASY DRIVERS

Select cheat codes from the options menu and enter race the pack.

WALMART CAR AND TRACK

Select cheat codes from the options menu and enter walmart everyday.

NBA 07

2006 CHARLOTTE BOBCATS ALTERNATE JERSEY

Select NBA.com from the Trophy Room. Press ● to bring up the Enter Code screen. Enter JKL846ETK5.

2006 NOK HORNETS ALTERNATE JERSEY

Select NBA.com from the Trophy Room. Press ● to bring up the Enter Code screen. Enter EL2E3T8H58.

2006 NEW JERSEY NETS ALTERNATE JERSEY

Select NBA.com from the Trophy Room. Press ● to bring up the Enter Code screen. Enter NB79D965D2.

2006 UTAH JAZZ ALTERNATE JERSEY

Select NBA.com from the Trophy Room. Press ◉ to bring up the Enter Code screen. Enter 228GG7585G.

2006 WAS WIZARDS ALTERNATE JERSEY

Select NBA.com from the Trophy Room. Press ◉ to bring up the Enter Code screen. Enter PL5285F37F.

2007 EASTERN ALL STARS

Select NBA.com from the Trophy Room. Press ◉ to bring up the Enter Code screen. Enter 5F89RE3H8G.

2007 WESTERN ALL STARS

Select NBA.com from the Trophy Room. Press ◉ to bring up the Enter Code screen. Enter 2H5E89EH8C.

NBA 2K7

ABA BALL

Select Codes from the Features menu and enter payrespect.

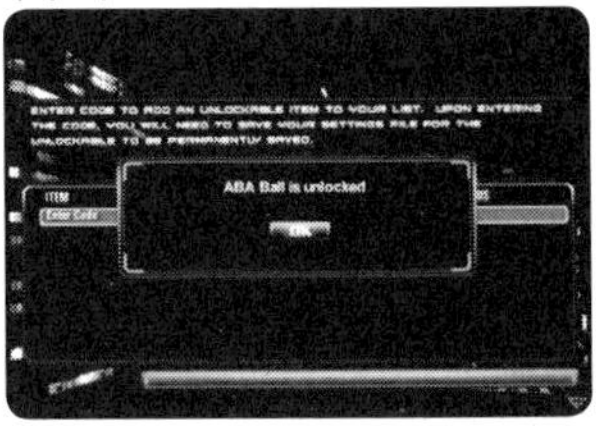

ALL-STAR BALL

Select Codes from the Features menu and enter ply8mia.

MAXIMUM DURABILITY

Select Codes from the Features menu and enter ironman.

UNLIMITED STAMINA

Select Codes from the Features menu and enter norest.

+10 DEFENSIVE AWARENESS

Select Codes from the Features menu and enter getstops.

+10 OFFENSIVE AWARENESS

Select Codes from the Features menu and enter inthezone.

2007 ALL-STAR UNIFORMS

Select Codes from the Features menu and enter syt6cii.

BOBCATS SECONDARY

Select Codes from the Features menu and enter bcb8sta.

JAZZ SECONDARY

Select Codes from the Features menu and enter zjb3lau.

NETS SECONDARY

Select Codes from the Features menu and enter nrd4esj.

WIZARDS SECONDARY

Select Codes from the Features menu and enter zw9idla.

ST. PATRICK'S DAY UNIFORMS

Select Codes from the Features menu and enter tpk7sgn.

VALENTINE'S DAY UNIFORMS

Select Codes from the Features menu and enter vdr5lya.

INTERNATIONAL ALL-STARS

Select Codes from the Features menu and enter tns9roi.

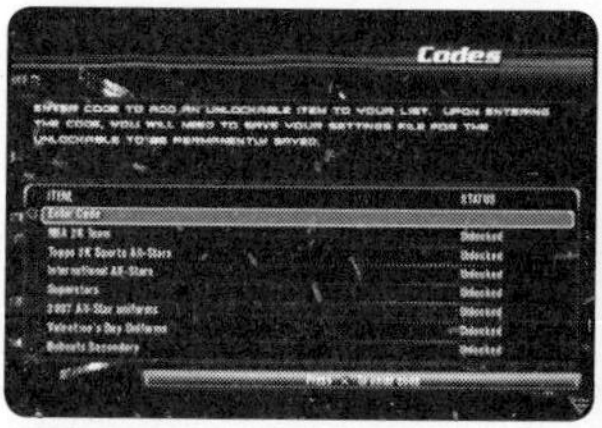

NBA 2K TEAM

Select Codes from the Features menu and enter bestsim.

SUPERSTARS

Select Codes from the Features menu and enter rta1spe

TOPPS 2K SPORTS ALL-STARS

Select Codes from the Features menu and enter topps2ksports.

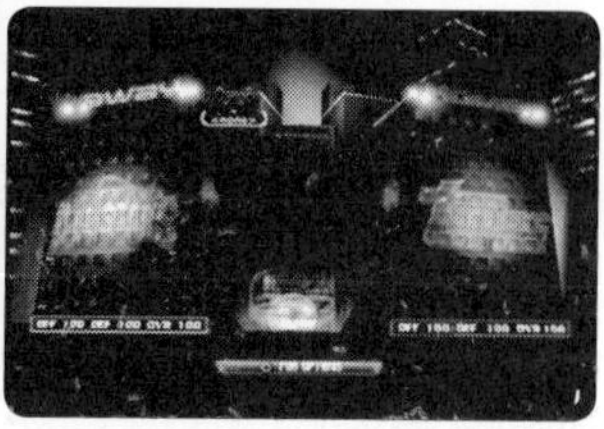

NBA 2K8

ABA BALL

Select Codes from the Features menu and enter Payrespect.

2KSPORTS TEAM

Select Codes from the Features menu and enter 2ksports.

NBA DEVELOPMENT TEAM

Select Codes from the Features menu and enter nba2k.

SUPERSTARS TEAM

Select Codes from the Features menu and enter llmohffaae.

VISUAL CONCEPTS TEAM

Select Codes from the Features menu and enter Vcteam.

2008 ALL-STAR NBA JERSEYS

Select Codes from the Features menu and enter haeitgyebs.

BOBCATS RACING JERSEY

Select Codes from the Features menu and enter agtaccsinr.

PACERS SECOND ROAD JERSEY

Select Codes from the Features menu and enter cpares.

ST. PATRICK'S DAY JERSEYS

Select Codes from the Features menu and enter uclerehanp.

VALENTINE'S DAY JERSEYS

Select Codes from the Features menu and enter amcnreo.

NBA 2K9

2K SPORTS TEAM
Select Codes from the Features menu and enter 2ksports.

NBA 2K TEAM
Select Codes from the Features menu and enter nba2k.

SUPERSTARS
Select Codes from the Features menu and enter llmohffaae.

VC TEAM
Select Codes from the Features menu and enter vcteam.

ABA BALL
Select Codes from the Features menu and enter payrespect.

NBA LIVE 08

ADIDAS GIL-ZERO - ALL-STAR EDITION
Select NBA Codes from My NBA and enter 23DN1PPOG4.

ADIDAS TIM DUNCAN STEALTH - ALL-STAR EDITION
Select NBA Codes from My NBA and enter FE454DFJCC.

NBA LIVE 07

AIR JORDAN V
Select NBA Codes from My NBA Live 07 and enter PNBBX1EVT5.

AIR JORDAN V
Select NBA Codes from My NBA Live 07 and enter VIR13PC451.

AIR JORDAN V
Select NBA Codes from My NBA Live 07 and enter IB7G8NN91Z.

JORDAN MELO M3
Select NBA Codes from My NBA Live 07 and enter JUL38TC485.

C-BILLUPS ALL-STAR EDITION
Select NBA Codes from My NBA Live 07 and enter BV6877HB9N.

ADIDAS C-BILLUPS VEGAS EDITION

Select NBA Codes from My NBA Live 07 and enter 85NVLDMWS5.

ADIDAS GARNETT BOUNCE ALL-STAR EDITION

Select NBA Codes from My NBA Live 07 and enter HYIOUHCAAN.

ADIDAS GARNETT BOUNCE VEGAS EDITION

Select NBA Codes from My NBA Live 07 and enter KDZ2MQL17W.

ADIDAS GIL-ZERO ALL-STAR EDITION

Select NBA Codes from My NBA Live 07 and enter 23DN1PPOG4.

ADIDAS GIL-ZERO VEGAS EDITION

Select NBA Codes from My NBA Live 07 and enter QQQ3JCUYQ7.

ADIDAS GIL-ZERO MID

Select NBA Codes from My NBA Live 07 and enter 1GSJC8JWRL.

ADIDAS GIL-ZERO MID

Select NBA Codes from My NBA Live 07 and enter 369V6RVU3G.

ADIDAS STEALTH ALL-STAR EDITION

Select NBA Codes from My NBA Live 07 and enter FE454DFJCC.

ADIDAS T-MAC 6 ALL-STAR EDITION

Select NBA Codes from My NBA Live 07 and enter MCJK843NNC.

ADIDAS T-MAC 6 VEGAS EDITION

Select NBA Codes from My NBA Live 07 and enter 84GF7EJG8V.

CHARLOTTE BOBCATS SECOND ROAD JERSEY

Select NBA Codes from My NBA Live 07 and enter WEDX671H7S.

UTAH JAZZ SECOND ROAD JERSEY

Select NBA Codes from My NBA Live 07 and enter VCBI89FK83.

NEW JERSEY NETS SECOND ROAD JERSEY

Select NBA Codes from My NBA Live 07 and enter D4SAA98U5H.

WASHINGTON WIZARDS SECOND ROAD JERSEY

Select NBA Codes from My NBA Live 07 and enter QV93NLKXQC.

EASTERN ALL-STARS 2007 ROAD JERSEY

Select NBA Codes from My NBA Live 07 and enter WOCNW4KL7L.

EASTERN ALL-STARS 2007 HOME JERSEY

Select NBA Codes from My NBA Live 07 and enter 5654ND43N6.

WESTERN ALL-STARS 2007 ROAD JERSEY

Select NBA Codes from My NBA Live 07 and enter XX93BVL20U.

WESTERN ALL-STARS 2007 HOME JERSEY

Select NBA Codes from My NBA Live 07 and enter 993NSKL199.

NBA STREET HOMECOURT

ALL TEAMS

At the Main menu, hold **R1** + **L1** and press Left, Right, Left, Right.

ALL COURTS

At the Main menu, hold **R1** + **L1** and press Up, Right, Down, Left.

BLACK/RED BALL

At the Main menu, hold **R1** + **L1** and press Up, Down, Left, Right.

NEED FOR SPEED PROSTREET

$2,000

Select Career and then choose Code Entry. Enter 1MA9X99.

$4,000

Select Career and then choose Code Entry. Enter W2IOLL01.

$8,000

Select Career and then choose Code Entry. Enter L1IS97A1.

$10,000

Select Career and then choose Code Entry. Enter 1MI9K7E1.

$10,000

Select Career and then choose Code Entry. Enter CASHMONEY.

$10,000

Select Career and then choose Code Entry. Enter REGGAME.

AUDI TT

Select Career and then choose Code Entry. Enter ITSABOUTYOU.

CHEVELLE SS

Select Career and then choose Code Entry. Enter HORSEPOWER.

COKE ZERO GOLF GTI

Select Career and then choose Code Entry. Enter COKEZERO.

DODGE VIPER

Select Career and then choose Code Entry. Enter WORLDSLONGESTLASTING.

MITSUBISHI LANCER EVOLUTION

Select Career and then choose Code Entry. Enter MITSUBISHIGOFAR.

UNLOCK ALL BONUSES

Select Career and then choose Code Entry. Enter UNLOCKALLTHINGS.

5 REPAIR MARKERS

Select Career and then choose Code Entry. Enter SAFETYNET.

ENERGIZER VINYL

Select Career and then choose Code Entry. Enter ENERGIZERLITHIUM.

CASTROL SYNTEC VINYL

Select Career and then choose Code Entry. Enter CASTROLSYNTEC. This also gives you $10,000.

NHL 08

ALL RBK EDGE JERSEYS

At the RBK Edge Code option, enter h3oyxpwksf8ibcgt.

RATATOUILLE

Select Gusteau's Shop from the Extras menu. Choose Secrets, select the appropriate code number, and then enter the code. Once the code is entered, select the cheat you want to activate it.

CODE NUMBER	CODE	EFFECT
1	Pieceocake	Very Easy difficulty mode
2	Myhero	no impact and no damage from enemies
3	Shielded	No damage from enemies
4	Spyagent	Move undetected by any enemy
5	Ilikeonions	Fart every time Remy jumps
6	Hardfeelings	Head butt when attacking instead of tailswipe
7	Slumberparty	Multiplayer mode
8	Gusteauart	All Concept Art
9	Gusteauship	All four championship modes
10	Mattelme	All single player and multiplayer minigames
11	Gusteauvid	All Videos
12	Gusteaures	All Bonus Artworks
13	Gusteaudream	All Dream Worlds in Gusteau's Shop
14	Gusteauslide	All Slides in Gusteau's Shop
15	Gusteaulevel	All single player minigames
16	Gusteaucombo	All items in Gusteau's Shop
17	Gusteaupot	5,000 Gusteau points
18	Gusteaujack	10,000 Gusteau points
19	Gusteauomni	50,000 Gusteau points

RATCHET & CLANK FUTURE: TOOLS OF DESTRUCTION

CHALLENGE MODE

After defeating the game, you can replay the game in Challenge Mode with all of Ratchet's current upgraded weapons and armor.

SKILL POINTS

Complete the following objectives to earn skill points. Each one is worth 10 to 40 points and you can use these points to unlock Cheats in the Cheats Menu. The following table lists the skill points with a location and description.

SKILL POINT	LOCATION	DESCRIPTION
Smashing Good Time	Cobalia	Destroy all crates and consumer bots in the trade port and gel factory.
I Should Have Gone Down in a Barrel	Cobalia	Jump into each of the two gel waterfall areas in Cobalia gel factory.

SKILL POINT	LOCATION	DESCRIPTION
Giant Hunter	Cobalia	Kill several Basilisk Leviathans in the Cobalia wilderness.
Wrench Ninja 3	Stratus City	Use only the Omniwrench to get through the level to the Robo-Wings segment.
We Don't Need No Stinkin' Bridges!	Stratus City	Cross the tri-pad sequence using gel-cube bounces.
Surface-to-Air Plasma Beasts	Stratus City	Take out several flying targets using a specific weapon.
Been Around	Stratus City	Take off from every Robo-wing launch pad in Stratus City.
Collector's Addition	Voron	Be very thorough in your collection of goodies.
Minesweeper	Voron	Clear out a bunch of mines.
What's That, R2?	Voron	Barrel roll multiple times.
I Think I'm Gonna Be Sick	IFF	Ride the Ferris wheel for 5 loops without getting off or taking damage.
Fast and the Fire-ious	IFF	Use the Charge Boots to cross the bridge to the arena without being burned.
One Heckuva Peephole	IFF	Return after receiving the Geo-laser and complete the Geo-laser setup.
Alphabet City	Apogee	Teleport to each of the six asteroids in alphabetical order.
Knock You Down to Size	Apogee	Wrench Slam 5 centipedes.
Dancin' with the Stars	Apogee	Make 5 enemies dance at once on an asteroid.
Taste o' Yer Own Medicine	Pirate Base	Destroy all of the Shooter Pirates with the Combuster.
Preemptive Strike	Pirate Base	Destroy all of the "sleeping bats" while they are still sleeping.
It's Mutant-E Cap'n!	Pirate Base	Change 5 pirates into penguins in one blast.
You Sunk My Battleship!	Rakar	Shoot down a large percentage of the big destroyers.
Pretty Lights	Rakar	Complete the level without destroying any of the snatchers that fire beams at Ratchet.
I've Got Places To Be	Rakar	Destroy the boss in under 2:30.
The Consumer Is Not (Always) Right	Rykan V	Destroy a bunch of consumer bots in the level.
Live Strong	Rykan V	Complete the Gryo Cycle in 1:45.
Untouchable	Rykan V	Don't take damage in the Gyro-Cycle.
It Sounded Like a Freight Train	Sargasso	Get 10 Swarmers in one tornado.
Head Examiner	Sargasso	Land on all of the dinosaur heads in Sargasso.
Extinction	Sargasso	Kill all of the Sargasso Predators.
Lombaxes Don't Like Cold	Iris	Break all the breakable icicles.
Mow Down Ho-Down	Iris	Use turrets to destroy 10 dancing pirates.
Dancin' on the Ceiling	Zordoom	Successfully use a Groovitron while on a Magboot surface.
Seared Ahi	Zordoom	Use the Pyroblaster on 3 Drophid creatures after freeing them from their robotic suits.
Shocking Ascent	Zordoom	Destroy all enemies on the elevator using just the Shock Ravager.
Expert Marksman	Boraq	Kill 75% of all of the enemies.
Can't Touch This	Boraq	Don't take damage before fighting the boss.
Pyoo, Pyoo!	Boraq	Complete the level without secondary fire.
Dead Aim	Kerchu	Destroy several destructible towers while on the pirate barge.
Fire With Fire	Kerchu	Kill a few Kerchu Flamethrowers with the Pyro Blaster.
Rocket Jump	Kerchu	Successfully jump over a row of three rockets while on the grindrail during the boss fight in Kerchu City.
Your Friendly Neighborhood…	Slag Fleet	Destroy 5 enemies while on the grav ramp before Slag's ship.

SKILL POINT	LOCATION	DESCRIPTION
Turret Times Two	Slag Fleet	Destroy at least 2 pirates with each turret in the level.
Six Gun Salute	Slag Fleet	Get six pirates in a row to salute Ratchet while in the Pirate Disguise.
Gotta Catch 'Em All	Cragmite Ruins	Hit all Cragmite soldiers with the Mag-Net Launcher.
Ratchet and Goliath	Cragmite Ruins	Destroy multiple walkers using just the Nano-Swarmers.
Ratchet &...Not Clank?!	Cragmite Ruins	Use Mr. Zurkon in Cragmite's Ratchet-only segment.
Stay Still So I Can Shoot You!	Meridian	Use strafe-flip 10 times while fighting the Cragmite soldiers.
Now Boarding...	Meridian	Complete the Gyro-Cycle in 55 seconds.
Low Flying Howls	Meridian	Fly under an electrified barrier in the Robo-wings segment.
Extreme Alien Makeover	Fastoon2	Turn 10 Cragmites into penguins.
Empty Bag o' Tricks	Fastoon2	Complete the level without using any devices.
Nowhere to Hide	Fastoon2	Destroy every piece of breakable cover.
No, Up Your Arsenal	Global	Upgrade every weapon to the max.
Roflcopter	Global	Turn enemies into penguins, then use the Visicopter to destroy the penguins.
Stir Fry	Global	Kill 2 different enemy types using the Shock Ravager while they are trapped in a tornado.
Golden Children	Overall	Find all of the Gold Bolts.
Sacagawea	Global	Complete all of the maps 100%, leaving no area undiscovered.
Cheapskate	Global	Purchase a single Combustor round.
Everybody Dance Now	Global	Make every type of enemy in the game dance.
F5 on the Fujita Scale	Global	Pick up more than 10 enemies with one tornado.
Chorus line	Global	Get 10+ enemies to dance together.
Happy Feet	Global	Get several penguins to dance on-screen.
Disco Inferno	Global	Use the Groovitron followed by the Pyro Blaster.
Bolts in the Bank	Global	Sell a bunch of Leviathan Souls to the Smuggler.
It's Like the North Pole Here	Global	Have at least 12-15 enemies and/or citizens turned into penguins at one time.
Say Hello to My Little Friend	Global	Kill 15 enemies with one RYNO shot.
For the Hoard!	Global	Get every item.
Promoted to Inspector	Global	Get every gadget.
Global Thermonuclear War	Global	Get every weapon.
It's Even Better the Second Time!	Global	Complete Challenge Mode.
The Hardest of Core	Global	Get all skill points and everything else in the game.

SEGA SUPERSTARS TENNIS

UNLOCK CHARACTERS

Complete the following missions to unlock the corresponding character.

CHARACTER	MISSION TO COMPLETE
Alex Kidd	Mission 1 of Alex Kidd's World
Amy Rose	Mission 2 of Sonic the Hedgehog's World
Gilius	Mission 1 of Golden Axe's World
Gum	Mission 12 of Jet Grind Radio's World
Meemee	Mission 8 of Super Monkey Ball's World
Pudding	Mission 1 of Space Channel 5's World
Reala	Mission 2 of NiGHTs' World
Shadow The Hedgehog	Mission 14 of Sonic the Hedgehog's World

THE SIMPSONS GAME

After unlocking the following, the outfits can be changed at the downstairs closet in the Simpson's house. The Trophies can be viewed at different locations in the house: Bart's room, Lisa's room, Marge's room, and the garage.

BART'S OUTFITS AND TROPHIES (POSTER COLLECTION)

At the main menu, press Right, Left, ■, ■, ▲, R3.

HOMER'S OUTFITS AND TROPHIES (BEER BOTTLE COLLECTION)

At the main menu, press Left, Right, ▲, ▲, ■, L3.

LISA'S OUTFITS AND TROPHIES (DOLLS)

At the main menu, press ■, ▲, ■, ■, ■, Triangle, L3.

MARGE'S OUTFITS AND TROPHIES (HAIR PRODUCTS)

At the main menu, press ▲, ■, ▲, ▲, ■, R3.

SKATE

BEST BUY CLOTHES

At the Main menu, press Up, Down, Left, Right, ■, **R1**, ▲, **L1**.

STAR WARS: THE FORCE UNLEASHED

CHEAT CODES

Pause the game and select Input Code. Here you can enter the following codes. Activating any of the following cheat codes will disable some unlockables, and you will be unable to save your progress.

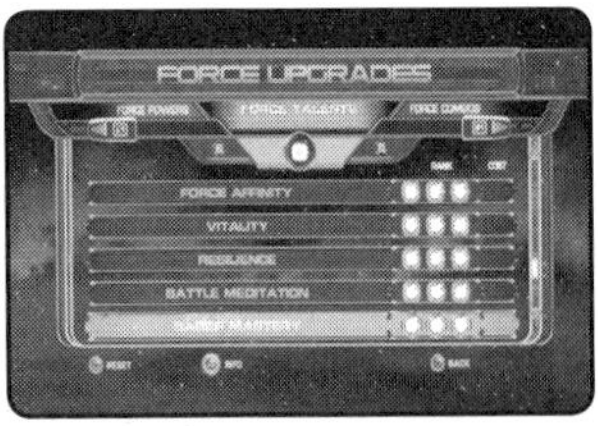

CHEAT	CODE
All Force Powers at Max Power	KATARN
All Force Push Ranks	EXARKUN
All Saber Throw Ranks	ADEGAN
All Repulse Ranks	DATHOMIR
All Saber Crystals	HURRIKANE
All Talents	JOCASTA
Deadly Saber	LIGHTSABER

COMBOS

Pause the game and select Input Code. Here you can enter the following codes. Activating any of the following cheat codes will disable some unlockables, and you will be unable to save your progress.

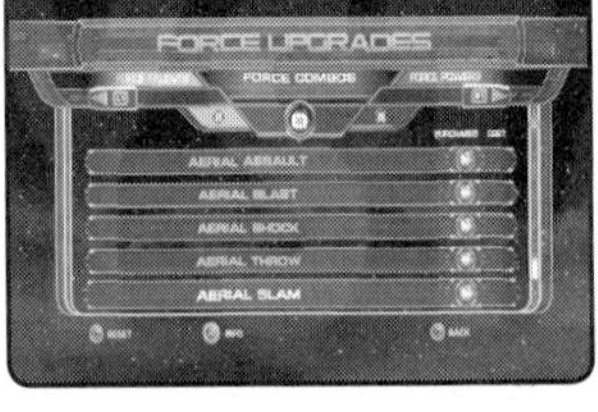

COMBO	CODE
All Combos	MOLDYCROW
Aerial Ambush	VENTRESS
Aerial Assault	EETHKOTH
Aerial Blast	YADDLE
Impale	BRUTALSTAB
Lightning Bomb	MASSASSI
Lightning Grenade	RAGNOS
Saber Slam	PLOKOON
Saber Sling	KITFISTO
Sith Saber Flurry	LUMIYA
Sith Slash	DARAGON
Sith Throw	SAZEN
New Combo	FREEDON
New Combo	MARAJADE

ALL DATABANK ENTRIES

Pause the game and select Input Code. Enter OSSUS.

MIRRORED LEVEL

Pause the game and select Input Code. Enter MINDTRICK. Re-enter the code to return level to normal.

SITH MASTER DIFFICULTY

Pause the game and select Input Code. Enter SITHSPAWN.

COSTUMES

Pause the game and select Input Code. Here you can enter the following codes.

COSTUME	CODE
All Costumes	SOHNDANN
Bail Organa	VICEROY
Ceremonial Jedi Robes	DANTOOINE
Drunken Kota	HARDBOILED
Emperor	MASTERMIND
Incinerator Trooper	PHOENIX
Jedi Adventure Robe	HOLOCRON
Kashyyyk Trooper	TK421GREEN
Kota	MANDALORE
Master Kento	WOOKIEE
Proxy	PROTOTYPE
Scout Trooper	FERRAL
Shadow Trooper	BLACKHOLE
Sith Stalker Armor	KORRIBAN
Snowtrooper	SNOWMAN
Stormtrooper	TK421WHITE
Stormtrooper Commander	TK421BLUE

STUNTMAN IGNITION

3 PROPS IN STUNT CREATOR MODE
Select Cheats from Extras and enter COOLPROP.

ALL ITEMS UNLOCKED FOR CONSTRUCTION MODE
Select Cheats from Extras and enter NOBLEMAN.

MVX SPARTAN
Select Cheats from Extras and enter fastride.

ALL CHEATS
Select Cheats from Extras and enter Wearefrozen.

This unlocks the following cheats: Slo-mo Cool, Thrill Cam, Vision Switcher, Nitro Addiction, Freaky Fast, and Ice Wheels.

ALL CHEATS
Select Cheats from Extras and enter Kungfoopete.

ICE WHEELS CHEAT
Select Cheats from Extras and enter IceAge.

NITRO ADDICTION CHEAT
Select Cheats from Extras and enter TheDuke.

VISION SWITCHER CHEAT
Select Cheats from Extras and enter GFXMODES.

SUPER PUZZLE FIGHTER II TURBO HD REMIX

PLAY AS AKUMA
At the character select, highlight Hsien-Ko and press Down.

PLAY AS DAN
At the character select, highlight Donovan and press Down.

PLAY AS DEVILOT
At the character select, highlight Morrigan and press Down.

PLAY AS ANITA
At the character select, hold **L1** + **R1** and choose Donovan.

PLAY AS HSIEN-KO'S TALISMAN
At the character select, hold **L1** + **R1** and choose Hsien-Ko.

PLAY AS MORRIGAN AS A BAT
At the character select, hold **L1** + **R1** and choose Morrigan.

SURF'S UP

ALL CHAMPIONSHIP LOCATIONS
Select Cheat Codes from the Extras menu and enter FREEVISIT.

ALL LEAF SLIDE STAGES
Select Cheat Codes from the Extras menu and enter GOINGDOWN.

ALL MULTIPLAYER LEVELS
Select Cheat Codes from the Extras menu and enter MULTIPASS.

ALL BOARDS
Select Cheat Codes from the Extras menu and enter MYPRECIOUS.

ASTRAL BOARD
Select Cheat Codes from the Extras menu and enter ASTRAL.

MONSOON BOARD
Select Cheat Codes from the Extras menu and enter MONSOON.

TINE SHOCKWAVE BOARD
Select Cheat Codes from the Extras menu and enter TINYSHOCKWAVE.

ALL CHARACTER CUSTOMIZATIONS
Select Cheat Codes from the Extras menu and enter TOPFASHION.

PLAY AS ARNOLD
Select Cheat Codes from the Extras menu and enter TINYBUTSTRONG.

PLAY AS ELLIOT
Select Cheat Codes from the Extras menu and enter SURPRISEGUEST.

PLAY AS GEEK
Select Cheat Codes from the Extras menu and enter SLOWANDSTEADY.

PLAY AS TANK EVANS
Select Cheat Codes from the Extras menu and enter IMTHEBEST.

PLAY AS TATSUHI KOBAYASHI
Select Cheat Codes from the Extras menu and enter KOBAYASHI.

PLAY AS ZEKE TOPANGA
Select Cheat Codes from the Extras menu and enter THELEGEND.

ALL VIDEOS AND SPEN GALLERY
Select Cheat Codes from the Extras menu and enter WATCHAMOVIE.

ART GALLERY
Select Cheat Codes from the Extras menu and enter NICEPLACE.

TIGER WOODS PGA TOUR 08

ALL COURSES
Select Password from EA Sports Extras and enter greensfees.

ALL GOLFERS
Select Password from EA Sports Extras and enter allstars.

WAYNE ROONEY
Select Password from EA Sports Extras and enter playfifa08.

INFINITE MONEY
Select Password from EA Sports Extras and enter cream.

TONY HAWK'S PROJECT 8

SPONSOR ITEMS

As you progress through Career mode and move up the rankings, you gain sponsors and each comes with its own Create-a-skater item.

RANK REQUIRED	CAS ITEM UNLOCKED
Rank 040	Adio Kenny V2 Shoes
Rank 050	Quiksilver Hoody 3
Rank 060	Birdhouse Tony Hawk Deck
Rank 080	Vans No Skool Gothic Shoes
Rank 100	Volcom Scallero Jacket
Rank 110	eS Square One Shoes
Rank 120	Almost Watch What You Say Deck
Rank 140	DVS Adage Shoe
Rank 150	Element Illuminate Deck
Rank 160	Etnies Sheckler White Lavender Shoes
Complete Skateshop Goal	Stereo Soundwave Deck

SKATERS

All of the skaters, except for Tony Hawk, must be unlocked by completing challenges in the Career Mode. They are useable in Free Skate and 2 Player modes.

SKATER	HOW TO UNLOCK
Tony Hawk	Always Unlocked
Lyn-z Adams Hawkins	Complete Pro Challenge
Bob Burquist	Complete Pro Challenge
Dustin Dollin	Complete Pro Challenge
Nyjah Huston	Complete Pro Challenge
Bam Margera	Complete Pro Challenge
Rodney Mullen	Complete Pro Challenge
Paul Rodriguez	Complete Pro Challenge
Ryan Sheckler	Complete Pro Challenge
Daewon Song	Complete Pro Challenge
Mike Vallely	Complete Pro Challenge
Stevie Willams	Complete Pro Challenge
Travis Barker	Complete Pro Challenge
Kevin Staab	Complete Pro Challenge
Zombie	Complete Pro Challenge
Christaian Hosoi	Rank #1
Jason Lee	Complete Final Tony Hawk Goal
Photographer	Unlock Shops
Security Guard	Unlock School
Bum	Unlock Car Factory
Beaver Mascot	Unlock High School
Real Estate Agent	Unlock Downtown
Filmer	Unlock High School
Skate Jam Kid	Rank #4
Dad	Rank #1
Colonel	All Gaps
Nerd	Complete School Spirit Goal

CHEAT CODES

Select Cheat Codes from the Options and enter the following codes. In game you can access some codes from the Options menu.

CHEAT CODE	RESULTS
plus44	Unlocks Travis Barker
hohohosoi	Unlocks Christian Hosoi
notmono	Unlocks Jason Lee
mixitup	Unlocks Kevin Staab
strangefellows	Unlocks Dad & Skater Jam Kid
themedia	Unlocks Photog Girl & Filmer
militarymen	Unlocks Colonel & Security Guard
jammypack	Unlocks Always Special
balancegalore	Unlocks Perfect Rail
frontandback	Unlocks Perect Manual
shellshock	Unlocks Unlimited Focus
shescaresme	Unlocks Big Realtor
birdhouse	Unlocks Inkblot deck
allthebest	Full stats
needaride	All decks unlocked and free, except for Inkblot Deck and Gamestop Deck
yougotitall	All specials unlocked and in player's special list and set as owned in skate shop
wearelosers	Unlocks Nerd and a Bum
manineedadate	Unlocks Beaver Mascot
suckstobedead	Unlocks Officer Dick
HATEDANDPROUD	Unlocks the Vans item

TONY HAWK'S PROVING GROUND

Select Cheat Codes from the Options and enter the following cheats. Some codes need to be enabled by selecting Cheats from the Options during a game.

UNLOCK	CHEAT
Unlocks Boneman	CRAZYBONEMAN
Unlocks Bosco	MOREMILK
Unlocks Cam	NOTACAMERA
Unlocks Cooper	THECOOP
Unlocks Eddie X	SKETCHY
Unlocks El Patinador	PILEDRIVER
Unlocks Eric	FLYAWAY
Unlocks Mad Dog	RABBIES
Unlocks MCA	INTERGALACTIC
Unlocks Mel	NOTADUDE
Unlocks Rube	LOOKSSMELLY
Unlocks Spence	DAPPER
Unlocks Shayne	MOVERS
Unlocks TV Producer	SHAKER
Unlock FDR	THEPREZPARK
Unlock Lansdowne	THELOCALPARK
Unlock Air & Space Museum	THEINDOORPARK

UNLOCK	CHEAT
Unlocks all Fun Items	OVERTHETOP
Unlocks all CAS items	GIVEMESTUFF
Unlocks all Decks	LETSGOSKATE
Unlock all Game Movies	WATCHTHIS
Unlock all Lounge Bling Items	SWEETSTUFF
Unlock all Lounge Themes	LAIDBACKLOUNGE
Unlock all Rigger Pieces	IMGONNABUILD
Unlock all Video Editor Effects	TRIPPY
Unlock all Video Editor Overlays	PUTEMONTOP
All specials unlocked and in player's special list	LOTSOFTRICKS
Full Stats	BEEFEDUP
Give player +50 skill points	NEEDSHELP

The following cheats lock you out of the Leaderboards:

UNLOCK	CHEAT
Unlocks Perfect Manual	STILLAINTFALLIN
Unlocks Perfect Rail	AINTFALLIN
Unlock Super Check	BOOYAH
Unlocks Unlimited Focus	MYOPIC
Unlock Unlimited Slash Grind	SUPERSLASHIN
Unlocks 100% branch completion in NTT	FOREVERNAILED
No Bails	ANDAINTFALLI

You can not use the Video Editor with the following cheats:

UNLOCK	CHEAT
Unlocks Invisible Man	THEMISSING
Mini Skater	TINYTATER
No Board	MAGICMAN

TRANSFORMERS: THE GAME

INFINITE HEALTH

At the Main menu, press Left, Left, Up, Left, Right, Down, Right.

INFINITE AMMO

At the Main menu, press Up, Down, Left, Right, Up, Up, Down.

NO MILITARY OR POLICE

At the Main menu, press Right, Left, Right, Left, Right, Left, Right.

ALL MISSIONS

At the Main menu, press Down, Up, Left, Right, Right, Right, Up, Down.

BONUS CYBERTRON MISSIONS

At the Main menu, press Right, Up, Up, Down, Right, Left, Left.

GENERATION 1 SKIN: JAZZ

At the Main menu, press Left, Up, Down, Down, Left, Up, Right.

GENERATION 1 SKIN: MEGATRON

At the Main menu, press Down, Left, Left, Down, Right, Right, Up.

GENERATION 1 SKIN: OPTIMUS PRIME

At the Main menu, press Down, Right, Left, Up, Down, Down, Left.

GENERATION 1 SKIN: ROBOVISION OPTIMUS PRIME

At the Main menu, press Down, Down, Up, Up, Right, Right, Right.

GENERATION 1 SKIN: STARSCREAM

At the Main menu, press Right, Down, Left, Left, Down, Up, Up.

WALL-E

The following cheats will disable saving. The five possible characters starting with Wall-E and going down are: Wall-E, Auto, EVE, M-O, GEL-A Steward.

ALL BONUS FEATURES UNLOCKED

Select Cheats from the Bonus Features menu and enter Wall-E, Auto, EVE, GEL-A Steward.

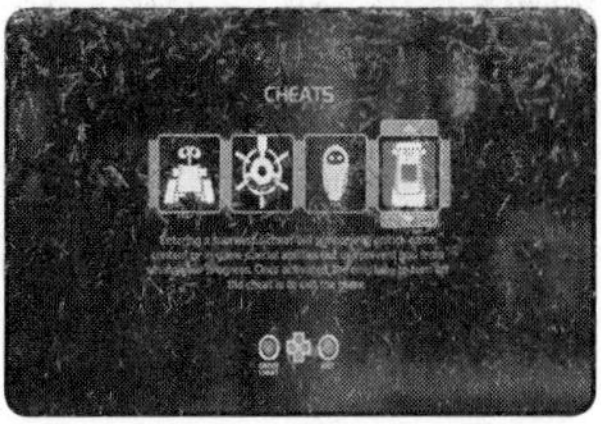

ALL GAME CONTENT UNLOCKED

Select Cheats from the Bonus Features menu and enter M-O, Auto, GEL-A Steward, EVE.

ALL SINGLE-PLAYER LEVELS UNLOCKED

Select Cheats from the Bonus Features menu and enter Auto, GEL-A Steward, M-O, Wall-E.

ALL MULTIPLAYER MAPS UNLOCKED

Select Cheats from the Bonus Features menu and enter EVE, M-O, Wall-E, Auto.

ALL HOLIDAY COSTUMES UNLOCKED

Select Cheats from the Bonus Features menu and enter Auto, Auto, GEL-A Steward, GEL-A Steward.

ALL MULTIPLAYER COSTUMES UNLOCKED

Select Cheats from the Bonus Features menu and enter GEL-A Steward, Wall-E, M-O, Auto.

UNLIMITED HEALTH UNLOCKED

Select Cheats from the Bonus Features menu and enter Wall-E, M-O, Auto, M-O.

WALL-E: MAKE ANY CUBE AT ANY TIME

Select Cheats from the Bonus Features menu and enter Auto, M-O, Auto, M-O.

WALL-EVE: MAKE ANY CUBE AT ANY TIME

Select Cheats from the Bonus Features menu and enter M-O, GEL-A Steward, EVE, EVE.

WALL-E WITH A LASER GUN AT ANY TIME

Select Cheats from the Bonus Features menu and enter Wall-E, EVE, EVE, Wall-E.

WALL-EVE WITH A LASER GUN AT ANY TIME

Select Cheats from the Bonus Features menu and enter GEL-A Steward, EVE, M-O, Wall-E.

WALL-E: PERMANENT SUPER LASER UPGRADE

Select Cheats from the Bonus Features menu and enter Wall-E, Auto, EVE, M-O.

EVE: PERMANENT SUPER LASER UPGRADE

Select Cheats from the Bonus Features menu and enter EVE, Wall-E, Wall-E, Auto.

CREDITS

Select Cheats from the Bonus Features menu and enter Auto, Wall-E, GEL-A Steward, M-O.

WORLD SERIES OF POKER 2008: BATTLE FOR THE BRACELETS

PHILLIP J. HELLMUTH

Enter BEATTHEBRAT as the player name.

WWE SMACKDOWN! VS. RAW 2008

HBK AND HHH'S DX OUTFIT

Select Cheat Codes from the Options and enter DXCostume69K2.

KELLY KELLY'S ALTERNATE OUTFIT

Select Cheat Codes from the Options and enter KellyKG12R.

BRET HART

Complete the March 31, 1996 Hall of Fame challenge by defeating Bret Hart with Shawn Michaels in a One-On-One 30-Minute Iron Man Match on Legend difficulty. Purchase from WWE Shop for $210,000.

MICK FOLEY

Complete the June 28, 1998 Hall of Fame challenge by defeating Mick Foley with The Undertaker in a H*** In a Cell Match on Legend difficulty. Purchase from WWE Shop for $210,000.

MR. MCMAHON

Win or successfully defend a championship (WWE or World Heavyweight) at WrestleMania in WWE 24/7 GM Mode. Purchase from WWE Shop for $110,000.

THE ROCK

Complete the April 1, 2001 Hall of Fame challenge by defeating The Rock with Steve Austin in a Single Match on Legend Difficulty. Purchase from WWE Shop for $210,000.

STEVE AUSTIN

Complete the March 23, 1997 Hall of Fame challenge by defeating Steve Austin with Bret Hart in a Submission Match on Legend Difficulty. Purchase from WWE Shop for $210,000.

TERRY FUNK

Complete the April 13, 1997 Hall of Fame challenge by defeating Tommy Dreamer, Sabu and Sandman with any Superstar in an ECW Extreme Rules 4-Way Match on Legend difficulty. Purchase from WWE Shop for $210,000.

MR. MCMAHON BALD

Must unlock Mr. McMahon as a playable character first. Purchase from WWE Shop for $60,000.

VIRTUA FIGHTER 5

WATCH MODE

Select Exhibition Mode, then at the character select, hold **L1** + **R1** and press ⊗.

NINTENDO Wii™

CONTENTS

NINTENDO Wii™ VIRTUAL CONSOLE GAMES

CONTENTS

AVATAR: THE LAST AIRBENDER

UNLIMITED HEALTH

Select Code Entry from Extras and enter 94677.

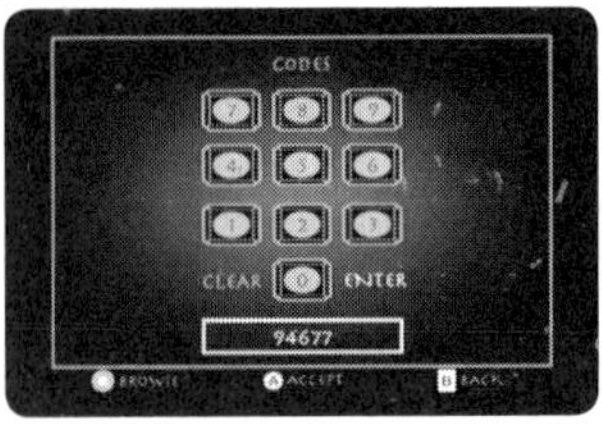

UNLIMITED CHI

Select Code Entry from Extras and enter 24463.

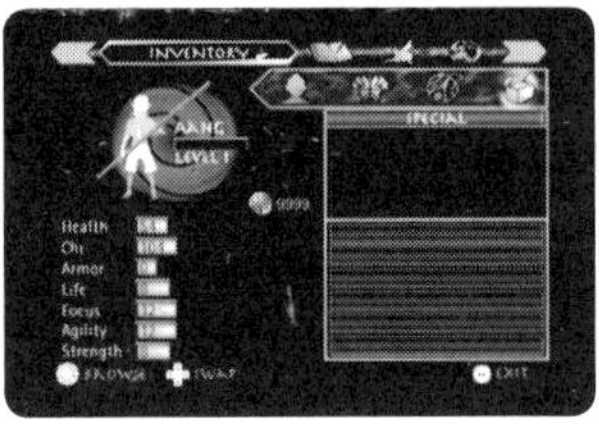

UNLIMITED COPPER

Select Code Entry from Extras and enter 23637.

NEVERENDING STEALTH

Select Code Entry from Extras and enter 53467.

1 HIT DISHONOR

Select Code Entry from Extras and enter 54641.

DOUBLE DAMAGE

Select Code Entry from Extras and enter 34743.

ALL TREASURE MAPS

Select Code Entry from Extras and enter 37437.

THE CHARACTER CONCEPT ART GALLERY

Select Code Entry from Extras and enter 97831.

AVATAR: THE LAST AIRBENDER–THE BURNING EARTH

DOUBLE DAMAGE

Go to the code entry section and enter 90210.

INFINITE LIFE

Go to the code entry section and enter 65049.

INFINITE SPECIAL ATTACKS

Go to the code entry section and enter 66206.

MAX LEVEL

Go to the code entry section and enter 89121.

ONE-HIT DISHONOR

Go to the code entry section and enter 28260.

ALL BONUS GAMES

Go to the code entry section and enter 99801.

ALL GALLERY ITEMS

Go to the code entry section and enter 85061.

BEN 10: PROTECTOR OF EARTH

INVINCIBILITY

Select a game from the Continue option. Go to the Map Selection screen, press Plus and choose Extras. Select Enter Secret Code and enter XLR8, Heatblast, Wildvine, Fourarms.

ALL COMBOS

Select a game from the Continue option. Go to the Map Selection screen, press Plus and choose Extras. Select Enter Secret Code and enter Cannonblot, Heatblast, Fourarms, Heatblast.

ALL LOCATIONS

Select a game from the Continue option. Go to the Map Selection screen, press Plus and choose Extras. Select Enter Secret Code and enter Heatblast, XLR8, XLR8, Cannonblot.

DNA FORCE SKINS

Select a game from the Continue option. Go to the Map Selection screen, press Plus and choose Extras. Select Enter Secret Code and enter Wildvine, Fourarms, Heatblast, Cannonbolt.

DARK HEROES SKINS

Select a game from the Continue option. Go to the Map Selection screen, press Plus and choose Extras. Select Enter Secret Code and enter Cannonbolt, Cannonbolt, Fourarms, Heatblast.

ALL ALIEN FORMS

Select a game from the Continue option. Go to the Map Selection screen, press Plus and choose Extras. Select Enter Secret Code and enter Wildvine, Fourarms, Heatblast, Wildvine.

MASTER CONTROL

Select a game from the Continue option. Go to the Map Selection screen, press Plus and choose Extras. Select Enter Secret Code and enter Cannonbolt, Heatblast, Wildvine, Fourarms.

BLAZING ANGELS: SQUADRONS OF WWII

ALL AIRCRAFT AND CAMPAIGNS

After you have chosen a pilot, hold Minus + Plus and press Left, Right, 1, 2, 2, 1.

GOD MODE

Pause the game, hold Minus and press 1, 2, 1, 2.

WEAPON DAMAGE INCREASED

Pause the game, hold Minus and press 2, 1, 1, 2.

BOOM BLOX

ALL TOYS IN CREATE MODE

At the title screen, press Up, Right, Down, Left to bring up a cheats menu. Enter Tool Pool.

SLOW-MO IN SINGLE PLAYER

At the title screen, press Up, Right, Down, Left to bring up a cheats menu. Enter Blox Time.

CHEERLEADERS BECOME PROFILE CHARACTER

At the title screen, press Up, Right, Down, Left to bring up a cheats menu. Enter My Team.

FLOWER EXPLOSIONS

At the title screen, press Up, Right, Down, Left to bring up a cheats menu. Enter Flower Power.

JINGLE BLOCKS

At the title screen, press Up, Right, Down, Left to bring up a cheats menu. Enter Maestro.

CARS MATER-NATIONAL

ALL ARCADE RACES, MINI-GAMES, AND WORLDS

Select Codes/Cheats from the options and enter PLAYALL.

ALL CARS

Select Codes/Cheats from the options and enter MATTEL07.

ALTERNATE LIGHTNING MCQUEEN COLORS

Select Codes/Cheats from the options and enter NCEDUDZ.

ALL COLORS FOR OTHERS

Select Codes/Cheats from the options and enter PAINTIT.

UNLIMITED TURBO

Select Codes/Cheats from the options and enter ZZOOOOM.

EXTREME ACCELERATION

Select Codes/Cheats from the options and enter OTO200X.

EXPERT MODE

Select Codes/Cheats from the options and enter VRYFAST.

ALL BONUS ART

Select Codes/Cheats from the options and enter BUYTALL.

CODE LYOKO: QUEST FOR INFINITY

UNLOCK EVERYTHING

Pause the game and press 2, 1, C, Z, 2, 1.

UNLIMITED HEALTH AND POWER

Pause the game and press 2, 2, Z, Z, 1, 1.

INCREASE SPEED

Pause the game and press Z, 1, 2, 1 (x3).

INCREASE DAMAGE

Pause the game and press 1, Z, Z, C (x3).

CONFIGURATION A

Pause the game and press 2, Z, 1, Z, C, Z.

CONFIGURATION B

Pause the game and press C, C, 1, C, Z, C.

ALL ABILITIES

Pause the game and press Z, C, Z, C (x3).

ALL BONUSES

Pause the game and press 1, 2, C, 2 (x3).

ALL GOODIES

Pause the game and press C, 2, 2, Z, C, Z.

DE BLOB

INVULNERABILITY

During a game, hold C and press 1, 1, 1, 1.
Re-enter the code to disable.

LIFE UP

During a game, hold C and press 1, 1, 2, 2

TIME BONUS

During a game, hold C and press 1, 2, 1, 2.
This adds 10 minutes to your time.

ALL MOODS

At the main menu, hold C and press B, B, 1, 2, 1, 2, B, B.

ALL MULTIPLAYER LEVELS

At the main menu, hold C and press 2, 2, B, B, 1, 1, B, B.

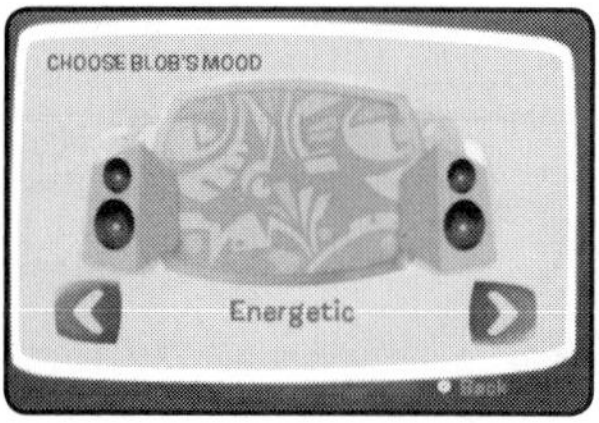

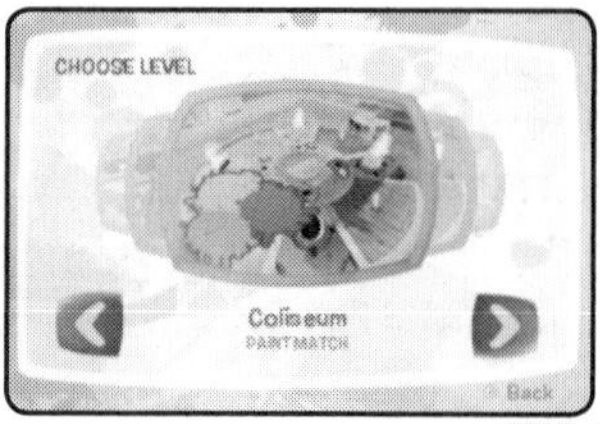

DEFEND YOUR CASTLE

CATAPULTS ONLY

Show the credits and click on IM IN UR CONSOLZ DFENDIN UR CASLEZ when it shows up.

GIANT STICK FIGURE

Show the credits and click on SMB3W4 when it shows up.

TINY UNITS

Show the credits and click on Chuck Norris when it shows up.

DISNEY'S CHICKEN LITTLE: ACE IN ACTION

ALL LEVELS

Select the Cheats option and enter Right, Up, Left, Right, Up.

ALL WEAPONS

Select the Cheats option and enter Right, Down, Right, Left.

UNLIMITED SHIELD

Select the Cheats option and enter Right, Down, Right, Down, Right.

DISNEY PRINCESS: ENCHANTED JOURNEY

BELLE'S KINGDOM

Select Secrets and enter GASTON.

GOLDEN SET

Select Secrets and enter BLUEBIRD.

FLOWER WAND

Select Secrets and enter SLEEPY.

HEART WAND

Select Secrets and enter BASHFUL.

SHELL WAND

Select Secrets and enter RAJAH.

SHIELD WAND

Select Secrets and enter CHIP.

STAR WAND

Select Secrets and enter SNEEZY.

DONKEY KONG COUNTRY 2: DIDDY'S KONG QUEST

SOUND TEST

Highlight Two Player and press Down (x5).

CHEAT MODE

Press Down (x5) again after getting Sound Test to access the cheat mode. Now you can enter the following:

50 LIVES

Press Y, A, Select, A, Down, Left, A, Down.

HARD MODE

Press B, A, Right, Right, A, Left, A, X. This gets rid of the barrels.

DRAGON BALL Z: BUDOKAI TENKAICHI 3

SURVIVAL MODE

Clear 30 missions in Mission 100 mode.

DRAGON BLADE: WRATH OF FIRE

ALL LEVELS

At the title screen, hold Plus + Minus and select New Game or Load game. Hold the buttons until the stage select appears.

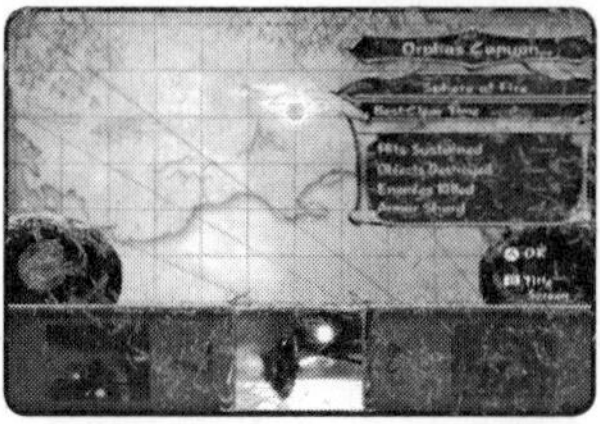

EASY DIFFICULTY

At the title screen, hold Z + 2 when selecting "New Game."

HARD DIFFICLUTY

At the title screen, hold C + 2 when selecting "New Game."

To clear the following codes, hold Z at the stage select.

DRAGON HEAD

At the stage select, hold Z and press Plus. Immediately Swing Wii Remote Right, swing Wii Remote Down, swing Nunchuk Left, swing Nunchuk Right.

DRAGON WINGS

At the stage select, hold Z and press Plus. Immediately Swing Nunchuk Up + Wii Remote Up, swing Nunchuk Down + Wii Remote Down, swing Nunchuk Right + Wii Remote Left, swing Nunchuk Left + Wii Remote Right.

TAIL POWER

At the stage select, hold Z and press Plus. Immediately Swing your Wii Remote Down, Up, Left, and Right.

DOUBLE FIST POWER

At the stage select, hold Z and press Plus. Immediately swing your Nunchuk Right; swing your Wii Remote left; swing your Nunchuk right while swinging your Wii Remote left; swing both the Wii Remote and the Nunchuk down.

GHOST SQUAD

COSTUMES

Reach the following levels in single-player to unlock the corresponding costume.

LEVEL	COSTUME
07	Desert Camouflage
10	Policeman
15	Tough Guy
18	Sky Camouflage
20	World War II
23	Cowboy

LEVEL	COSTUME
30	Urban Camouflage
34	Virtua Cop
38	Future Warrior
50	Ninja
60	Panda Suit
99	Gold Uniform

NINJA MODE

Play through Arcade Mode.

PARADISE MODE

Play through Ninja Mode.

GODZILLA UNLEASHED

UNLOCK ALL

At the main menu, press A + Up to bring up the cheat entry screen. Enter 204935.

90000 STORE POINTS

At the main menu, press A + Up to bring up the cheat entry screen. Enter 031406.

SET DAY

At the main menu, press A + Up to bring up the cheat entry screen. Enter 0829XX, where XX represents the day. Use 00 for day one.

SHOW MONSTER MOVES

At the main menu, press A + Up to bring up the cheat entry screen. Enter 411411.

VERSION NUMBER

At the main menu, press A + Up to bring up the cheat entry screen. Enter 787321.

MOTHERSHIP LEVEL

Playing as the Aliens, destroy the mothership in the Invasion level.

THE GRIM ADVENTURES OF BILLY & MANDY

CONCEPT ART

At the Main menu, hold 1 and press Up, Up, Down, Down, Left, Right, Left, Right.

ICE AGE 2: THE MELTDOWN

INFINITE PEBBLES

Pause the game and press Down, Down, Left, Up, Up, Right, Up, Down.

INFINITE ENERGY

Pause the game and press Down, Left, Right, Down, Down, Right, Left, Down.

INFINITE HEALTH

Pause the game and press Up, Right, Down, Up, Left, Down, Right, Left.

IRON MAN

ARMOR SELECTION

Iron Man's different armor suits are unlocked by completing certain missions. Refer to the following tables for when each is unlocked. After selecting a mission to play, you get the opportunity to pick the armor you wish to use.

COMPLETE MISSION	SUIT UNLOCKED
1: Escape	Mark I
2: First Flight	Mark II
3: Fight Back	Mark III
6: Flying Fortress	Comic Tin Can
9: Home Front	Classic
13: Showdown	Silver Centurion

CONCEPT ART

Concept Art is unlocked after finding certain numbers of Weapon Crates.

CONCEPT ART UNLOCKED	NUMBER OF WEAPON CRATES FOUND
Environments Set 1	6
Environments Set 2	12
Iron Man	18
Environments Set 3	24
Enemies	30
Environments Set 4	36
Villains	42
Vehicles	48
Covers	50

KUNG FU PANDA

INFINITE CHI

Select Cheats from the Extra menu and press Down, Right, Left, Up, Down.

INVINCIBILITY

Select Cheats from the Extra menu and press Down, Down, Right, Up, Left.

4X DAMAGE MULTIPLYER

Select Cheats from the Extra menu and press Up, Down, Up, Right, Left.

ALL MULTIPLAYER CHARACTERS

Select Cheats from the Extra menu and press Left, Down, Left, Right, Down.

DRAGON WARRIOR OUTFIT IN MULTIPLAYER

Select Cheats from the Extra menu and press Left, Down, Right, Left, Up.

LEGO BATMAN

BATCAVE CODES

Using the computer in the Batcave, select Enter Code and enter the following codes.

CHARACTERS

CHARACTER	CODE
Alfred	ZAQ637
Batgirl	JKR331
Bruce Wayne	BDJ327
Catwoman (Classic)	M1AAWW
Clown Goon	HJK327
Commissioner Gordon	DDP967
Fishmonger	HGY748
Freeze Girl	XVK541
Joker Goon	UTF782
Joker Henchman	YUN924
Mad Hatter	JCA283
Man-Bat	NYU942
Military Policeman	MKL382
Nightwing	MVY759
Penguin Goon	NKA238

CHARACTER	CODE
Penguin Henchman	BJH782
Penguin Minion	KJP748
Poison Ivy Goon	GTB899
Police Marksman	HKG984
Police Officer	JRY983
Riddler Goon	CRY928
Riddler Henchman	XEU824
S.W.A.T.	HTF114
Sailor	NAV592
Scientist	JFL786
Security Guard	PLB946
The Joker (Tropical)	CCB199
Yeti	NJL412
Zoo Sweeper	DWR243

VEHICLES

VEHICLE	CODE
Bat-Tank	KNTT4B
Bruce Wayne's Private Jet	LEA664
Catwoman's Motorcycle	HPL826
Garbage Truck	DUS483
Goon Helicopter	GCH328
Harbor Helicopter	CHP735
Harley Quinn's Hammer Truck	RDT637
Mad Hatter's Glider	HS000W
Mad Hatter's Steamboat	M4DM4N
Mr. Freeze's Iceberg	ICYICE
The Joker's Van	JUK657

VEHICLE	CODE
Mr. Freeze's Kart	BCT229
Penguin Goon Submarine	BTN248
Police Bike	LJP234
Police Boat	PLC999
Police Car	KJL832
Police Helicopter	CWR732
Police Van	MAC788
Police Watercraft	VJD328
Riddler's Jet	HAHAHA
Robin's Submarine	TTF453
Two-Face's Armored Truck	EFE933

CHEATS

CHEAT	CODE
Always Score Multiply	9LRGNB
Fast Batarangs	JRBDCB
Fast Walk	ZOLM6N
Flame Batarang	D8NYWH
Freeze Batarang	XPN4NG
Extra Hearts	ML3KHP
Fast Build	EVG26J
Immune to Freeze	JXUDY6
Invincibility	WYD5CP
Minikit Detector	ZXGH9J

CHEAT	CODE
More Batarang Targets	XWP645
Piece Detector	KHJ554
Power Brick Detector	MMN786
Regenerate Hearts	HJH7HJ
Score x2	N4NR3E
Score x4	CX9MAT
Score x6	MLVNF2
Score x8	WCCDB9
Score x10	18HW07

LEGO INDIANA JONES: THE ORIGINAL ADVENTURES

CHARACTERS

Approach the blackboard in the Classsroom and enter the following codes.

CHARACTER	CODE
Bandit	12N68W
Bandit Swordsman	1MK4RT
Barranca	04EM94
Bazooka Trooper (Crusade)	MK83R7
Bazooka Trooper (Raiders)	S93Y5R
Belloq	CHN3YU
Belloq (Jungle)	TDR197
Belloq (Robes)	VEO29L
British Commander	B73EUA
British Officer	VJ5TI9
British Soldier	DJ5I2W
Captain Katanga	VJ3TT3
Chatter Lal	ENW936
Chatter Lal (Thuggee)	CNH4RY
Chen	3NK48T
Colonel Dietrich	2K9RKS
Colonel Vogel	8EAL4H
Dancing Girl	C7EJ21
Donovan	3NFTU8

CHARACTER	CODE
Elsa (Desert)	JSNRT9
Elsa (Officer)	VMJ5US
Enemy Boxer	8246RB
Enemy Butler	VJ48W3
Enemy Guard	VJ7R51
Enemy Guard (Mountains)	YR47WM
Enemy Officer	572E61
Enemy Officer (Desert	2MK450
Enemy Pilot	B84ELP
Enemy Radio Operator	1MF94R
Enemy Soldier (Desert)	4NSU7Q
Fedora	V75YSP
First Mate	0GIN24
Grail Knight	NE6THI
Hovitos Tribesman	HOV1SS
Indiana Jones (Desert Disguise)	4J8S4M
Indiana Jones (Officer)	VJ850S
Jungle Guide	24PF34
Kao Kan	WM046L

CHARACTER	CODE
Kazim	NRH23J
Kazim (Desert)	3M29TJ
Lao Che	2NK479
Maharajah	NFK5N2
Major Toht	13NS01
Masked Bandit	N48SF0
Mola Ram	FJUR31
Monkey Man	3RF6YJ
Pankot Assassin	2NKT72
Pankot Guard	VN28RH
Sherpa Brawler	VJ37WJ

CHARACTER	CODE
Sherpa Gunner	ND762W
Slave Child	0E3ENW
Thuggee	VM683E
Thuggee Acolyte	T2R3F9
Thuggee Slave Driver	VBS7GW
Village Dignitary	KD48TN
Village Elder	4682E1
Willie (Dinner Suit)	VK93R7
Willie (Pajamas)	MEN4IP
Wu Han	3NSLT8

EXTRAS

Approach the blackboard in the Classsroom and enter the following codes. Some cheats need to be enabled by selecting Extras from the pause menu.

CHEAT	CODE
Artifact Detector	VIKED7
Beep Beep	VNF59Q
Character Treasure	VIES2R
Disarm Enemies	VKRNS9
Disguises	4ID1N6
Fast Build	V83SL0
Fast Dig	378RS6
Fast Fix	FJ59WS
Fertilizer	B1GW1F
Ice Rink	33GM7J
Parcel Detector	VUT673
Poo Treasure	WWQ1SA

CHEAT	CODE
Regenerate Hearts	MDLP69
Secret Characters	3X44AA
Silhouettes	3HE85H
Super Scream	VN3R7S
Super Slap	0P1TA5
Treasure Magnet	H86LA2
Treasure x10	VI3PS8
Treasure x2	VM4TS9
Treasure x4	VLWEN3
Treasure x6	V84RYS
Treasure x8	A72E1M

LEGO STAR WARS: THE COMPLETE SAGA

The following still need to be purchase after entering the codes.

CHARACTERS

ADMIRAL ACKBAR

At the bar in Mos Eisley Cantina, select Enter Code and enter ACK646.

BATTLE DROID (COMMANDER)

At the bar in Mos Eisley Cantina, select Enter Code and enter KPF958.

BOBA FETT (BOY)

At the bar in Mos Eisley Cantina, select Enter Code and enter GGF539.

BOSS NASS

At the bar in Mos Eisley Cantina, select Enter Code and enter HHY697.

CAPTAIN TARPALS

At the bar in Mos Eisley Cantina, select Enter Code and enter QRN714.

COUNT DOOKU

At the bar in Mos Eisley Cantina, select Enter Code and enter DDD748.

DARTH MAUL

At the bar in Mos Eisley Cantina, select Enter Code and enter EUK421.

EWOK

At the bar in Mos Eisley Cantina, select Enter Code and enter EWK785.

GENERAL GRIEVOUS

At the bar in Mos Eisley Cantina, select Enter Code and enter PMN576.

GREEDO

At the bar in Mos Eisley Cantina, select Enter Code and enter ZZR636.

IG-88

At the bar in Mos Eisley Cantina, select Enter Code and enter GIJ989.

IMPERIAL GUARD

At the bar in Mos Eisley Cantina, select Enter Code and enter GUA850.

JANGO FETT

At the bar in Mos Eisley Cantina, select Enter Code and enter KLJ897.

KI-ADI MUNDI

At the bar in Mos Eisley Cantina, select Enter Code and enter MUN486.

LUMINARA

At the bar in Mos Eisley Cantina, select Enter Code and enter LUM521.

PADMÉ

At the bar in Mos Eisley Cantina, select Enter Code and enter VBJ322.

R2-Q5

At the bar in Mos Eisley Cantina, select Enter Code and enter EVILR2.

STORMTROOPER

At the bar in Mos Eisley Cantina, select Enter Code and enter NBN431.

TAUN WE

At the bar in Mos Eisley Cantina, select Enter Code and enter PRX482.

VULTURE DROID

At the bar in Mos Eisley Cantina, select Enter Code and enter BDC866.

WATTO

At the bar in Mos Eisley Cantina, select Enter Code and enter PLL967.

ZAM WESELL

At the bar in Mos Eisley Cantina, select Enter Code and enter 584HJF.

SKILLS

DISGUISE

At the bar in Mos Eisley Cantina, select Enter Code and enter BRJ437.

FORCE GRAPPLE LEAP

At the bar in Mos Eisley Cantina, select Enter Code and enter CLZ738.

VEHICLES

DROID TRIFIGHTER

At the bar in Mos Eisley Cantina, select Enter Code and enter AAB123.

IMPERIAL SHUTTLE

At the bar in Mos Eisley Cantina, select Enter Code and enter HUT845.

TIE INTERCEPTOR

At the bar in Mos Eisley Cantina, select Enter Code and enter INT729.

TIE FIGHTER

At the bar in Mos Eisley Cantina, select Enter Code and enter DBH897.

ZAM'S AIRSPEEDER

At the bar in Mos Eisley Cantina, select Enter Code and enter UUU875.

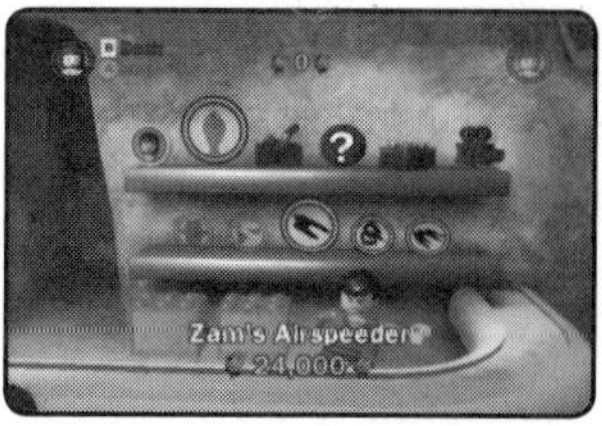

MADDEN NFL 07

MADDEN CARDS

Select Madden Cards from My Madden. Then select Madden Codes and enter the following:

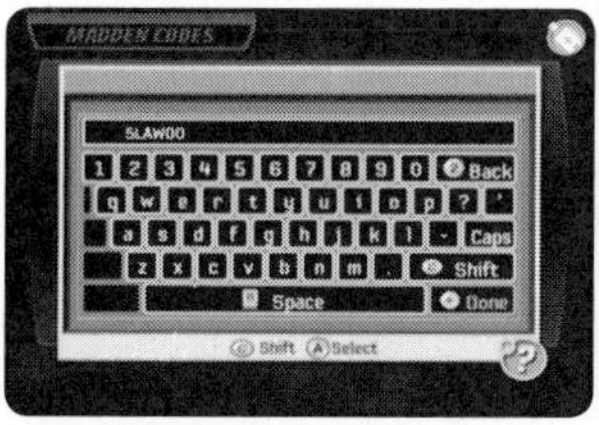

CARD	PASSWORD
#199 Gold Lame Duck Cheat	5LAWOO
#200 Gold Mistake Free Cheat	XL7SP1
#210 Gold QB on Target Cheat	WROAOR
#220 Super Bowl XLI Gold	RLA9R7
#221 Super Bowl XLII Gold	WRLUF8
#222 Super Bowl XLIII Gold	NIEV4A
#223 Super Bowl XLIV Gold	M5AB7L
#224 Aloha Stadium Gold	YI8P8U
#225 1958 Colts Gold	B57QLU
#226 1966 Packers Gold	1PL1FL
#227 1968 Jets Gold	MIE6WO
#228 1970 Browns Gold	CL2TOE

CARD	PASSWORD
#229 1972 Dolphins Gold	NOEB7U
#230 1974 Steelers Gold	YOOFLA
#231 1976 Raiders Gold	MOA11I
#232 1977 Broncos Gold	C8UM7U
#233 1978 Dolphins Gold	VIU007
#234 1980 Raiders Gold	NLAPH3
#235 1981 Chargers Gold	COAGI4
#236 1982 Redskins Gold	WL8BRI
#237 1983 Raiders Gold	H0EW71
#238 1984 Dolphins Gold	M1AM1E
#239 1985 Bears Gold	QOET08
#240 1986 Giants Gold	ZI8S2L

CARD	PASSWORD
#241 1988 49ers Gold	SP2A8H
#242 1990 Eagles Gold	2L4TRO
#243 1991 Lions Gold	J1ETRI
#244 1992 Cowboys Gold	W9UVI9
#245 1993 Bills Gold	DLA3I7
#246 1994 49ers Gold	DR7EST
#247 1996 Packers Gold	F8LUST
#248 1998 Broncos Gold	FIES95
#249 1999 Rams Gold	S9OUSW
#250 Bears Pump Up the Crowd	B1OUPH
#251 Bengals Cheerleader	DRL2SW
#252 Bills Cheerleader	1PLUYO
#253 Broncos Cheerleader	3ROUJO
#254 Browns Pump Up the Crowd	T1UTOA
#255 Buccaneers Cheerleader	S9EWRI
#256 Cardinals Cheerleader	57IEPI

CARD	PASSWORD
#257 Chargers Cheerleader	F7UHL8
#258 Chiefs Cheerleader	PRI5SL
#259 Colts Cheerleader	1R5AMI
#260 Cowboys Cheerleader	Z2ACHL
#261 Dolphins Cheerleader	C5AHLE
#262 Eagles Cheerleader	PO7DRO
#263 Falcons Cheerleader	37USPO
#264 49ers Cheerleader	KLOCRL
#265 Giants Pump Up the Crowd	C4USPI
#266 Jaguars Cheerleader	MIEH7E
#267 Jets Pump Up the Crowd	COLUXI
#268 Lions Pump Up the Crowd	3LABLU
#269 Packers Pump Up the Crowd	4HO7VO
#270 Panthers Cheerleader	F2IASP
#282 All AFC Team Gold	PRO9PH
#283 All NFC Team Gold	RLATH7

MARIO & SONIC AT THE OLYMPIC GAMES

UNLOCK 4X100M RELAY EVENT

Medal in Mercury, Venus, Jupiter, and Saturn.

UNLOCK SINGLE SCULLS EVENT

Medal in Mercury, Venus, Jupiter, and Saturn.

UNLOCK DREAM RACE EVENT

Medal in Mercury, Venus, Jupiter, and Saturn.

UNLOCK ARCHERY EVENT

Medal in Moonlight Circuit.

UNLOCK HIGH JUMP EVENT

Medal in Stardust Circuit.

UNLOCK 400M EVENT

Medal in Planet Circuit.

UNLOCK DREAM FENCING EVENT

Medal in Comet Circuit.

UNLOCK DREAM TABLE TENNIS EVENT

Medal in Satellite Circuit.

UNLOCK 400M HURDLES EVENT

Medal in Sunlight Circuit.

UNLOCK POLE VAULT EVENT

Medal in Meteorite Circuit.

UNLOCK VAULT EVENT

Medal in Meteorite Circuit.

UNLOCK DREAM PLATFORM EVENT

Medal in Cosmos Circuit.

CROWNS

Get all gold medals in all events with a character to unlock their crown.

MARIO KART WII

CHARACTERS

CHARACTER	HOW TO UNLOCK
Baby Daisy	Earn 1 Star in 50cc for Mushroom, Flower, Star, and Special Cups
Baby Luigi	Unlock 8 Expert Staff Ghost Data in Time Trials
Birdo	Race 16 different courses in Time Trials or win 250 versus races
Bowser Jr.	Earn 1 Star in 100cc for Shell, Banana, Leaf, and Lightning Cups
Daisy	Win 150cc Special Cup
Diddy Kong	Win 50cc Lightning Cup
Dry Bones	Win 100cc Leaf Cup

CHARACTER	HOW TO UNLOCK
Dry Bowser	Earn 1 Star in 150cc for Mushroom, Flower, Star, and Special Cups
Funky Kong	Unlock 4 Expert Staff Ghost Data in Time Trials
King Boo	Win 50cc Star Cup
Mii Outfit A	Win 100cc Special Cup
Mii Outfit B	Unlock all 32 Expert Staff Ghost Data in Time Trials
Mii Outfit C	Get 15,000 points in Versus Mode
Rosalina	Have a Super Mario Galaxy save file and she is unlocked after 50 races or earn 1 Star in all Mirror Cups
Toadette	Race 32 different courses in Time Trials

KARTS

KART	HOW TO UNLOCK
Blue Falcon	Win Mirror Lightning Cup
Cheep Charger	Earn 1 Star in 50cc for Mushroom, Flower, Star, and Special Cups
Rally Romper	Unlock an Expert Staff Ghost Data in Time Trials
B Dasher Mk. 2	Unlock 24 Expert Staff Ghost Data in Time Trials
Royal Racer	Win 150cc Leaf Cup
Turbo Blooper	Win 50cc Leaf Cup
Aero Glider	Earn 1 Star in 150cc for Mushroom, Flower, Star, and Special Cups
Dragonetti	Win 150cc Lightning Cup
Piranha Prowler	Win 50cc Special Cup

BIKES

KART	HOW TO UNLOCK
Bubble Bike	Win Mirror Leaf Cup
Magikruiser	Race 8 different courses in Time Trials
Quacker	Win 150cc Star Cup
Dolphin Dasher	Win Mirror Star Cup
Nitrocycle	Earn 1 Star in 100cc for all cups
Rapide	Win 100cc Lightning Cup
Phantom	Win Mirror Special Cup
Torpedo	Unlock 12 Expert Staff Ghost Data in Time Trials
Twinkle Star	Win 100cc Star Cup

MARVEL ULTIMATE ALLIANCE

UNLOCK ALL SKINS

At the Team menu, press Up, Down, Left, Right, Left, Right, Plus.

UNLOCKS ALL HERO POWERS

At the Team menu, press Left, Right, Up, Down, Up, Down, Plus.

ALL HEROES TO LEVEL 99

At the Team menu, press Up, Left, Up, Left, Down, Right, Down, Right, Plus.

UNLOCK ALL HEROES

At the Team menu, press Up, Up, Down, Down, Left, Left, Left, Plus.

UNLOCK DAREDEVIL

At the Team menu, press Left, Left, Right, Right, Up, Down, Up, Down, Plus.

UNLOCK SILVER SURFER

At the Team menu, press Down, Left, Left, Up, Right, Up, Down, Left, Plus.

GOD MODE

During gameplay, press Up, Down, Up, Down, Up, Left, Down, Right, Plus.

TOUCH OF DEATH

During gameplay, press Left, Right, Down, Down, Right, Left, Plus.

SUPER SPEED

During gameplay, press Up, Left, Up, Right, Down, Right, Plus.

FILL MOMENTUM

During gameplay, press Left, Right, Right, Left, Up, Down, Down, Up, Plus.

UNLOCK ALL COMICS

At the Review menu, press Left, Right, Right, Left, Up, Up, Right, Plus.

UNLOCK ALL CONCEPT ART

At the Review menu, press Down, Down, Down, Right, Right, Left, Down, Plus.

UNLOCK ALL CINEMATICS

At the Review menu, press Up, Left, Left, Up, Right, Right, Up, Plus.

UNLOCK ALL LOAD SCREENS

At the Review menu, press Up, Down, Right, Left, Up, Up Down, Plus.

UNLOCK ALL COURSES

At the Comic Missions menu, press Up, Right, Left, Down, Up, Right, Left, Down, Plus.

MLB POWER PROS

EXTRA FORMS

At the main menu, press Right, Left, Up, Down, Down, Right, Right, Up, Up, Left, Down, Left.

VIEW MLB PLAYERS AT CUSTOM PLAYER MENU

Select View or Delete Custom Players/Password Display from My Data and press Up, Up, Down, Down, Left, Right, Left, Right, 1, 2.

MONSTER JAM

TRUCKS

As you collect monster points, they are tallied toward your Championship Score. Trucks are unlocked when you reach certain point totals.

TRUCK	POINTS
Destroyer	10,000
Blacksmith	50,000
El Toro Loco	70,000
Suzuki	110,000
Maximum Destruction	235,000

MYSIMS

PASSWORD SCREEN

Press the Minus button to bring up the pause screen. Then enter the following with the Wii Remote: 2, 1, Down, Up, Down, Up, Left, Left, Right, Right. Now you can enter the following passwords:

OUTFITS

Camouflage pants	N10ng5g
Diamond vest	Tglg0ca
Genie outfit	Gvsb3k1
Kimono dress	I3hkdvs
White jacket	R705aan

FURNITURE

Bunk bed	F3nevr0
Hourglass couch	Ghtymba
Modern couch	T7srhca
Racecar bed	Ahvmrva
Rickshaw bed	Itha7da

MYSIMS KINGDOM

DETECTIVE OUTFIT

Pause the game and press Left, Right, Left, Right, Left, Right.

TATTOO VEST OUTFIT

Pause the game and press C, Z, C, Z, B, A, B, A.

NBA LIVE 08

AGENT ZERO SHOES

At the extras menu, enter ADGILLIT6BE as a code.

CUBA SHOES

At the extras menu, enter ADGILLIT4BC as a code.

CUSTOMIZE SHOES

At the extras menu, enter ADGILLIT5BD as a code.

DUNCAN ALL STAR SHOES

At the extras menu, enter FE454DFJCC as a code.

GIL WOOD SHOES

At the extras menu, enter ADGILLIT1B9 as a code.

GIL ZERO ALL STAR SHOES

At the extras menu, enter 23DN1PPOG4 as a code.

TS LIGHTSWITCH AWAY SHOES

At the extras menu, enter ADGILLIT0B8 as a code.

TS LIGHTSWITCH HOME SHOES

At the extras menu, enter ADGILLIT2BA as a code.

NEED FOR SPEED CARBON

CASTROL CASH

At the Main menu, press Down, Up, Left, Down, Right, Up, Button 1, B. This gives you 10,000 extra cash.

INFINITE CREW CHARGE

At the Main menu, press Down, Up, Up, Right, Left, Left, Right, Button 1.

INFINITE NITROUS

At the Main menu, press Left, Up, Left, Down, Left, Down, Right, Button 1.

INFINITE SPEEDBREAKER

At the Main menu, press Down, Right, Right, Left, Right, Up, Down, Button 1.

NEED FOR SPEED CARBON LOGO VINYLS

At the Main menu, press Right, Up, Down, Up, Down, Left, Right, Button 1.

NEED FOR SPEED CARBON SPECIAL LOGO VINYLS

At the Main menu, press Up, Up, Down, Down, Down, Down, Up, Button 1.

NEED FOR SPEED PROSTREET

$2,000

Select Career and then choose Code Entry. Enter 1MA9X99.

$4,000

Select Career and then choose Code Entry. Enter W2IOLL01.

$8,000

Select Career and then choose Code Entry. Enter L1IS97A1.

$10,000

Select Career and then choose Code Entry. Enter 1MI9K7E1.

$10,000

Select Career and then choose Code Entry. Enter CASHMONEY.

$10,000

Select Career and then choose Code Entry. Enter REGGAME.

AUDI TT

Select Career and then choose Code Entry. Enter ITSABOUTYOU.

CHEVELLE SS

Select Career and then choose Code Entry. Enter HORSEPOWER.

COKE ZERO GOLF GTI

Select Career and then choose Code Entry. Enter COKEZERO.

DODGE VIPER

Select Career and then choose Code Entry. Enter WORLDSLONGESTLASTING.

MITSUBISHI LANCER EVOLUTION

Select Career and then choose Code Entry. Enter MITSUBISHIGOFAR.

UNLOCK ALL BONUSES

Select Career and then choose Code Entry. Enter UNLOCKALLTHINGS.

5 REPAIR MARKERS

Select Career and then choose Code Entry. Enter SAFETYNET.

ENERGIZER VINYL

Select Career and then choose Code Entry. Enter ENERGIZERLITHIUM.

CASTROL SYNTEC VINYL

Select Career and then choose Code Entry. Enter CASTROLSYNTEC. This also gives you $10,000.

NICKTOONS: ATTACK OF THE TOYBOTS

DAMAGE BOOST

Select Cheats from the Extras menu. Choose Enter Cheat Code and enter 456645.

INVULNERABILITY

Select Cheats from the Extras menu. Choose Enter Cheat Code and enter 313456.

UNLOCK EXO-HUGGLES 9000

Select Cheats from the Extras menu. Choose Enter Cheat Code and enter 691427.

UNLOCK MR. HUGGLES

Select Cheats from the Extras menu. Choose Enter Cheat Code and enter 654168.

UNLIMITED LOBBER GOO

Select Cheats from the Extras menu. Choose Enter Cheat Code and enter 118147.

UNLIMITED SCATTER GOO

Select Cheats from the Extras menu. Choose Enter Cheat Code and enter 971238.

UNLIMITED SPLITTER GOO

Select Cheats from the Extras menu. Choose Enter Cheat Code and enter 854511.

PRINCE OF PERSIA RIVAL SWORDS

BABY TOY WEAPON

Pause the game and enter the following code. Use the D-pad for the directions.
Left, Left, Right, Right, Z, Nunchuck down, Nunchuck down, Z, Up, Down

CHAINSAW

Pause the game and enter the following code. Use the D-pad for the directions.
Up, Up, Down, Down, Left, Right, Left, Right, Z, Nunchuck down, Z, Nunchuck down

SWORDFISH

Pause the game and enter the following code. Use the D-pad for the directions.
Up, Down, Up, Down, Left, Right, Left, Right, Z, Nunchuck down, Z, Nunchuck down

TELEPHONE SWORD

Pause the game and enter the following code. Use the D-pad for the directions.
Right, Left, Right, Left, Down, Down, Up, Up, Z, Nunchuck Down, Z, Z, Nunchuck Down, Nunchuck Down

RATATOUILLE

Select Gusteau's Shop from the Extras menu. Choose Secrets, select the appropriate code number, and then enter the code. Once the code is entered, select the cheat you want to activate it.

CODE NO.	CODE	EFFECT
1	Pieceocake	Very Easy difficulty mode
2	Myhero	No impact and no damage from enemies
3	Shielded	No damage from enemies
4	Spyagent	Move undetected by any enemy
5	Ilikeonions	Fart every time Remy jumps
6	Hardfeelings	Head butt when attacking instead of tailswipe
7	Slumberparty	Multiplayer mode
8	Gusteauart	All concept art
9	Gusteauship	All four championship modes
10	Mattelme	All single-player and multiplayer minigames
11	Gusteauvid	All videos
12	Gusteaures	All bonus artworks
13	Gusteaudream	All dream worlds in Gusteau's shop
14	Gusteauslide	All slides in Gusteau's shop
15	Gusteaulevel	All single-player minigames
16	Gusteaucombo	All items in Gusteau's shop
17	Gusteaupot	5,000 Gusteau points
18	Gusteaujack	10,000 Gusteau points
19	Gusteauomni	50,000 Gusteau points

RAYMAN RAVING RABBIDS 2

FUNKYTOWN

Play each game at least once.

RABBID COSTUMES

Costumes are unlocked as you score 12,000 points in certain games and when you shoot the correct rabbid in the shooting games.

COSTUME	MINIGAME	HOW TO UNLOCK
Cossack	Chess	Earn 12,000 points
Crash Test Dummy	Shopping Cart Downhill	Earn 12,000 points
Cupid	Burgerinnii	Earn 12,000 points
Doctor	Anesthetics	Earn 12,000 points
Fireman	Paris, Pour Troujours	Shoot fireman rabbid
French Maid	Little Chemist	Earn 12,000 points
Fruit-Hat Dancer	Year of the Rabbids	Shoot rabbid wearing fruit hat
Gingerbread	Hot Cake	Earn 12,000 points
HAZE Armor	Big City Fights	Shoot rabbid with armor
Indiana Jones	Rolling Stone	Earn 12,000 points
Jet Trooper	Greatest Hits	Earn 12,000 points
Ken	RRR Xtreme Beach Volleyball	Earn 12,000 points
Martian	Bumper Cars	Earn 12,000 points
Party Girl	Paris, Mon Amour	Once inside boat, shoot girl rabbid
Raider's	American Football	Earn 12,000 points
Sam Fisher	Rabbid School	Earn 12,000 points
Samurai	The Office	Earn 12,000 points

COSTUME	MINIGAME	HOW TO UNLOCK
Space	Year of the Rabbids	Earn 12,000 points
Spider-	Spider Rabbid	Play the "Spider Rabbid" Game
TMNT, Leonardo	Usual Rabbids	Earn 12,000 points
Transformer	Plumber Rabbids	Earn 12,000 points
Vegas Showgirl	Burp	Earn 12,000 points
Voodoo	Voodoo Rabbids	Earn 12,000 points
Wrestler	Greatest Hits	Shoot rabbid in green outfit

SHREK THE THIRD

10,000 GOLD COINS

At the gift shop, press Up, Up, Down, Up, Right, Left.

SIMCITY CREATOR

EGYPTIAN BUILDING SET

Name your city Mummy's desert.

GREEK BUILDING SET

Name your city Ancient culture.

JUNGLE BUILDING SET

Name your city Become wild.

SCI-FI BUILDING SET

Name your city Future picture.

THE SIMS 2: CASTAWAY

CHEAT GNOME

During a game, press B, Z, Up, Down, B. You can now use this Gnome to get the following:

MAX ALL MOTIVES

During a game, press Minus, Plus, Z, Z, A.

MAX CURRENT INVENTORY

During a game, press Left, Right, Left, Right, A.

MAX RELATIONSHIPS

During a game, press Z, Plus, A, B, 2.

ALL RESOURCES

During a game, press A, A, Down, Down, A.

ALL CRAFTING PLANS

During a game, press Plus, Plus, Minus, Minus, Z.

ADD 1 TO SKILL

During a game, press 2, Up, Right, Z, Right.

THE SIMPSONS GAME

UNLIMITED POWER FOR ALL CHARACTERS

At the Extras menu, press Plus, Left, Right, Plus, Minus, Z.

ALL MOVIES

At the Extras menu, press Minus, Left, Minus, Right, Plus, C.

ALL CLICHÉS

At the Extras menu, press Left, Minus, Right, Plus, Right, Z.

SPACE HARRIER

CONTINUE AFTER GAME OVER

At the Game Over screen, press Up, Up, Down, Down, Left, Right, Left, Right, Down, Up, Down, Up.

SPEED RACER

INVULNERABILITY

Select Enter Code from the Options menu and enter A, B, A, Up, Left, Down, Right.

UNLIMITED BOOST

Select Enter Code from the Options menu and enter B, A, Down, Up, B, A, Down.

LAST 3 CARS

Select Enter Code from the Options menu and enter 1, 2, 1, 2, B, A, Plus.

GRANITE CAR

Select Enter Code from the Options menu and enter B, Up, Minus, Plus, 1, Up, Plus.

MONSTER TRUCK

Select Enter Code from the Options menu and enter B, Up, Minus, 2, B, Up, Minus.

AGGRESSIVE OPPONENTS

Select Enter Code from the Options menu and enter Up, Left, Down, Right, Up, Left, Down.

PACIFIST OPPONENTS

Select Enter Code from the Options menu and enter Up, Right, Down, Left, Up, Right, Down.

TINY OPPONENTS

Select Enter Code from the Options menu and enter B, A, Left, Down, Minus, Up, Minus.

HELIUM

Select Enter Code from the Options menu and enter Minus, Up, Minus, 2, Minus, Up, Minus.

MOON GRAVITY

Select Enter Code from the Options menu and enter Up, Plus, Up, Right, Minus, Up, Minus.

OVERKILL

Select Enter Code from the Options menu and enter A, Minus, Plus, Down, Up, Plus, 1.

PSYCHEDELIC

Select Enter Code from the Options menu and enter Left, A, Right, Down, B, Up, Minus.

SPIDER-MAN: FRIEND OR FOE

NEW GREEN GOBLIN AS A SIDEKICK

While standing in the Helicarrier between levels, press Left, Down, Right, Right, Down, Left.

SANDMAN AS A SIDEKICK

While standing in the Helicarrier between levels, press Right, Right, Right, Up, Down, Left.

VENOM AS A SIDEKICK

While standing in the Helicarrier between levels, press Left, Left, Right, Up, Down, Down.

5000 TECH TOKENS

While standing in the Helicarrier between levels, press Up, Up, Down, Down, Left, Right.

SPONGEBOB SQUAREPANTS FEATURING NICKTOONS: GLOBS OF DOOM

When entering the following codes, the order of the characters going down is: SpongeBob SquarePants, Nicolai Technus, Danny Phantom, Dib, Zim, Tlaloc, Tak, Beautiful Gorgeous, Jimmy Neutron, Plankton. These names are shortened to the first name in the following.

ATTRACT COINS

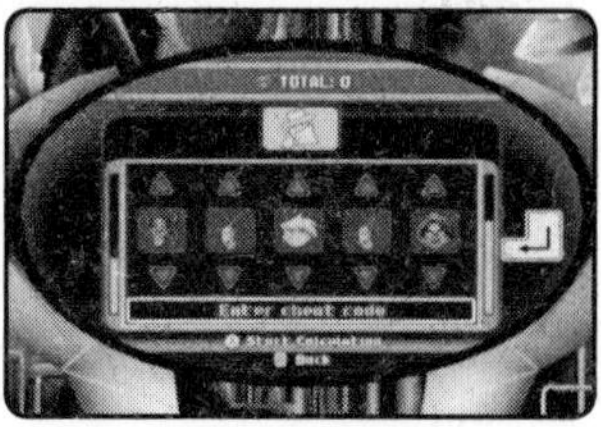

Using the Upgrade Machine on the bottom level of the lair, select "Input cheat codes here". Enter Tlaloc, Plankton, Danny, Plankton, Tak. Coins are attracted to you making them much easier to collect.

DON'T LOSE COINS

Using the Upgrade Machine on the bottom level of the lair, select "Input cheat codes here". Enter Plankton, Jimmy, Beautiful, Jimmy, Plankton. You don't lose coins when you get knocked out.

GOO HAS NO EFFECT

Using the Upgrade Machine on the bottom level of the lair, select "Input cheat codes here". Enter Danny, Danny, Danny, Nicolai, Nicolai. Goo does not slow you down.

MORE GADGET COMBO TIME

Using the Upgrade Machine on the bottom level of the lair, select "Input cheat codes here". Enter SpongeBob, Beautiful, Danny, Plankton, Nicolai. You have more time to perform gadget combos.

PATRICK TUX IN STARFISHMAN TO THE RESCUE

Select Cheat Codes from the Extras menu and enter PATRICK. Select Activate Bonus Items to enable this bonus item.

SPONGEBOB PLANKTON IN SUPER-SIZED PATTY

Select Cheat Codes from the Extras menu and enter PANTS. Select Activate Bonus Items to enable this bonus item.

PATRICK LASER COLOR IN ROCKET RODEO

Select Cheat Codes from the Extras menu and enter ROCKET. Select Activate Bonus Items to enable this bonus item.

PATRICK ROCKET SKIN COLOR IN ROCKET RODEO

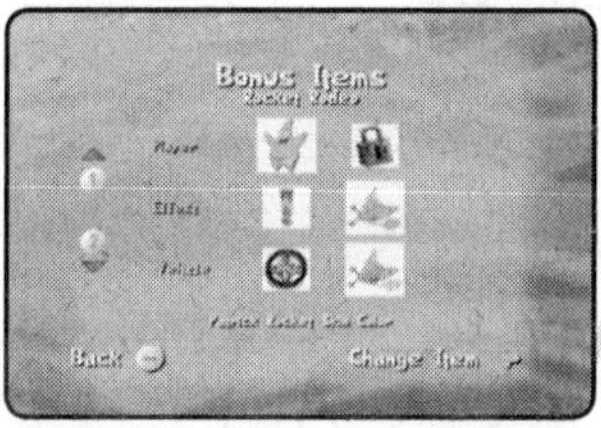

Select Cheat Codes from the Extras menu and enter SPACE. Select Activate Bonus Items to enable this bonus item.

PLANKTON ASTRONAUT SUIT IN REVENGE OF THE GIANT PLANKTON MONSTER

Select Cheat Codes from the Extras menu and enter ROBOT. Select Activate Bonus Items to enable this bonus item.

PLANKTON EYE LASER COLOR IN REVENGE OF THE GIANT PLANKTON MONSTER

Select Cheat Codes from the Extras menu and enter LASER. Select Activate Bonus Items to enable this bonus item.

PIRATE PATRICK IN ROOFTOP RUMBLE

Select Cheat Codes from the Extras menu and enter PIRATE. Select Activate Bonus Items to enable this bonus item.

HOVERCRAFT VEHICLE SKIN IN HYPNOTIC HIGHWAY—PLANKTON

Select Cheat Codes from the Extras menu and enter HOVER. Select Activate Bonus Items to enable this bonus item.

SSX BLUR

ALL CHARACTERS

Select Cheats from the Options menu and enter NoHolds.

ENTIRE MOUNTAIN UNLOCKED

Select Cheats from the Options menu and enter MasterKey.

ALL OUTFITS

Select Cheats from the Options menu and enter ClothShop.

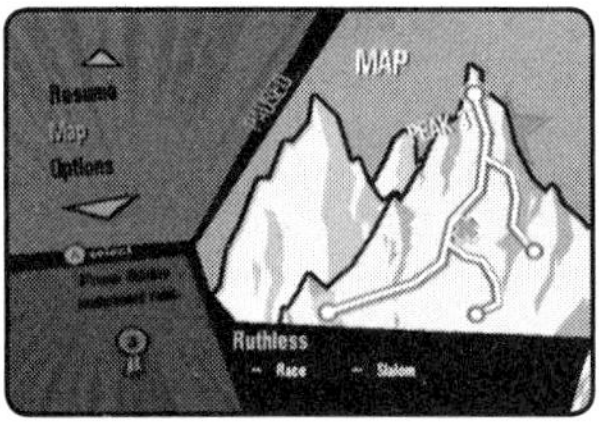

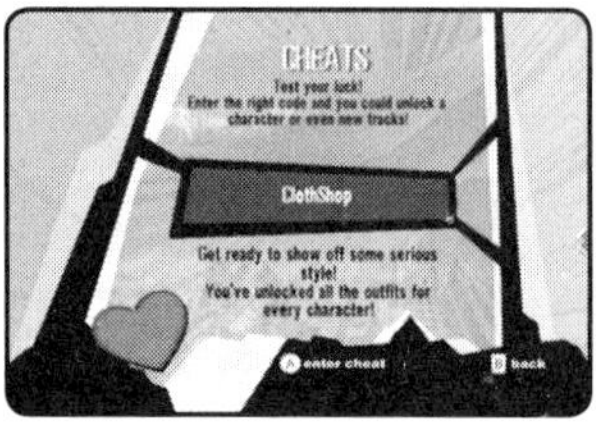

YETI OUTFIT

Select Cheats from the Options menu and enter WildFur.

ALL CHAMPIONSHIP LOCATIONS

Select Cheat Codes from the Extras menu and enter FREEVISIT.

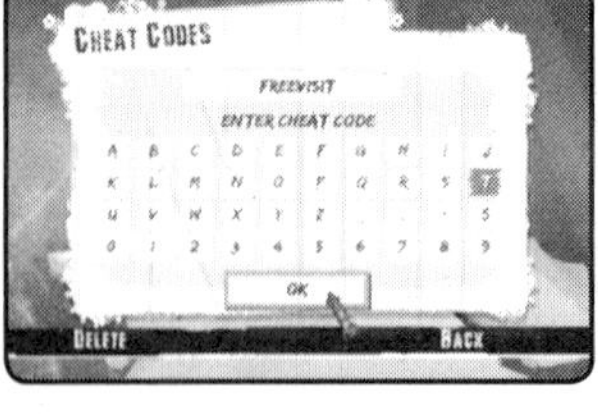

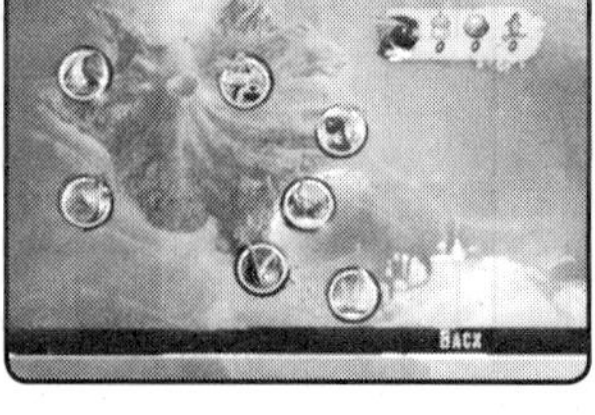

ALL LEAF SLIDE STAGES

Select Cheat Codes from the Extras menu and enter GOINGDOWN.

ALL MULTIPLAYER LEVELS

Select Cheat Codes from the Extras menu and enter MULTIPASS.

ALL BOARDS

Select Cheat Codes from the Extras menu and enter MYPRECIOUS.

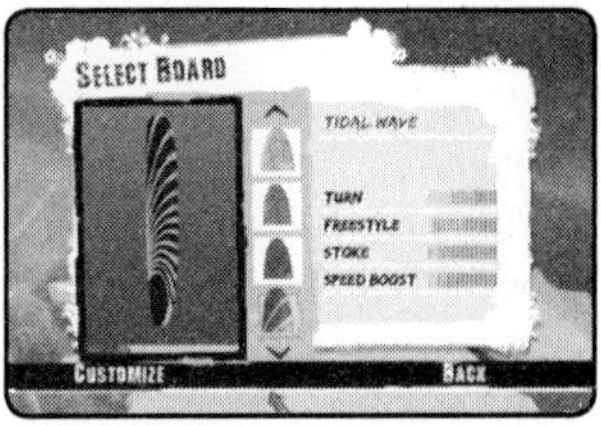

ASTRAL BOARD

Select Cheat Codes from the Extras menu and enter ASTRAL.

MONSOON BOARD

Select Cheat Codes from the Extras menu and enter MONSOON.

TINE SHOCKWAVE BOARD

Select Cheat Codes from the Extras menu and enter TINYSHOCKWAVE.

ALL CHARACTER CUSTOMIZATIONS

Select Cheat Codes from the Extras menu and enter TOPFASHION.

PLAY AS ARNOLD

Select Cheat Codes from the Extras menu and enter TINYBUTSTRONG.

PLAY AS ELLIOT

Select Cheat Codes from the Extras menu and enter SURPRISEGUEST.

PLAY AS GEEK

Select Cheat Codes from the Extras menu and enter SLOWANDSTEADY.

PLAY AS TANK EVANS

Select Cheat Codes from the Extras menu and enter IMTHEBEST.

PLAY AS TATSUHI KOBAYASHI

Select Cheat Codes from the Extras menu and enter KOBAYASHI.

PLAY AS ZEKE TOPANGA

Select Cheat Codes from the Extras menu and enter THELEGEND.

ALL VIDEOS AND SPEN GALLERY

Select Cheat Codes from the Extras menu and enter WATCHAMOVIE.

ART GALLERY

Select Cheat Codes from the Extras menu and enter NICEPLACE.

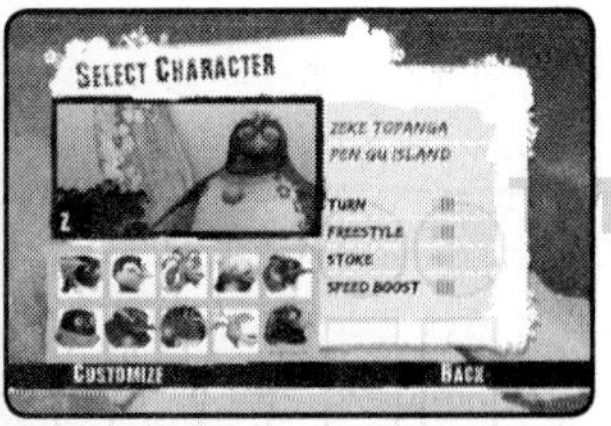

STAR WARS: THE FORCE UNLEASHED

CHEATS

Once you have accessed the Rogue Shadow, select Enter Code from the Extras menu. Now you can enter the following codes:

CHEAT	CODE
Invincibility	CORTOSIS
Unlimited Force	VERGENCE
1,000,000 Force Points	SPEEDER
All Force Powers	TYRANUS
Max Force Power Level	KATARN
Max Combo Level	COUNTDOOKU
Stronger Lightsaber	LIGHTSABER

COSTUMES

Once you have accessed the Rogue Shadow, select Enter Code from the Extras menu. Now you can enter the following codes:

COSTUME	CODE
All Costumes	GRANDMOFF
501st Legion	LEGION
Aayla Secura	AAYLA
Admiral Ackbar	ITSATWAP
Anakin Skywalker	CHOSENONE
Asajj Ventress	ACOLYTE
Ceremonial Jedi Robes	DANTOOINE
Chop'aa Notimo	NOTIMO
Classic stormtrooper	TK421
Count Dooku	SERENNO
Darth Desolous	PAUAN
Darth Maul	ZABRAK
Darth Phobos	HIDDENFEAR
Darth Vader	SITHLORD
Drexl Roosh	DREXLROOSH
Emperor Palpatine	PALPATINE
General Rahm Kota	MANDALORE
Han Solo	NERFHERDER
Heavy trooper	SHOCKTROOP

COSTUME	CODE
Juno Eclipse	ECLIPSE
Kento's Robe	WOOKIEE
Kleef	KLEEF
Lando Calrissian	SCOUNDREL
Luke Skywalker	T16WOMPRAT
Luke Skywalker (Yavin)	YELLOWJCKT
Mace Windu	JEDIMASTER
Mara Jade	MARAJADE
Maris Brook	MARISBROOD
Navy commando	STORMTROOP
Obi Wan Kenobi	BENKENOBI
Proxy	HOLOGRAM
Qui Gon Jinn	MAVERICK
Shaak Ti	TOGRUTA
Shadow trooper	INTHEDARK
Sith Robes	HOLOCRON
Sith Stalker Armor	KORRIBAN
Twi'lek	SECURA

STRONG BAD'S COOL GAME FOR ATTRACTIVE PEOPLE EPISODE 1: HOMESTAR RUINER

COBRA MODE IN SNAKE BOXER 5

At the Snake Boxer 5 title screen, press Up, Up, Down, Up, Plus.

SUPER MARIO GALAXY

PLAY AS LUIGI

Collect all 120 stars and fight Bowser. After the credits you will get a message that Luigi is playable.

GRAND FINALE GALAXY

Collect all 120 stars with Luigi and beat Bowser.

STAR 121

Collect 100 purple coins.

THRILLVILLE: OFF THE RAILS

$50,000
During a game, press C, Z, B, C, Z, B, A.

500 THRILL POINTS
During a game, press Z, C, B, Z, C, B, C.

ALL MISSIONS
During a game, press C, Z, B, C, Z, B, Z.

ALL PARKS
During a game, press C, Z, B, C, Z, B, C.

ALL RIDES
During a game, press C, Z, B, C, Z, B, B.

ALL MINIGAMES
During a game, press C, Z, B, C, Z, B, Right.

TIGER WOODS PGA TOUR 09 ALL-PLAY

SPECTATORS BIG HEAD MODE
Select EA SPORTS Extras from My Tiger '09, choose Password and enter cephalus.

TIGER WOODS PGA TOUR 08

ALL CLUBS
Select Passwords from the Options and enter PROSHOP.

ALL GOLFERS
Select Passwords from the Options and enter GAMEFACE.

BRIDGESTONE ITEMS
Select Passwords from the Options and enter NOTJUSTTIRES.

BUICK ITEMS
Select Passwords from the Options and enter THREESTRIPES.

CLEVELAND GOLF ITEMS
Select Passwords from the Options and enter CLEVELAND.

COBRA ITEMS
Select Passwords from the Options and enter SNAKEKING.

EA ITEMS
Select Passwords from the Options and enter INTHEGAME.

GRAFALLOY ITEMS
Select Passwords from the Options and enter JUSTSHAFTS.

MIZUNO ITEMS
Select Passwords from the Options and enter RIHACHINRIZO.

NIKE ITEMS
Select Passwords from the Options and enter JUSTDOIT.

PRECEPT ITEMS
Select Passwords from the Options and enter GUYSAREGOOD.

TONY HAWK'S PROVING GROUND

Select Cheat Codes from the Options and enter the following cheats. Some codes need to be enabled by selecting Cheats from the Options during a game.

UNLOCK	CHEAT
Unlocks Bosco	MOREMILK
Unlocks Cam	NOTACAMERA
Unlocks Cooper	THECOOP
Unlocks Eddie X	SKETCHY
Unlocks El Patinador	PILEDRIVER
Unlocks Eric	FLYAWAY

UNLOCK	CHEAT
Unlocks Judy Nails	LOVEROCKNROLL
Unlocks Mad Dog	RABBIES
Unlocks MCA	INTERGALACTIC
Unlocks Mel	NOTADUDE
Unlocks Rube	LOOKSSMELLY
Unlocks Spence	DAPPER

UNLOCK	CHEAT
Unlocks Shayne	MOVERS
Unlocks TV Producer	SHAKER
Unlock FDR	THEPREZPARK
Unlock Lansdowne	THELOCALPARK
Unlock Air & Space Museum	THEINDOORPARK
Unlocks all Fun Items	OVERTHETOP

UNLOCK	CHEAT
Unlock all Game Movies	WATCHTHIS
Unlock all Rigger Pieces	IMGONNABUILD
All specials unlocked and in player's special list	LOTSOFTRICKS
Full Stats	BEEFEDUP
Give player +50 skill points	NEEDSHELP

The following cheats lock you out of the Leaderboards:

Unlocks Perfect Manual	STILLAINTFALLIN
Unlocks Perfect Rail	AINTFALLIN
Unlocks Unlimited Focus	MYOPIC

You cannot use the Video Editor with the following cheats:

Invisible Man	THEMISSING
Mini Skater	TINYTATER

TRANSFORMERS: THE GAME

INFINITE HEALTH

At the Main menu, press Left, Left, Up, Left, Right, Down, Right.

INFINITE AMMO

At the Main menu, press Up, Down, Left, Right, Up, Up, Down.

NO MILITARY OR POLICE

At the Main menu, press Right, Left, Right, Left, Right, Left, Right.

ALL MISSIONS

At the Main menu, press Down, Up, Left, Right, Right, Right, Up, Down.

BONUS CYBERTRON MISSIONS

At the Main menu, press Right, Up, Up, Down, Right, Left, Left.

GENERATION 1 SKIN: JAZZ

At the Main menu, press Left, Up, Down, Down, Left, Up, Right.

GENERATION 1 SKIN: MEGATRON

At the Main menu, press Down, Left, Left, Down, Right, Right, Up.

GENERATION 1 SKIN: OPTIMUS PRIME

At the Main menu, press Down, Right, Left, Up, Down, Down, Left.

GENERATION 1 SKIN: ROBOVISION OPTIMUS PRIME

At the Main menu, press Down, Down, Up, Up, Right, Right, Right.

GENERATION 1 SKIN: STARSCREAM

At the Main menu, press Right, Down, Left, Left, Down, Up, Up.

WALL-E

The following cheats will disable saving. The five possible characters starting with Wall-E and going down are: Wall-E, Auto, EVE, M-O, GEL-A Steward.

ALL BONUS FEATURES UNLOCKED

Select Cheats from the Bonus Features menu and enter Wall-E, Auto, EVE, GEL-A Steward.

ALL GAME CONTENT UNLOCKED

Select Cheats from the Bonus Features menu and enter M-O, Auto, GEL-A Steward, EVE.

ALL SINGLE-PLAYER LEVELS UNLOCKED

Select Cheats from the Bonus Features menu and enter Auto, GEL-A Steward, M-O, Wall-E.

ALL MULTIPLAYER MAPS UNLOCKED

Select Cheats from the Bonus Features menu and enter EVE, M-O, Wall-E, Auto.

ALL HOLIDAY COSTUMES UNLOCKED

Select Cheats from the Bonus Features menu and enter Auto, Auto, GEL-A Steward, GEL-A Steward.

ALL MULTIPLAYER COSTUMES UNLOCKED

Select Cheats from the Bonus Features menu and enter GEL-A Steward, Wall-E, M-O, Auto.

UNLIMITED HEALTH UNLOCKED

Select Cheats from the Bonus Features menu and enter Wall-E, M-O, Auto, M-O.

WALL-E: MAKE ANY CUBE AT ANY TIME

Select Cheats from the Bonus Features menu and enter Auto, M-O, Auto, M-O.

WALL-EVE: MAKE ANY CUBE AT ANY TIME

Select Cheats from the Bonus Features menu and enter M-O, GEL-A Steward, EVE, EVE.

WALL-E WITH A LASER GUN AT ANY TIME

Select Cheats from the Bonus Features menu and enter Wall-E, EVE, EVE, Wall-E.

WALL-EVE WITH A LASER GUN AT ANY TIME

Select Cheats from the Bonus Features menu and enter GEL-A Steward, EVE, M-O, Wall-E.

WALL-E: PERMANENT SUPER LASER UPGRADE

Select Cheats from the Bonus Features menu and enter Wall-E, Auto, EVE, M-O.

EVE: PERMANENT SUPER LASER UPGRADE

Select Cheats from the Bonus Features menu and enter EVE, Wall-E, Wall-E, Auto.

CREDITS

Select Cheats from the Bonus Features menu and enter Auto, Wall-E, GEL-A Steward, M-O.

WII SPORTS

BOWLING BALL COLOR

After selecting your Mii, hold the following direction on the D-pad and press A at the warning screen:

DIRECTION	COLOR
Up	Blue
Right	Gold
Down	Green
Left	Red

NO HUD IN GOLF

Hold 2 as you select a course to disable the power meter, map, and wind speed meter.

BLUE TENNIS COURT

After selecting your Mii, hold 2 and press A at the warning screen.

WWE SMACKDOWN! VS. RAW 2008

HBK AND HHH'S DX OUTFIT

Select Cheat Codes from the Options and enter DXCostume69K2.

KELLY KELLY'S ALTERNATE OUTFIT

Select Cheat Codes from the Options and enter KellyKG12R.

Nintendo Wii™: Virtual Console

For the Virtual Console games, a Classic Controller may be needed to enter some codes.

ALTERED BEAST

LEVEL SELECT

At the Title screen, press B + Start.

BEAST SELECT

At the Title screen, hold A + B + C + Down/Left and press Start.

SOUND TEST

At the Title screen, hold A + C + Up/Right and press Start.

CHEW MAN FU

GAME COMPLETE PASSWORDS

Select Password and enter 573300 or 441300.

COMIX ZONE

STAGE SELECT

At the Jukebox menu, press C on the following numbers:

14, 15, 18, 5, 13, 1, 3, 18, 15, 6

A voice says "Oh Yeah" when entered correctly. Then, press C on 1 through 6 to warp to that stage.

INVINCIBLE

At the Jukebox menu, press C on the following numbers:

3, 12, 17, 2, 2, 10, 2, 7, 7, 11

A voice says "Oh Yeah" when entered correctly.

CREDITS

At the Options menu press A + B + C.

DR. ROBOTNIK'S MEAN BEAN MACHINE

EASY PASSWORDS

STAGE	PASSWORD
02: Frankly	Red Bean, Red Bean, Red Bean, Has Bean
03: Humpty	Clear Bean, Purple Bean, Clear Bean, Green Bean
04: Coconuts	Red Bean, Clear Bean, Has Bean, Yellow Bean
05: Davy Sprocket	Clear Bean, Blue Bean, Blue Bean, Purple Bean
06: Skweel	Clear Bean, Red Bean, Clear Bean, Purple Bean
07: Dynamight	Purple Bean, Yellow Bean, Red Bean, Blue Bean
08: Grounder	Yellow Bean, Purple Bean, Has Bean, Blue Bean
09: Spike	Yellow Bean, Purple Bean, Has Bean, Blue Bean
10: Sir Ffuzy-Logik	Red Bean, Yellow Bean, Clear Bean, Has Bean
11: Dragon Breath	Green Bean, Purple Bean, Blue Bean, Clear Bean
12: Scratch	Red Bean, Has Bean, Has Bean, Yellow Bean
13: Dr. Robotnik	Yellow Bean, Has Bean, Blue Bean, Blue Bean

NORMAL PASSWORDS

STAGE	PASSWORD
02: Frankly	Has Bean, Clear Bean, Yellow Bean, Yellow Bean
03: Humpty	Blue Bean, Clear Bean, Red Bean, Yellow Bean
04: Coconuts	Yellow Bean, Blue Bean, Clear Bean, Purple Bean
05: Davy Sprocket	Has Bean, Green Bean, Blue Bean, Yellow Bean
06: Skweel	Green Bean, Purple Bean, Purple Bean, Yellow Bean
07: Dynamight	Purple Bean, Blue Bean, Green Bean, Has Bean
08: Grounder	Green Bean, Has Bean, Clear Bean, Yellow Bean
09: Spike	Blue Bean, Purple Bean, Has Bean, Has Bean
10: Sir Ffuzy-Logik	Has Bean, Red Bean, Yellow Bean, Clear Bean
11: Dragon Breath	Clear Bean, Red Bean, Red Bean, Blue Bean
12: Scratch	Green Bean, Green Bean, Clear Bean, Yellow Bean
13: Dr. Robotnik	Purple Bean, Yellow Bean, Has Bean, Clear Bean

HARD PASSWORDS

STAGE	PASSWORD
02: Frankly	Clear Bean, Green Bean, Yellow Bean, Yellow Bean
03: Humpty	Yellow Bean, Purple Bean, Clear Bean, Purple Bean
04: Coconuts	Blue Bean, Green Bean, Clear Bean, Blue Bean
05: Davy Sprocket	Red Bean, Purple Bean, Green Bean, Green Bean
06: Skweel	Yellow Bean, Yellow Bean, Clear Bean, Green Bean
07: Dynamight	Purple Bean, Clear Bean, Blue Bean, Blue Bean
08: Grounder	Clear Bean, Yellow Bean, Has Bean, Yellow Bean
09: Spike	Purple Bean, Blue Bean, Blue Bean, Green Bean
10: Sir Ffuzy-Logik	Clear Bean, Green Bean, Red Bean, Yellow Bean
11: Dragon Breath	Blue Bean, Yellow Bean, Yellow Bean, Has Bean
12: Scratch	Green Bean, Clear Bean, Clear Bean, Blue Bean
13: Dr. Robotnik	Has Bean, Clear Bean, Purple Bean, Has Bean

HARDEST PASSWORDS

STAGE	PASSWORD
02: Frankly	Blue Bean, Blue Bean, Green Bean, Yellow Bean
03: Humpty	Green Bean, Yellow Bean, Green Bean, Clear Bean
04: Coconuts	Purple Bean, Purple Bean, RedBean, Has Bean
05: Davy Sprocket	Green Bean, Red Bean, Purple Bean, Blue Bean
06: Skweel	Purple Bean, Clear Bean, Green Bean, Yellow Bean
07: Dynamight	Blue Bean, Purple Bean, Green Bean, Has Bean
08: Grounder	Clear Bean, Purple Bean, Yellow Bean, Has Bean
09: Spike	Purple Bean, Green Bean, Has Bean, Clear Bean
10: Sir Ffuzy-Logik	Green Bean, Blue Bean, Yellow Bean, Has Bean
11: Dragon Breath	Green Bean, Purple Bean, Has Bean, Red Bean
12: Scratch	Red Bean, Green Bean, Has Bean, Blue Bean
13: Dr. Robotnik	Red Bean, Red Bean, Clear Bean, Yellow Bean

ECCO THE DOLPHIN

DEBUG MENU

Pause the game with Ecco facing the screen and press Right, B, C, B, C, Down, C, Up.

INFINITE AIR

Enter LIFEFISH as a password.

PASSWORDS

LEVEL	PASSWORD
The Undercaves	WEFIDNMP
The Vents	BQDPXJDS

LEVEL	PASSWORD
The Lagoon	JNSBRIKY
Ridge Water	NTSBZTKB

LEVEL	PASSWORD
Open Ocean	YWGTTJNI
Ice Zone	HZIFZBMF
Hard Water	LRFJRQLI
Cold Water	UYNFRQLC
Island Zone	LYTIOQLZ
Deep Water	MNOPOQLR
The Marble	RJNTQQLZ
The Library	RTGXQQLE
Deep City	DDXPQQLJ
City of Forever	MSDBRQLA

LEVEL	PASSWORD
Jurassic Beach	IYCBUNLB
Pteranodon Pond	DMXEUNLI
Origin Beach	EGRIUNLB
Trilobite Circle	IELMUNLB
Dark Water	RKEQUNLN
City of Forever 2	HPQIGPLA
The Tube	JUMFKMLB
The Machine	GXUBKMLF
The Last Fight	TSONLMLU

F-ZERO X

ALL TRACKS, VEHICLES, AND DIFFICULTIES

At the Mode Select screen, press Up on the D-pad, L, R, Up on the Right control stick, X, Y, ZR, Plus.

GOLDEN AXE

LEVEL SELECT

At the Character Select screen, in Arcade mode, hold Down/Left and press B + Start.

START WITH 9 CONTINUES

At the Character Select screen, in Arcade mode, hold Down/Left and then hold A + C. Release the buttons and select a character.

GRADIUS

MAX OUT WEAPONS

Pause the game and press Up, Up, Down, Down, Left, Right, Left, Right, B, A.

GRADIUS III

FULL POWER-UP

Pause the game and press Up, Up, Down, Down, L, R, L, R, B, A.

SUICIDE

Pause the game and press Up, Up, Down, Down, Left, Right, Left, Right, B, A.

MILITARY MADNESS

PASSWORDS

LEVEL	PASSWORD
01	REVOLT
02	ICARUS
03	CYRANO
04	RAMSEY
05	NEWTON
06	SENECA

LEVEL	PASSWORD
07	SABINE
08	ARATUS
09	GALIOS
10	DARWIN
11	PASCAL
12	HALLEY

LEVEL	PASSWORD
13	BORMAN
14	APOLLO
15	KAISER
16	NECTOR
17	MILTON
18	IRAGAN
19	LIPTUS
20	INAKKA
21	TETROS
22	ARBINE

LEVEL	PASSWORD
23	RECTOS
24	YEANTA
25	MONOGA
26	ATTAYA
27	DESHTA
28	NEKOSE
29	ERATIN
30	SOLCIS
31	SAGINE
32	WINNER

SOUND TEST

Enter ONGAKU as a password.

RISTAR

Select Passwords from the Options menu and enter the following:

LEVEL SELECT

ILOVEU

BOSS RUSH MODE

MUSEUM

TIME ATTACK MODE

DOFEEL

TOUGHER DIFFICULTY

SUPER

ONCHI MUSIC

MAGURO. Activate this from the Sound Test.

CLEARS PASSWORD

XXXXXX

GAME COPYRIGHT INFO

AGES

SONIC THE HEDGEHOG

LEVEL SELECT

At the Title screen, press Up, Down, Left, Right. A sound of a ring being collected plays if the code is entered correctly. Hold A and press Start to access the Level Select.

CONTROL MODE

At the Title screen, press Up, C, Down, C, Left, C, Right, C. Then, hold A and press Start.

DEBUG MODE

After entering the Control Mode, hold A and press Start. Press A to change Sonic into another sprite. Press B to change back to Sonic. Press C to place that sprite. Pause the game and press A to restart. Hold B for slow motion and press C to advance a frame.

CHANGE DEMO

During the demo, hold C and Sonic will start making mistakes.

WARIO'S WOODS

HARD BATTLES

Highlight VS. Computer Mode, hold Left and press Start.

XBOX 360™

TABLE OF CONTENTS

AMPED 3

ALL SLEDS

Select Cheat Codes from the Options screen and press Right Trigger, X, Left Trigger, Down, Right, Left Bumper, Left Trigger, Right Trigger, Y, X.

ALL GEAR

Select Cheat Codes from the Options and press Y, Down, Up, Left, Right, Left Bumper, Right, Right Trigger, Right Trigger, Right Bumper.

ALL TRICKS

Select Cheat Codes from the Options screen and press Left Bumper, Right Trigger, Y, Up, Down, X, Left Trigger, Left, Right Bumper, Right Trigger.

ALL LEVELS

Select Cheat Codes from the Options screen and press X, Y, Up, Left, Left Bumper, Left Bumper, Right Trigger, X, Y, Left Trigger.

ALL CONFIGS

Select Cheat Codes from the Options screen and press Down, X, Right, Left Bumper, Right, Right Bumper, X, Right Trigger, Left Trigger, Y.

SUPER SPINS

Select Cheat Codes from the Options screen and press X(x4), Y(x3), X.

AWESOME METER ALWAYS FULL

Select Cheat Codes from the Options screen and press Up, Right Trigger, X, Y Left Bumper, X, Down, Left Bumper, Right Trigger, Right Bumper.

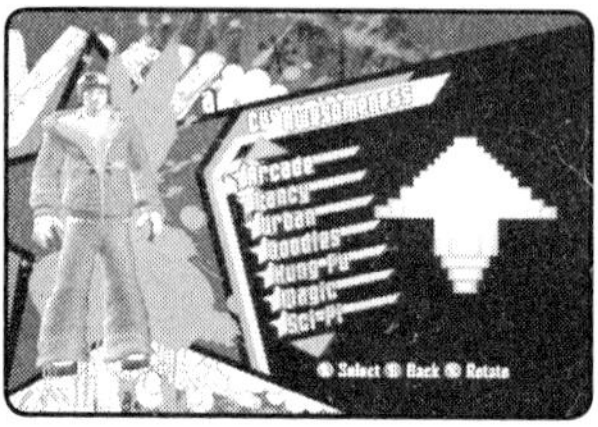

ALL AWESOMENESS

Select Cheat Codes from the Options screen and press Right Bumper, Right Bumper, Down, Left, Up, Right Trigger, X, Right Bumper, X, X.

ALL BUILD LICENSES

Select Cheat Codes from the Options screen and press Left, Right Trigger, Left Bumper, Right Trigger, X, X, Y, Down, Up, X.

ALL BUILD OBJECTS

Select Cheat Codes from the Options screen and press Left Trigger, Right Trigger, Up, Up, Right Bumper, Left, Right, X, Y, Left Bumper.

ALL CHALLENGES

Select Cheat Codes from the Options screen and press Right, Left Bumper, Left Trigger, X, Left, Right Bumper, Right Trigger, Y, Left Trigger, X.

LOUD SPEAKERS

Select Cheat Codes from the Options screen and press Y. Right Trigger, Right Trigger, Left Bumper, Down, Down, Left, Left, Right, Left Bumper.

LOW GRAVITY BOARDERS

Select Cheat Codes from the Options screen and press Right Trigger, Down, Down, Up, X, Left Bumper, Y, Right Trigger, Y, Down.

NO AI

Select Cheat Codes from the Options screen and press X, X, Left Bumper, Down, Right, Right, Up, Y, Y, Left Trigger.

ALL MUSIC

Select Cheat Codes from the Options screen and press Up, Left, Right Trigger, Right Bumper, Right Trigger, Up, Down, Left, Y, Left Trigger.

AVATAR: THE LAST AIRBENDER – THE BURNING EARTH

UNLIMITED HEALTH

Select Code Entry from the Extras menu and enter 65049.

DOUBLE DAMAGE

Select Code Entry from the Extras menu and enter 90210.

MAXIMUM LEVEL

Select Code Entry from the Extras menu and enter 89121.

UNLIMITED SPECIALS

Select Code Entry from the Extras menu and enter 66206.

ONE-HIT DISHONOR

Select Code Entry from the Extras menu and enter 28260.

ALL BONUS GAMES

Select Code Entry from the Extras menu and enter 99801.

UNLOCKS GALLERY

Select Code Entry from the Extras menu and enter 85061.

BAJA: EDGE OF CONTROL

ALL VEHICLES AND TRACKS

Select Cheat Codes from the Options menu and enter SHOWTIME.

ALL PARTS

Select Cheat Codes from the Options menu and enter SUPERMAX.

BATTLESTATIONS: MIDWAY

ALL CAMPAIGN AND CHALLENGE MISSIONS

At the mission select, hold Right Bumper + Left Bumper + Right Trigger + Left Trigger and press Ⓧ.

BEAT'N GROOVY

ALTERNATE CONTROLS

At the title screen, press Up, Up, Down, Down, Left, Right, Left, Right, Ⓑ, Ⓐ.

BLAZING ANGELS: SQUADRONS OF WWII

ALL MISSIONS, MEDALS, & PLANES

At the Main menu hold Left Trigger + Right Trigger and press Ⓧ, Left Bumper, Right Bumper, Ⓨ, Ⓨ Right Bumper, Left Bumper, Ⓧ.

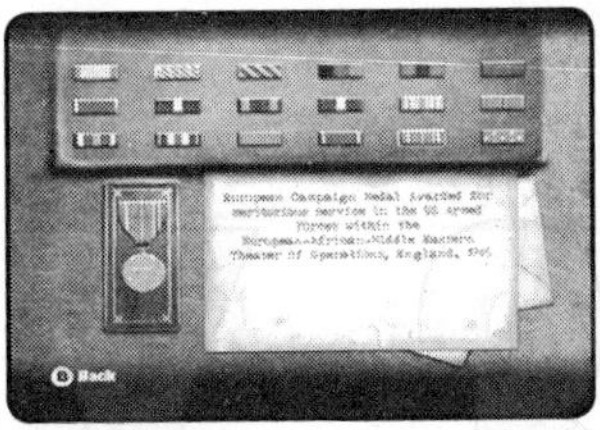

GOD MODE

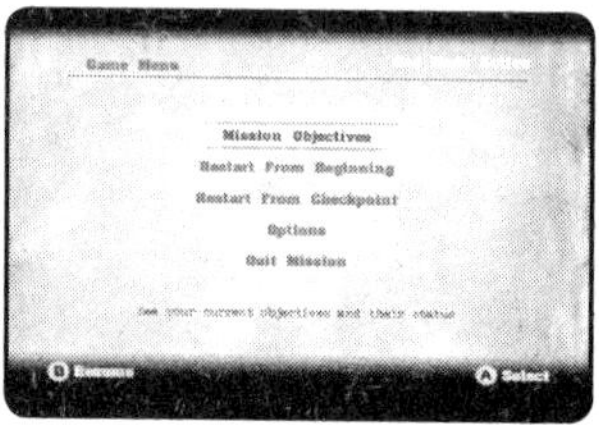

Pause the game, hold Left Trigger and press X, Y, Y, X Release Left Trigger, hold Right Trigger and press Y, X, X, Y. Re-enter the code to disable it.

INCREASED DAMAGE

Pause the game, hold Left Trigger and press Left Bumper, Left Bumper, Right Bumper. Release Left Trigger, hold Right Trigger and press Right Bumper, Right Bumper, Left Bumper. Re-enter the code to disable it.

BLAZING ANGELS 2: SECRET MISSIONS OF WWII

Achievements are disabled when using these codes.

ALL MISSIONS AND PLANES UNLOCKED

At the Main menu, hold Left Trigger + Right Trigger, and press X, Left Bumper, Right Bumper, Y, Y, Right Bumper, Left Bumper, X.

GOD MODE

Pause the game, hold Left Trigger, and press X, Y, Y, X. Release Left Trigger, hold Right Trigger and press Y, X, X, Y. Re-enter the code to disable it.

INCREASED DAMAGE WITH ALL WEAPONS

Pause the game, hold Left Trigger, and press Left Bumper, Left Bumper, Right Bumper. Release Left Trigger, hold Right Trigger, and press Right Bumper, Right Bumper, Left Bumper. Re-enter the code to disable it.

BURNOUT PARADISE

BEST BUY CAR

Pause the game and select Sponsor Product Code from the Under the Hood menu. Enter Bestbuy. Need A License to use this car offline.

CIRCUIT CITY CAR

Pause the game and select Sponsor Product Code from the Under the Hood menu. Enter Circuitcity. Need Burnout Paradise License to use this car offline.

GAMESTOP CAR

Pause the game and select Sponsor Product Code from the Under the Hood menu. Enter Gamestop. Need A License to use this car offline.

WALMART CAR

Pause the game and select Sponsor Product Code from the Under the Hood menu. Enter Walmart. Need Burnout Paradise License to use this car offline.

"STEEL WHEELS" GT

Pause the game and select Sponsor Product Code from the Under the Hood menu. Enter G23X 5K8Q GX2V 04B1 or E60J 8Z7T MS8L 51U6.

LICENSES

LICENSE	NUMBER OF WINS NEEDED
D	2
C	7
B	16
A	26
Burnout Paradise	45
Elite License	All events

CARS

UNLOCK EVERYTHING

Select Cheat Codes from the Options and enter IF900HP.

ALL CHARACTERS

Select Cheat Codes from the Options and enter YAYCARS.

ALL CHARACTER SKINS

Select Cheat Codes from the Options and enter R4MONE.

ALL MINI-GAMES AND COURSES

Select Cheat Codes from the Options and enter MATTL66.

FAST START

Select Cheat Codes from the Options and enter IMSPEED.

INFINITE BOOST

Select Cheat Codes from the Options and enter VROOOOM.

ART

Select Cheat Codes from the Options and enter CONC3PT.

VIDEOS

Select Cheat Codes from the Options and enter WATCHIT.

CARS MATER-NATIONAL

ALL ARCADE RACES, MINI-GAMES, AND WORLDS

Select Codes/Cheats from the options and enter PLAYALL.

ALL CARS

Select Codes/Cheats from the options and enter MATTEL07.

ALTERNATE LIGHTNING MCQUEEN COLORS

Select Codes/Cheats from the options and enter NCEDUDZ.

ALL COLORS FOR OTHERS

Select Codes/Cheats from the options and enter PAINTIT.

UNLIMITED TURBO

Select Codes/Cheats from the options and enter ZZOOOOM.

EXTREME ACCELERATION

Select Codes/Cheats from the options and enter 0TO200X.

EXPERT MODE

Select Codes/Cheats from the options and enter VRYFAST.

ALL BONUS ART

Select Codes/Cheats from the options and enter BUYTALL.

CASTLEVANIA: SYMPHONY OF THE NIGHT

Before using the following codes, complete the game with 170%.

PLAY AS RICHTER BELMONT

Enter RICHTER as your name.

ALUCARD WITH AXELORD ARMOR

Enter AXEARMOR as your name.

ALUCARD WITH 99 LUCK AND OTHER STATS ARE LOW

Enter X-X!V"Q as your name.

CRASH OF THE TITANS

BIG HEAD CRASH

Pause the game, hold the Right Trigger, and press X, X, Y, A.

SHADOW CRASH

Pause the game, hold the Right Trigger, and press Y, X, Y, A.

DON KING PRESENTS: PRIZEFIGHTER

UNLOCK RICARDO MAYORGA

Select Enter Unlock Code from the Extras menu and enter potsemag.

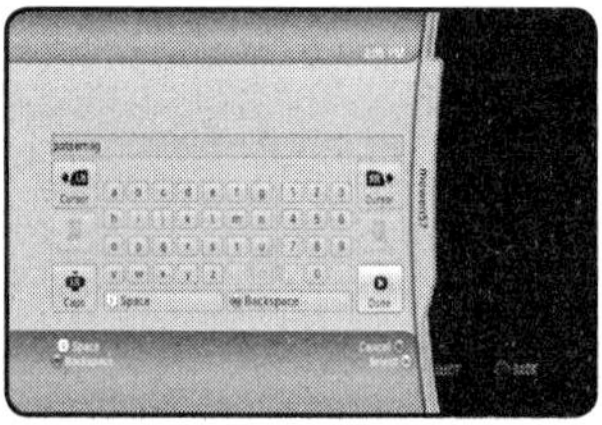

EXCLUSIVE BEST BUY FIGHT FOOTAGE

Select Enter Unlock Code from the Extras menu and enter 1bestbuybest. Select Watch Videos from the Extras menu to find video.

ERAGON

UNLIMITED FURY MODE

Pause the game, hold Left Bumper + Left Trigger + Right Bumper + Right Trigger and press X, X, B, B.

EVERY EXTEND EXTRA EXTREME

FINE ADJUSTMENT MENU

At the Start screen, press Left Bumper, Right Bumper, Left Bumper, Right Bumper, Left Bumper, Right Bumper, Left Bumper, Right Bumper.

FATAL FURY SPECIAL

CHEAT MENU

During a game, hold Start and push A + X + Y.

FIGHT NIGHT ROUND 3

ALL VENUES

Create a champ with a first name of NEWVIEW.

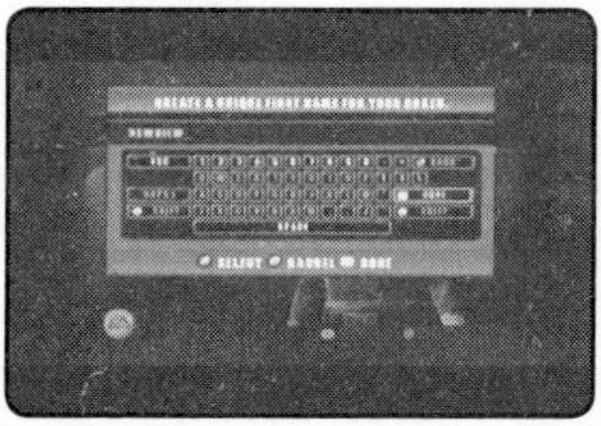

FLATOUT: ULTIMATE CARNAGE

MOB CAR IN SINGLE EVENTS

Select Enter Code from Extras and enter BIGTRUCK.

PIMPSTER IN SINGLE EVENTS

Select Enter Code from Extras and enter RUTTO.

ROCKET IN SINGLE EVENTS

Select Enter Code from Extras and enter KALJAKOPPA.

FROGGER

BIG FROGGER

At the one/two player screen, press Up, Up, Down, Down, Left, Right, Left, Right, B, A.

FULL AUTO

ALL TRACKS, VEHICLES, & WEAPONS

Create a new profile with the name magicman.

GRID

ALL DRIFT CARS

Select Bonus Codes from the Options. Then choose Enter Code and enter TUN58396.

ALL MUSCLE CARS

Select Bonus Codes from the Options. Then choose Enter Code and enter MUS59279.

BUCHBINDER EMOTIONAL ENGINEERING BMW 320SI

Select Bonus Codes from the Options. Then choose Enter Code and enter F93857372. You can use this in Race Day or in GRID World once you've started your own team.

EBAY

Select Bonus Codes from the Options. Then choose Enter Code and enter DAFJ55E01473M0. You can use this in Race Day or in GRID World once you've started your own team.

GAMESTATION BMW 320SI

Select Bonus Codes from the Options. Then choose Enter Code and enter G29782655. You can use this in Race Day or in GRID World once you've started your own team.

MICROMANIA PAGANI ZONDA R

Select Bonus Codes from the Options. Then choose Enter Code and enter M38572343. You can use this in Race Day or in GRID World once you've started your own team.

PLAY.COM ASTON MARTIN DBR9

Select Bonus Codes from the Options. Then choose Enter Code and enter P47203845. You can use this in Race Day or in GRID World once you've started your own team.

IDOLMASTER: LIVE FOR YOU!

MAMI

At the character select, press R3 while on Ami.

SHORT-HAIRED MIKI

At the character select, press R3 while on Miki.

IRON MAN

CLASSIC ARMOR

Clear One Man Army vs. Mercs.

EXTREMIS ARMOR

Clear One Man Army vs. Maggia.

MARK II ARMOR

Clear One Man Army vs. Ten Rings.

HULKBUSTER ARMOR

Clear One Man Army vs. AIM-X. Can also be unlocked when clear game save data from Incredible Hulk is stored on the same console.

SILVER CENTURION ARMOR

Clear Mission 13: Showdown.

CLASSIC MARK I ARMOR

Clear One Man Army vs. AIM.

JUICED 2: HOT IMPORT NIGHTS

FRITO-LAY INFINITY G35 CAR

Select Cheats and Codes from the DNA Lab menu and enter MNCH.

HIDDEN CHALLENGE AND AN AUDI TT 1.8 QUATTRO

Select Cheats and Codes from the DNA Lab menu and enter YTHZ. Defeat the challenge to earn the Audi TT 1.8 Quattro.

HIDDEN CHALLENGE AND A BMW Z4

Select Cheats and Codes from the DNA Lab menu and enter GVDL. Defeat the challenge to earn the BMW Z4.

HIDDEN CHALLENGE AND A HOLDEN MONARO

Select Cheats and Codes from the DNA Lab menu and enter RBSG. Defeat the challenge to earn the Holden Monaro.

HIDDEN CHALLENGE AND A HYUNDAI COUPE 2.7 V6

Select Cheats and Codes from the DNA Lab menu and enter BSLU. Defeat the challenge to earn the Hyundai Coupe 2.7 V6.

HIDDEN CHALLENGE AND AN INFINITY G35

Select Cheats and Codes from the DNA Lab menu and enter MRHC. Defeat the challenge to earn the Infinity G35.

HIDDEN CHALLENGE AND A KOENIGSEGG CCX

Select Cheats and Codes from the DNA Lab menu and enter KDTR. Defeat the challenge to earn the Koenigsegg CCX.

HIDDEN CHALLENGE AND A MITSUBISHI PROTOTYPE X

Select Cheats and Codes from the DNA Lab menu and enter DOPX. Defeat the challenge to earn the Mitsubishi Prototype X.

HIDDEN CHALLENGE AND A NISSAN 350Z

Select Cheats and Codes from the DNA Lab menu and enter PRGN. Defeat the challenge to earn the Nissan 350Z.

HIDDEN CHALLENGE AND A NISSAN SKYLINE R34 GT-R

Select Cheats and Codes from the DNA Lab menu and enter JWRS. Defeat the challenge to earn the Nissan Skyline R34 GT-R.

HIDDEN CHALLENGE AND A SALEEN S7

Select Cheats and Codes from the DNA Lab menu and enter WIKF. Defeat the challenge to earn the Saleen S7.

HIDDEN CHALLENGE AND A SEAT LEON CUPRA R

Select Cheats and Codes from the DNA Lab menu and enter FAMQ. Defeat the challenge to earn the Seat Leon Cupra R.

KUNG FU PANDA

INFINITE CHI

Select Cheats from the Extra menu and press Down, Right, Left, Up, Down.

INVINCIBILITY

Select Cheats from the Extra menu and press Down, Down, Right, Up, Left.

FULL UPGRADES

Select Cheats from the Extra menu and press Left, Right, Down, Left, Up.

4X DAMAGE MULTIPLIER

Select Cheats from the Extra menu and press Up, Down, Up, Right, Left.

ALL MULTIPLAYER CHARACTERS

Select Cheats from the Extra menu and press Left, Down, Left, Right, Down.

DRAGON WARRIOR OUTFIT IN MULTIPLAYER

Select Cheats from the Extra menu and press Left, Down, Right, Left, Up.

ALL OUTFITS

Select Cheats from the Extra menu and press Right, Left, Down, Up, Right.

THE LEGEND OF SPYRO: DAWN OF THE DRAGON

UNLIMITED LIFE

Pause the game, hold Left Bumper and press Right, Right, Down, Down, Left with the Left Control Stick.

UNLIMITED MANA

Pause the game, hold Right Bumper and press Up, Right, Up, Left, Down with the Left Control Stick.

MAXIMUM XP

Pause the game, hold Right Bumper and press Up, Left, Left, Down, Up with the Left Control Stick.

ALL ELEMENTAL UPGRADES

Pause the game, hold Left Bumper and press Left, Up, Down, Up, Right with the Left Control Stick.

LEGO BATMAN

BATCAVE CODES

Using the computer in the Batcave, select Enter Code and enter the following codes.

CHARACTERS

CHARACTER	CODE
Alfred	ZAQ637
Batgirl	JKR331
Bruce Wayne	BDJ327
Catwoman (Classic)	M1AAWW
Clown Goon	HJK327
Commissioner Gordon	DDP967
Fishmonger	HGY748
Freeze Girl	XVK541
Joker Goon	UTF782
Joker Henchman	YUN924
Mad Hatter	JCA283
Man-Bat	NYU942
Military Policeman	MKL382
Nightwing	MVY759
Penguin Goon	NKA238
Penguin Henchman	BJH782
Penguin Minion	KJP748
Poison Ivy Goon	GTB899
Police Marksman	HKG984
Police Officer	JRY983
Riddler Goon	CRY928
Riddler Henchman	XEU824
S.W.A.T.	HTF114
Sailor	NAV592
Scientist	JFL786
Security Guard	PLB946
The Joker (Tropical)	CCB199
Yeti	NJL412
Zoo Sweeper	DWR243

VEHICLES

VEHICLE	CODE
Bat-Tank	KNTT4B
Bruce Wayne's Private Jet	LEA664
Catwoman's Motorcycle	HPL826
Garbage Truck	DUS483
Goon Helicopter	GCH328
Harbor Helicopter	CHP735
Harley Quinn's Hammer Truck	RDT637
Mad Hatter's Glider	HS000W
Mad Hatter's Steamboat	M4DM4N
Mr. Freeze's Iceberg	ICYICE
The Joker's Van	JUK657
Mr. Freeze's Kart	BCT229
Penguin Goon Submarine	BTN248
Police Bike	LJP234
Police Boat	PLC999
Police Car	KJL832
Police Helicopter	CWR732
Police Van	MAC788
Police Watercraft	VJD328
Riddler's Jet	HAHAHA
Robin's Submarine	TTF453
Two-Face's Armored Truck	EFE933

CHEATS

CHEAT	CODE
Always Score Multiply	9LRGNB
Fast Batarangs	JRBDCB
Fast Walk	ZOLM6N
Flame Batarang	D8NYWH
Freeze Batarang	XPN4NG
Extra Hearts	ML3KHP
Fast Build	EVG26J
Immune to Freeze	JXUDY6
Invincibility	WYD5CP
Minikit Detector	ZXGH9J
More Batarang Targets	XWP645
Piece Detector	KHJ554
Power Brick Detector	MMN786
Regenerate Hearts	HJH7HJ
Score x2	N4NR3E
Score x4	CX9MAT
Score x6	MLVNF2
Score x8	WCCDB9
Score x10	18HW07

LEGO INDIANA JONES: THE ORIGINAL ADVENTURES

CHARACTERS

Approach the blackboard in the Classsroom and enter the following codes.

CHARACTER	CODE
Bandit	12N68W
Bandit Swordsman	1MK4RT
Barranca	04EM94
Bazooka Trooper (Crusade)	MK83R7
Bazooka Trooper (Raiders)	S93Y5R
Belloq	CHN3YU
Belloq (Jungle)	TDR197
Belloq (Robes)	VEO29L
British Commander	B73EUA
British Officer	VJ5TI9
British Soldier	DJ5I2W
Captain Katanga	VJ3TT3
Chatter Lal	ENW936
Chatter Lal (Thuggee)	CNH4RY
Chen	3NK48T
Colonel Dietrich	2K9RKS
Colonel Vogel	8EAL4H
Dancing Girl	C7EJ21
Donovan	3NFTU8
Elsa (Desert)	JSNRT9
Elsa (Officer)	VMJ5US
Enemy Boxer	8246RB
Enemy Butler	VJ48W3
Enemy Guard	VJ7R51
Enemy Guard (Mountains)	YR47WM
Enemy Officer	572E61
Enemy Officer (Desert	2MK450
Enemy Pilot	B84ELP
Enemy Radio Operator	1MF94R
Enemy Soldier (Desert)	4NSU7Q
Fedora	V75YSP
First Mate	0GIN24
Grail Knight	NE6THI
Hovitos Tribesman	HOV1SS
Indiana Jones (Desert Disguise)	4J8S4M
Indiana Jones (Officer)	VJ850S
Jungle Guide	24PF34
Kao Kan	WM046L
Kazim	NRH23J
Kazim (Desert)	3M29TJ
Lao Che	2NK479
Maharajah	NFK5N2
Major Toht	13NS01
Masked Bandit	N48SF0
Mola Ram	FJUR31
Monkey Man	3RF6YJ
Pankot Assassin	2NKT72
Pankot Guard	VN28RH
Sherpa Brawler	VJ37WJ
Sherpa Gunner	ND762W
Slave Child	0E3ENW
Thuggee	VM683E
Thuggee Acolyte	T2R3F9
Thuggee Slave Driver	VBS7GW
Village Dignitary	KD48TN
Village Elder	4682E1
Willie (Dinner Suit)	VK93R7
Willie (Pajamas)	MEN4IP
Wu Han	3NSLT8

EXTRAS

Approach the blackboard in the Classsroom and enter the following codes. Some cheats need to be enabled by selecting Extras from the pause menu.

CHEAT	CODE
Artifact Detector	VIKED7
Beep Beep	VNF59Q
Character Treasure	VIES2R
Disarm Enemies	VKRNS9
Disguises	4ID1N6
Fast Build	V83SL0
Fast Dig	378RS6
Fast Fix	FJ59WS
Fertilizer	B1GW1F
Ice Rink	33GM7J
Parcel Detector	VUT673
Poo Treasure	WWQ1SA

CHEAT	CODE
Regenerate Hearts	MDLP69
Secret Characters	3X44AA
Silhouettes	3HE85H
Super Scream	VN3R7S
Super Slap	0P1TA5
Treasure Magnet	H86LA2
Treasure x10	VI3PS8
Treasure x2	VM4TS9
Treasure x4	VLWEN3
Treasure x6	V84RYS
Treasure x8	A72E1M

LEGO STAR WARS II: THE ORIGINAL TRILOGY

BEACH TROOPER

At Mos Eisley Canteena, select Enter Code and enter UCK868. You still need to select Characters and purchase this character for 20,000 studs.

BEN KENOBI (GHOST)

At Mos Eisley Canteena, select Enter Code and enter BEN917. You still need to select Characters and purchase this character for 1,100,000 studs.

BESPIN GUARD

At Mos Eisley Canteena, select Enter Code and enter VHY832. You still need to select Characters and purchase this character for 15,000 studs.

BIB FORTUNA

At Mos Eisley Canteena, select Enter Code and enter WTY721. You still need to select Characters and purchase this character for 16,000 studs.

BOBA FETT

At Mos Eisley Canteena, select Enter Code and enter HLP221. You still need to select Characters and purchase this character for 175,000 studs.

DEATH STAR TROOPER

At Mos Eisley Canteena, select Enter Code and enter BNC332. You still need to select Characters and purchase this character for 19,000 studs.

EWOK

At Mos Eisley Canteena, select Enter Code and enter TTT289. You still need to select Characters and purchase this character for 34,000 studs.

GAMORREAN GUARD

At Mos Eisley Canteena, select Enter Code and enter YZF999. You still need to select Characters and purchase this character for 40,000 studs.

GONK DROID

At Mos Eisley Canteena, select Enter Code and enter NFX582. You still need to select Characters and purchase this character for 1,550 studs.

GRAND MOFF TARKIN

At Mos Eisley Canteena, select Enter Code and enter SMG219. You still need to select Characters and purchase this character for 38,000 studs.

GREEDO

At Mos Eisley Canteena, select Enter Code and enter NAH118. You still need to select Characters and purchase this character for 60,000 studs.

HAN SOLO (HOOD)

At Mos Eisley Canteena, select Enter Code and enter YWM840. You still need to select Characters and purchase this character for 20,000 studs.

IG-88

At Mos Eisley Canteena, select Enter Code and enter NXL973. You still need to select Characters and purchase this character for 30,000 studs.

IMPERIAL GUARD

At Mos Eisley Canteena, select Enter Code and enter MMM111. You still need to select Characters and purchase this character for 45,000 studs.

IMPERIAL OFFICER

At Mos Eisley Canteena, select Enter Code and enter BBV889. You still need to select Characters and purchase this character for 28,000 studs.

IMPERIAL SHUTTLE PILOT

At Mos Eisley Canteena, select Enter Code and enter VAP664. You still need to select Characters and purchase this character for 29,000 studs.

IMPERIAL SPY

At Mos Eisley Canteena, select Enter Code and enter CVT125. You still need to select Characters and purchase this character for 13,500 studs.

JAWA

At Mos Eisley Canteena, select Enter Code and enter JAW499. You still need to select Characters and purchase this character for 24,000 studs.

LOBOT

At Mos Eisley Canteena, select Enter Code and enter UUB319. You still need to select Characters and purchase this character for 11,000 studs.

PALACE GUARD

At Mos Eisley Canteena, select Enter Code and enter SGE549. You still need to select Characters and purchase this character for 14,000 studs.

REBEL PILOT

At Mos Eisley Canteena, select Enter Code and enter CYG336. You still need to select Characters and purchase this character for 15,000 studs.

REBEL TROOPER (HOTH)

At Mos Eisley Canteena, select Enter Code and enter EKU849. You still need to select Characters and purchase this character for 16,000 studs.

SANDTROOPER

At Mos Eisley Canteena, select Enter Code and enter YDV451. You still need to select Characters and purchase this character for 14,000 studs.

SKIFF GUARD

At Mos Eisley Canteena, select Enter Code and enter GBU888. You still need to select Characters and purchase this character for 12,000 studs.

SNOWTROOPER

At Mos Eisley Canteena, select Enter Code and enter NYU989. You still need to select Characters and purchase this character for 16,000 studs.

STROMTROOPER

At Mos Eisley Canteena, select Enter Code and enter PTR345. You still need to select Characters and purchase this character for 10,000 studs.

THE EMPEROR

At Mos Eisley Canteena, select Enter Code and enter HHY382. You still need to select Characters and purchase this character for 275,000 studs.

TIE FIGHTER

At Mos Eisley Canteena, select Enter Code and enter HDY739. You still need to select Characters and purchase this character for 60,000 studs.

TIE FIGHTER PILOT

At Mos Eisley Canteena, select Enter Code and enter NNZ316. You still need to select Characters and purchase this character for 21,000 studs.

TIE INTERCEPTOR

At Mos Eisley Canteena, select Enter Code and enter QYA828. You still need to select Characters and purchase this character for 40,000 studs.

TUSKEN RAIDER

At Mos Eisley Canteena, select Enter Code and enter PEJ821. You still need to select Characters and purchase this character for 23,000 studs.

UGNAUGHT

At Mos Eisley Canteena, select Enter Code and enter UGN694. You still need to select Characters and purchase this character for 36,000 studs.

LEGO STAR WARS: THE COMPLETE SAGA

The following still need to be purchase after entering the codes.

CHARACTERS

ADMIRAL ACKBAR

At the bar in Mos Eisley Cantina, select Enter Code and enter ACK646.

BATTLE DROID (COMMANDER)

At the bar in Mos Eisley Cantina, select Enter Code and enter KPF958.

BOBA FETT (BOY)

At the bar in Mos Eisley Cantina, select Enter Code and enter GGF539.

BOSS NASS

At the bar in Mos Eisley Cantina, select Enter Code and enter HHY697.

CAPTAIN TARPALS

At the bar in Mos Eisley Cantina, select Enter Code and enter QRN714.

COUNT DOOKU

At the bar in Mos Eisley Cantina, select Enter Code and enter DDD748.

DARTH MAUL

At the bar in Mos Eisley Cantina, select Enter Code and enter EUK421.

EWOK

At the bar in Mos Eisley Cantina, select Enter Code and enter EWK785.

GENERAL GRIEVOUS

At the bar in Mos Eisley Cantina, select Enter Code and enter PMN576.

GREEDO

At the bar in Mos Eisley Cantina, select Enter Code and enter ZZR636.

IG-88

At the bar in Mos Eisley Cantina, select Enter Code and enter GIJ989.

IMPERIAL GUARD

At the bar in Mos Eisley Cantina, select Enter Code and enter GUA850.

JANGO FETT

At the bar in Mos Eisley Cantina, select Enter Code and enter KLJ897.

KI-ADI MUNDI

At the bar in Mos Eisley Cantina, select Enter Code and enter MUN486.

LUMINARA

At the bar in Mos Eisley Cantina, select Enter Code and enter LUM521.

PADMÉ

At the bar in Mos Eisley Cantina, select Enter Code and enter VBJ322.

R2-Q5

At the bar in Mos Eisley Cantina, select Enter Code and enter EVILR2.

STORMTROOPER

At the bar in Mos Eisley Cantina, select Enter Code and enter NBN431.

TAUN WE

At the bar in Mos Eisley Cantina, select Enter Code and enter PRX482.

VULTURE DROID

At the bar in Mos Eisley Cantina, select Enter Code and enter BDC866.

WATTO

At the bar in Mos Eisley Cantina, select Enter Code and enter PLL967.

ZAM WESELL

At the bar in Mos Eisley Cantina, select Enter Code and enter 584HJF.

SKILLS

DISGUISE

At the bar in Mos Eisley Cantina, select Enter Code and enter BRJ437.

FORCE GRAPPLE LEAP

At the bar in Mos Eisley Cantina, select Enter Code and enter CLZ738.

VEHICLES

DROID TRIFIGHTER

At the bar in Mos Eisley Cantina, select Enter Code and enter AAB123.

IMPERIAL SHUTTLE

At the bar in Mos Eisley Cantina, select Enter Code and enter HUT845.

TIE INTERCEPTOR

At the bar in Mos Eisley Cantina, select Enter Code and enter INT729.

TIE FIGHTER

At the bar in Mos Eisley Cantina, select Enter Code and enter DBH897.

ZAM'S AIRSPEEDER

At the bar in Mos Eisley Cantina, select Enter Code and enter UUU875.

LOONEY TUNES: ACME ARSENAL

UNLMITED AMMO

At the cheat menu, press Down, Left, Up, Right, Down, Left, Up, Right, Down.

LOST PLANET: EXTREME CONDITION

The following codes are for Single Player Mode on Easy Difficulty only.

500 THERMAL ENERGY

Pause the game and press Up, Up, Down, Down, Left, Right, Left, Right, ⓧ, ⓨ, Right Bumper + Left Bumper.

INFINITE AMMUNITION

Pause the game and press Right Trigger, Right Bumper, ⓨ, ⓧ, Right, Down, Left, Left Bumper, Left Trigger, Right Trigger, Right Bumper, ⓨ, ⓧ, Right, Down, Left, Left Bumper, Left Trigger, Right Trigger, Left Trigger, Left Bumper, Right Bumper,ⓨ, Left, Down,ⓧ, Right Bumper + Left Bumper.

INFINITE HEALTH

Pause the game and press Down (x3), Up, ⓨ,Up, ⓨ,
Up, ⓨ, Up(x3), Down, ⓧ, Down, ⓧ, Down, ⓧ, Left, ⓨ, Right, ⓧ, –Left, ⓨ, Right, ⓧ, Right Bumper + Left Bumper.

CHANGE CAMERA ANGLE IN CUT SCENES

During a cut scene, press ⓑ, ⓐ,ⓧ,ⓨ, ⓑ, ⓐ,ⓧ,ⓨ, ⓑ, ⓐ,ⓧ, ⓨ.

MAJOR LEAGUE BASEBALL 2K6

UNLOCK EVERYTHING

Select Enter Cheat Code from the My 2K6 menu and enter Derek Jeter.

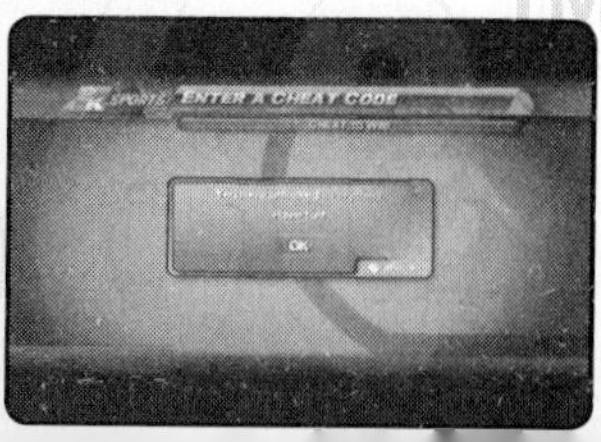

TOPPS 2K STARS

Select Enter Cheat Code from the My 2K6 menu and enter Dream Team.

SUPER WALL CLIMB

Select Enter Cheat Code from the My 2K6 menu and enter Last Chance. Enable the cheats by selecting My Cheats or selecting Cheat Codes from the in-game Options screen.

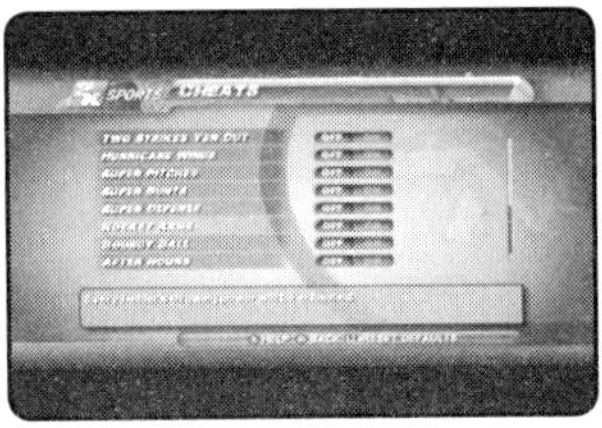

SUPER PITCHES

Select Enter Cheat Code from the My 2K6 menu and enter Unhittable. Enable the cheats by selecting My Cheats or selecting Cheat Codes from the in-game Options screen.

ROCKET ARMS

Select Enter Cheat Code from the My 2K6 menu and enter Gotcha. Enable the cheats by selecting My Cheats or selecting Cheat Codes from the in-game Options screen.

BOUNCY BALL

Select Enter Cheat Code from the My 2K6 menu and enter Crazy Hops. Enable the cheats by selecting My Cheats or selecting Cheat Codes from the in-game Options.

MAJOR LEAGUE BASEBALL 2K7

MICKEY MANTLE ON THE FREE AGENTS LIST

Select Enter Cheat Code from the My 2K7 menu and enter themick.

ALL CHEATS

Select Enter Cheat Code from the My 2K7 menu and enter Black Sox.

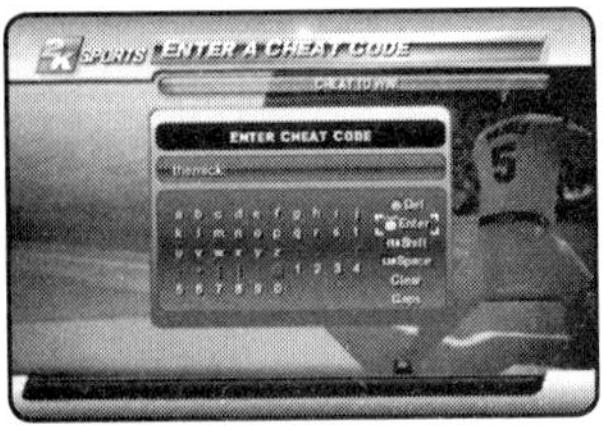

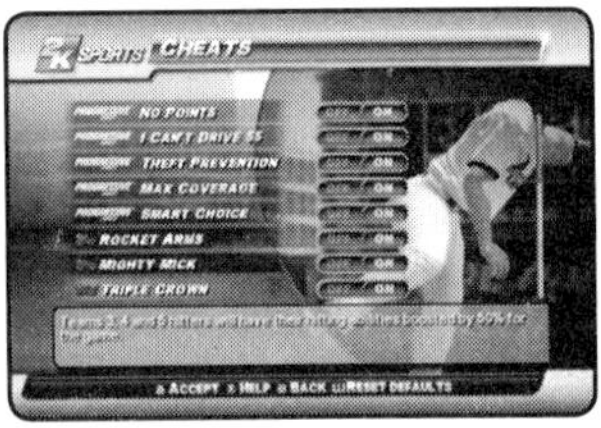

ALL EXTRAS

Select Enter Cheat Code from the My 2K7 menu and enter Game On.

UNLOCK EVERYTHING

Select Enter Cheat Code from the My 2K7 menu and enter Derek Jeter. This does not unlock the Topps cheats.

MIGHTY MICK CHEAT

Select Enter Cheat Code from the My 2K7 menu and enter mightymick.

TRIPLE CROWN CHEAT

Select Enter Cheat Code from the My 2K7 menu and enter triplecrown.

PINCH HIT MICK CHEAT

Select Enter Cheat Code from the My 2K7 menu and enter phmantle.

BIG BLAST CHEAT

Select Enter Cheat Code from the My 2K7 menu Rand enter m4murder.

MARVEL ULTIMATE ALLIANCE

UNLOCK ALL SKINS

At the Team menu, press Up, Down, Left, Right, Left, Right, Start.

UNLOCKS ALL HERO POWERS

At the Team menu, press Left, Right, Up, Down, Up, Down, Start.

ALL HEROES TO LEVEL 99

At the Team menu, press Up, Left, Up, Left, Down, Right, Down, Right, Start.

UNLOCK ALL HEROES

At the Team menu, press Up, Up, Down, Down, Left, Left, Left, Start.

UNLOCK DAREDEVIL

At the Team menu, press Left, Left, Right, Right, Up, Down, Up, Down, Start.

UNLOCK SILVER SURFER

At the Team menu, press Down, Left, Left, Up, Right, Up, Down, Left, Start.

GOD MODE

During gameplay, press Up, Down, Up, Down, Up, Left, Down, Right, Start.

TOUCH OF DEATH

During gameplay, press Left, Right, Down, Down, Right, Left, Start.

SUPER SPEED

During gameplay, press Up, Left, Up, Right, Down, Right, Start.

FILL MOMENTUM

During gameplay, press Left, Right, Right, Left, Up, Down, Down, Up, Start.

UNLOCK ALL COMICS

At the Review menu, press Left, Right, Right, Left, Up, Up, Right, Start.

UNLOCK ALL CONCEPT ART

At the Review menu, press Down, Down, Down, Right, Right, Left, Down, Start.

UNLOCK ALL CINEMATICS

At the Review menu, press Up, Left, Left, Up, Right, Right, Up, Start.

UNLOCK ALL LOAD SCREENS

At the Review menu, press Up, Down, Right, Left, Up, Up Down, Start.

UNLOCK ALL COURSES

At the Comic Missions menu, press Up, Right, Left, Down, Up, Right, Left, Down, Start.

X 360™

MONSTER MADNESS: BATTLE FOR SUBURBIA

Pause the game and press Up, Up, Down, Down, Left, Right, Left, Right, Ⓑ, Ⓐ. This brings up a screen where you can enter the following cheats. With the use of some cheats profile saving, level progression, and Xbox Live Achievements are disabled until you return to the Main menu.

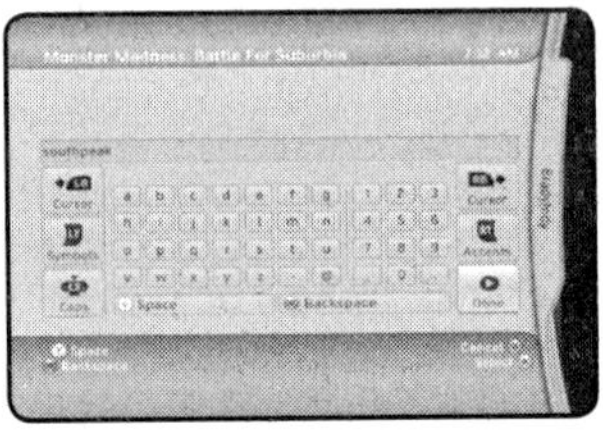

EFFECT	CHEAT
Animal Sounds	patrickdugan
Disable Tracking Cameras	ihatefunkycameras
Faster Music	upthejoltcola
First Person	morgythemole

EFFECT	CHEAT
Infinite Secondary Items	stevebrooks
Objects Move Away from Player	southpeak
Remove Film Grain	reverb

MOTOGP 07

ALL CHALLENGES

At the main menu, press Right, Up, B, A, B, A, Left, Down, Y.

ALL CHAMPIONSHIPS

At the main menu, press Right, Up, B, Y, Right, Up, B, Y, Right, Up, B, Y.

ALL LIVERIES

At the main menu, press Right, A, Left, Left, Y, Left, A, Down, Y.

ALL RIDERS

At the main menu, press Right, Up, B, B, A, Down, Up, B, Down, Up, B.

ALL TRACKS

At the main menu, press Left, A, Right, Down, Y, B, A, B, Y.

MX VS. ATV UNTAMED

ALL RIDING GEAR

Select Cheat Codes from the Options and enter crazylikea.

ALL HANDLEBARS

Select Cheat Codes from the Options and enter nohands.

27 GRAPHICS

Select Cheat Codes from the Options and enter STICKERS.

NASCAR 09

ALL FANTASY DRIVERS

Select EA Extras from My Nascar, choose Cheat Codes and enter CHECKERED FLAG.

WALMART TRACK AND THE WALMART CAR

Select EA Extras from My Nascar, choose Cheat Codes and enter Walmart Everyday.

NASCAR 08

ALL CHASE MODE CARS

Select Cheat Codes from the Options menu and enter checkered flag.

EA SPORTS CAR

Select Cheat Codes from the Options menu and enter ea sports car.

FANTASY DRIVERS

Select Cheat Codes from the Options menu and enter race the pack.

WALMART CAR AND TRACK

Select Cheat Codes from the Options menu and enter walmart everyday.

NBA 2K7

MAX DURABILITY

Select Codes from the Features menu and enter ironman.

UNLIMITED STAMINA

Select Codes from the Features menu and enter norest.

+10 DEFFENSIVE AWARENESS

Select Codes from the Features menu and enter getstops.

+10 OFFENSIVE AWARENESS

Select Codes from the Features menu and enter inthezone.

TOPPS 2K SPORTS ALL-STARS

Select Codes from the Features menu and enter topps2ksports.

ABA BALL

Select Codes from the Features menu and enter payrespect.

NBA 2K8

2KSPORTS TEAM

Select Codes from the Features menu and enter 2ksports.

VISUAL CONCEPTS TEAM

Select Codes from the Features menu and enter Vcteam.

ABA BALL

Select Codes from the Features menu and enter Payrespect.

NBA 2K9

2K SPORTS TEAM

Select Codes from the Features menu and enter 2ksports.

NBA 2K TEAM

Select Codes from the Features menu and enter nba2k.

SUPERSTARS

Select Codes from the Features menu and enter llmohffaae.

VC TEAM

Select Codes from the Features menu and enter vcteam.

ABA BALL

Select Codes from the Features menu and enter payrespect.

NBA LIVE 07

ADIDAS ARTILLERY II BLACK AND THE RBK ANSWER 9 VIDEO

Select NBA Codes from My NBA Live and enter 99B6356HAN.

ADIDAS ARTILLERY II

Select NBA Codes and enter NTGNFUE87H.

ADIDAS BTB LOW AND THE MESSAGE FROM ALLEN IVERSON VIDEO

Select NBA Codes and enter 7FB3KS9JQ0.

ADIDAS C-BILLUPS

Select NBA Codes and enter BV6877HB9N.

ADIDAS C-BILLUPS BLACK

Select NBA Codes and enter 85NVLDMWS5.

ADIDAS CAMPUS LT

Select NBA Codes and enter CLT2983NC8.

ADIDAS CRAZY 8

Select NBA Codes and enter CC98KKL814.

ADIDAS EQUIPMENT BBALL

Select NBA Codes and enter 220IUJKMDR.

ADIDAS GARNETT BOUNCE

Select NBA Codes and enter HYIOUHCAAN.

ADIDAS GARNETT BOUNCE BLACK

Select NBA Codes and enter KDZ2MQL17W.

ADIDAS GIL-ZERO

Select NBA Codes and enter 23DN1PPOG4.

ADIDAS GIL-ZERO BLACK

Select NBA Codes and enter QQQ3JCUYQ7.

ADIDAS GIL-ZERO MID

Select NBA Codes and enter 1GSJC8JWRL.

ADIDAS GIL-ZERO MID BLACK

Select NBA Codes and enter 369V6RVU3G.

ADIDAS STEALTH

Select NBA Codes and enter FE454DFJCC.

ADIDAS T-MAC 6

Select NBA Codes and enter MCJK843NNC.

ADIDAS T-MAC 6 WHITE

Select NBA Codes and enter 84GF7EJG8V.

CHARLOTTE BOBCATS 2006-2007 ALTERNATE JERSEY

Select NBA Codes and enter WEDX671H7S.

UTAH JAZZ 2006-2007 ALTERNATE JERSEY

Select NBA Codes and enter VCBI89FK83.

NEW JERSEY NETS 2006-2007 ALTERNATE JERSEY

Select NBA Codes and enter D4SAA98U5H.

WASHINGTON WIZARDS 2006-2007 ALTERNATE JERSEY

Select NBA Codes and enter QV93NLKXQC.

EASTERN ALL-STARS 2006-2007 AWAY JERSEY

Select NBA Codes and enter WOCNW4KL7L.

EASTERN ALL-STARS 2006-2007 HOME JERSEY

Select NBA Codes and enter 5654ND43N6.

WESTERN ALL-STARS 2006-2007 AWAY JERSEY

Select NBA Codes and enter XX93BVL20U.

WESTERN ALL-STARS 2006-2007 HOME JERSEY

Select NBA Codes and enter 993NSKL199.

NBA STREET HOMECOURT

ALL TEAMS

At the Main menu, hold Right Bumper + Left Bumper and press Left, Right, Left, Right.

ALL COURTS

At the Main menu, hold Right Bumper + Left Bumper and press Up, Right, Down, Left.

BLACK/RED BALL

At the Main menu, hold Right Bumper + Left Bumper and press Up, Down, Left, Right.

NCAA FOOTBALL 07

#16 BAYLOR

Select Pennant Collection from My NCAA. Press Select and enter Sic Em.

#16 NIKE SPEED TD

Select Pennant Collection from My NCAA. Press Select and enter Light Speed.

#63 ILLINOIS

Select Pennant Collection from My NCAA. Press Select and enter Oskee Wow.

#160 TEXAS TECH

Select Pennant Collection from My NCAA. Press Select and enter Fight.

#200 FIRST AND FIFTEEN

Select Pennant Collection from My NCAA. Press Select and enter Thanks.

#201 BLINK

Select Pennant Collection from My NCAA. Press Select and enter For.

#202 BOING

Select Pennant Collection from My NCAA. Press Select and enter Registering.

#204 BUTTER FINGERS

Select Pennant Collection from My NCAA. Press Select and enter With EA.

#205 CROSSED THE LINE

Select Pennant Collection from My NCAA. Press Select and enter Tiburon.

#206 CUFFED

Select Pennant Collection from My NCAA. Press Select and enter EA Sports.

#207 EXTRA CREDIT

Select Pennant Collection from My NCAA. Press Select and enter Touchdown.

#208 HELIUM

Select Pennant Collection from My NCAA. Press Select and enter In The Zone.

#209 HURRICANE

Select Pennant Collection from My NCAA. Press Select and enter Turnover.

#210 INSTANT FREPLAY

Select Pennant Collection from My NCAA. Press Select and enter Impact.

#211 JUMBALAYA

Select Pennant Collection from My NCAA. Press Select and enter Heisman.

#212 MOLASSES

Select Pennant Collection from My NCAA. Press Select and enter Game Time.

#213 NIKE FREE

Select Pennant Collection from My NCAA. Press Select and enter Break Free.

#214 NIKE MAGNIGRIP

Select Pennant Collection from My NCAA. Press Select and enter Hand Picked.

#215 NIKE PRO

Select Pennant Collection from My NCAA. Press Select and enter No Sweat.

#219 QB DUD

Select Pennant Collection from My NCAA. Press Select and enter Elite 11.

#221 STEEL TOE
Select Pennant Collection from My NCAA. Press Select and enter Gridiron.

#222 STIFFED
Select Pennant Collection from My NCAA. Press Select and enter NCAA.

#223 SUPER DIVE
Select Pennant Collection from My NCAA. Press Select and enter Upset.

#224 TAKE YOUR TIME
Select Pennant Collection from My NCAA. Press Select and enter Football.

#225 THREAD & NEEDLE
Select Pennant Collection from My NCAA. Press Select and enter 06.

#226 TOUGH AS NAILS
Select Pennant Collection from My NCAA. Press Select and enter Offense.

#227 TRIP
Select Pennant Collection from My NCAA. Press Select and enter Defense.

#228 WHAT A HIT
Select Pennant Collection from My NCAA. Press Select and enter Blitz.

#229 KICKER HEX
Select Pennant Collection from My NCAA. Press Select and enter Sideline.

#273 2004 ALL-AMERICANS
Select Pennant Collection from My NCAA. Press Select and enter Fumble.

#274 ALL-ALABAMA
Select Pennant Collection from My NCAA. Press Select and enter Roll Tide.

#276 ALL-ARKANSAS
Select Pennant Collection from My NCAA. Press Select and enter Woopigsooie.

#277 ALL-AUBURN
Select Pennant Collection from My NCAA. Press Select and enter War Eagle.

#278 ALL-CLEMSON
Select Pennant Collection from My NCAA. Press Select and enter Death Valley.

#279 ALL-COLORADO
Select Pennant Collection from My NCAA. Press Select and enter Glory.

#280 ALL-FLORIDA
Select Pennant Collection from My NCAA. Press Select and enter Great To Be.

#281 ALL-FSU
Select Pennant Collection from My NCAA. Press Select and enter Uprising.

#282 ALL-GEORGIA
Select Pennant Collection from My NCAA. Press Select and enter Hunker Down.

#283 ALL-IOWA
Select Pennant Collection from My NCAA. Press Select and enter On Iowa.

#284 ALL-KANSAS STATE
Select Pennant Collection from My NCAA. Press Select and enter Victory.

#285 ALL-LSU
Select Pennant Collection from My NCAA. Press Select and enter Geaux Tigers.

#286 ALL-MIAMI
Select Pennant Collection from My NCAA. Press Select and enter Raising Cane.

#287 ALL-MICHIGAN
Select Pennant Collection from My NCAA. Press Select and enter Go Blue.

#288 ALL-MISSISSIPPI STATE
Select Pennant Collection from My NCAA. Press Select and enter Hail State.

#289 ALL-NEBRASKA
Select Pennant Collection from My NCAA. Press Select and enter Go Big Red.

#290 ALL-NORTH CAROLINA
Select Pennant Collection from My NCAA. Press Select and enter Rah Rah.

#291 ALL-NOTRE DAME
Select Pennant Collection from My NCAA. Press Select and enter Golden Domer.

#292 ALL-OHIO STATE
Select Pennant Collection from My NCAA. Press Select and enter Killer Nuts.

#293 ALL-OKLAHOMA
Select Pennant Collection from My NCAA. Press Select and enter Boomer.

#294 ALL-OKLAHOMA STATE
Select Pennant Collection from My NCAA. Press Select and enter Go Pokes.

#295 ALL-OREGON
Select Pennant Collection from My NCAA. Press Select and enter Quack Attack.

#296 ALL-PENN STATE
Select Pennant Collection from My NCAA. Press Select and enter We Are.

#297 ALL-PITTSBURGH
Select Pennant Collection from My NCAA. Press Select and enter Lets Go Pitt.

#298 ALL-PURDUE
Select Pennant Collection from My NCAA. Press Select and enter Boiler Up.

#299 ALL-SYRACUSE
Select Pennant Collection from My NCAA. Press Select and enter Orange Crush.

#300 ALL-TENNESSEE
Select Pennant Collection from My NCAA. Press Select and enter Big Orange.

#301 ALL-TEXAS
Select Pennant Collection from My NCAA. Press Select and enter Hook Em.

#302 ALL-TEXAS A&M
Select Pennant Collection from My NCAA. Press Select and enter Gig Em.

#303 ALL-UCLA
Select Pennant Collection from My NCAA. Press Select and enter MIGHTY.

#304 ALL-USC
Select Pennant Collection from My NCAA. Press Select and enter Fight On.

#305 ALL-VIRGINIA
Select Pennant Collection from My NCAA. Press Select and enter Wahoos.

#306 ALL-VIRGINIA TECH
Select Pennant Collection from My NCAA. Press Select and enter Tech Triumph.

#307 ALL-WASHINGTON

Select Pennant Collection from My NCAA. Press Select and enter Bow Down.

#308 ALL-WISCONSIN

Select Pennant Collection from My NCAA. Press Select and enter U Rah Rah.

#311 ARK MASCOT

Select Pennant Collection from My NCAA. Press Select and enter Bear Down.

#329 GT MASCOT

Select Pennant Collection from My NCAA. Press Select and enter RamblinWreck.

#333 ISU MASCOT

Select Pennant Collection from My NCAA. Press Select and enter Red And Gold.

#335 KU MASCOT

Select Pennant Collection from My NCAA. Press Select and enter Rock Chalk.

#341 MINN MASCOT

Select Pennant Collection from My NCAA. Press Select and enter Rah Rah Rah.

#344 MIZZOU MASCOT

Select Pennant Collection from My NCAA. Press Select and enter Mizzou Rah.

#346 MSU MASCOT

Select Pennant Collection from My NCAA. Press Select and enter Go Green.

#349 NCSU MASCOT

Select Pennant Collection from My NCAA. Press Select and enter Go Pack.

#352 NU MASCOT

Select Pennant Collection from My NCAA. Press Select and enter Go Cats.

#360 S CAR MASCOT

Select Pennant Collection from My NCAA. Press Select and enter Go Carolina.

#371 UK MASCOT

Select Pennant Collection from My NCAA. Press Select and enter On On UK.

#382 WAKE FOREST

Select Pennant Collection from My NCAA. Press Select and enter Go Deacs Go.

#385 WSU MASCOT

Select Pennant Collection from My NCAA. Press Select and enter All Hail.

#386 WVU MASCOT

Select Pennant Collection from My NCAA. Press Select and enter Hail WV.

NEED FOR SPEED CARBON

CASTROL CASH

At the Main menu, press Down, Up, Left, Down, Right, Up, Ⓧ, Ⓑ. This will give you 10,000 extra cash.

INFINITE CREW CHARGE

At the Main menu, press Down, Up, Up, Right, Left, Left, Right, Ⓧ.

INFINITE NITROUS

At the Main menu, press Left, Up, Left, Down, Left, Down, Right, Ⓧ.

INFINITE SPEEDBREAKER

At the Main menu, press Down, Right, Right, Left, Right, Up, Down, ⊗.

NEED FOR SPEED CARBON LOGO VINYLS

At the Main menu, press Right, Up, Down, Up, Down, Left, Right, ⊗.

NEED FOR SPEED CARBON SPECIAL LOGO VINYLS

At the Main menu, press Up, Up, Down, Down, Down, Down, Up, ⊗.

NEED FOR SPEED PROSTREET

$2,000

Select Career and then choose Code Entry. Enter 1MA9X99.

$4,000

Select Career and then choose Code Entry. Enter W2IOLL01.

$8,000

Select Career and then choose Code Entry. Enter L1IS97A1.

$10,000

Select Career and then choose Code Entry. Enter 1MI9K7E1.

$10,000

Select Career and then choose Code Entry. Enter CASHMONEY.

$10,000

Select Career and then choose Code Entry. Enter REGGAME.

AUDI TT

Select Career and then choose Code Entry. Enter ITSABOUTYOU.

CHEVELLE SS

Select Career and then choose Code Entry. Enter HORSEPOWER.

COKE ZERO GOLF GTI

Select Career and then choose Code Entry. Enter COKEZERO.

DODGE VIPER

Select Career and then choose Code Entry. Enter WORLDSLONGESTLASTING.

MITSUBISHI LANCER EVOLUTION

Select Career and then choose Code Entry. Enter MITSUBISHIGOFAR.

UNLOCK ALL BONUSES

Select Career and then choose Code Entry. Enter UNLOCKALLTHINGS.

5 REPAIR MARKERS

Select Career and then choose Code Entry. Enter SAFETYNET.

ENERGIZER VINYL

Select Career and then choose Code Entry. Enter ENERGIZERLITHIUM.

CASTROL SYNTEC VINYL

Select Career and then choose Code Entry. Enter CASTROLSYNTEC. This also gives you $10,000.

NHL 08

ALL RBK EDGE JERSEYS

At the RBK Edge Code option, enter h3oyxpwksf8ibcgt.

NHL 2K8

2007–2008 NHL REEBOK EDGE JERSEYS

From the Features menu, select Unlock 2007-2008/Enter Password. Enter S6j83RMk01.

PETER JACKSON'S KING KONG: THE OFFICIAL GAME OF THE MOVIE

At the Main menu hold Left Bumper + Right Bumper + Left Trigger + Right Trigger and press Down, Up, Y, X, Down, Down, Y, Y. Release the buttons to access the Cheat option. The Cheat option will also be available on the pause menu. You cannot record your scores using cheat codes.

GOD MODE

Select Cheat and enter 8wonder.

ALL CHAPTERS

Select Cheat and enter KKst0ry.

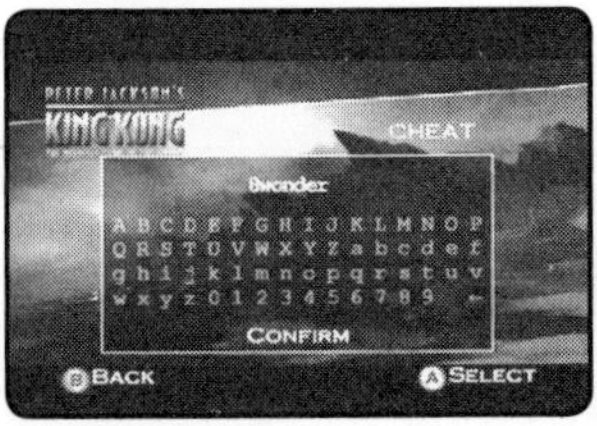

AMMO 999

Select Cheat and enter KK 999 mun.

MACHINE GUN

Select Cheat and enter KKcapone.

REVOLVER

Select Cheat and enter KKtigun.

SNIPER RIFLE

Select Cheat and enter KKsn1per.

INFINITE SPEARS

Select Cheat and enter lance 1nf.

ONE-HIT KILLS

Select Cheat and enter GrosBras.

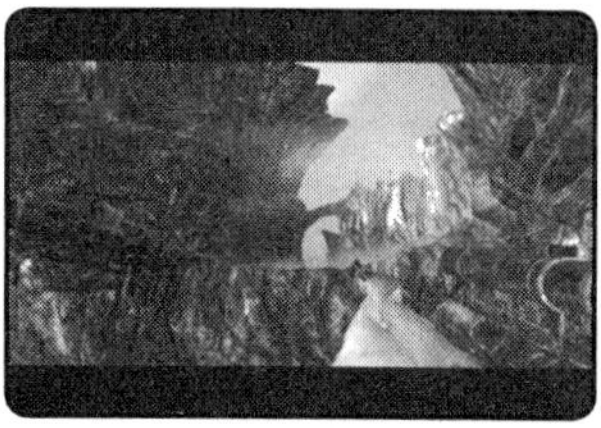

EXTRAS

Select Cheat and enter KKmuseum.

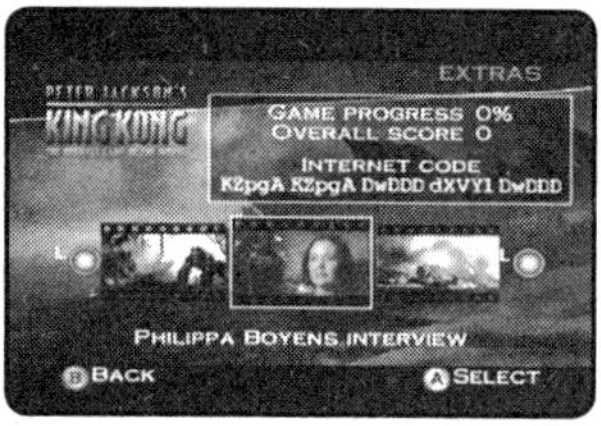

RATATOUILLE

UNLIMITED RUNNING

At the Cheat Code screen, enter SPEEDY.

ALL MULTIPLAYER AND SINGLE PLAYER MINI GAMES

At the Cheat Code screen, enter MATTELME.

ROCKSTAR GAMES PRESENTS TABLE TENNIS

Use of the following codes will disable achievements.

SWEATY CHARACTER VIEWER

After loading the map and before accepting the match, press Right Trigger, Up, Down, Left Trigger, Left, Right, Y, X, X, Y.

SMALL CROWD AUDIO

After loading the map and before accepting the match, press Down, Down, Down, Left Bumper, Left Trigger, Left Bumper, Left Trigger.

BIG BALL

After loading the map and before accepting the match, press Left, Right, Left, Right, Up, Up, Up, X.

COLORBLIND SPINDICATOR (ONLY IN NEWER PATCH)

After loading the map and before accepting the match, press Up, Down, X, X, Y, Y.

SILHOUETTE MODE

After loading the map and before accepting the match, press Up, Down, Y, Y, Left Bumper, Left Trigger, Right Trigger, Right Bumper.

BIG PADDLES CHEAT (ONLY IN NEWER PATCH)

After loading the map and before accepting the match, press Up, Left, Up, Right, Up, Down, Up, Up, X, X.

UNLOCK ALL

After loading the map and before accepting the match, press Up, Right, Down, Left, Left Bumper, Right, Up, Left, Down, Right Bumper.

VINTAGE AUDIO

After loading the map and before accepting the match, press Up, Up, Down, Down, Left, Right, Left, Right, Left Bumper, Right Bumper.

BIG CROWD AUDIO

After loading the map and before accepting the match, press Up, Up, Up, Right Bumper, Right Trigger, Right Bumper, Right Trigger.

OFFLINE GAMERTAGS

After loading the map and before accepting the match, press X, Y, X, Y, X, Y, Left Trigger, Right Trigger, Down, Down, Down.

SAMURAI SHODOWN 2

PLAY AS KUROKO IN 2-PLAYER

At the character select, press Up, Down, Left, Up, Down, Right + X.

SEGA SUPERSTARS TENNIS

UNLOCK CHARACTERS

Complete the following missions to unlock the corresponding character.

CHARACTER	MISSION TO COMPLETE
Alex Kidd	Mission 1 of Alex Kidd's World
Amy Rose	Mission 2 of Sonic the Hedgehog's World
Gilius	Mission 1 of Golden Axe's World
Gum	Mission 12 of Jet Grind Radio's World
Meemee	Mission 8 of Super Monkey Ball's World
Pudding	Mission 1 of Space Channel 5's World
Reala	Mission 2 of NiGHTs' World
Shadow The Hedgehog	Mission 14 of Sonic the Hedgehog's World

SHREK THE THIRD

10,000 GOLD COINS

At the gift shop, press Up, Up, Down, Up, Right, Left.

THE SIMPSONS GAME

After unlocking the following, the outfits can be changed at the downstairs closet in the Simpson's house. The Trophies can be viewed at different locations in the house: Bart's room, Lisa's room, Marge's room, and the garage.

BART'S OUTFITS AND TROPHIES (POSTER COLLECTION)

At the main menu, press Right, Left, X, X, Y, Right Thumb Stick.

HOMER'S OUTFITS AND TROPHIES (BEER BOTTLE COLLECTION)

At the main menu, press Left, Right, Ⓨ, Ⓨ, Ⓧ, Left Thumb Stick.

LISA'S OUTFITS AND TROPHIES (DOLLS)

At the main menu, press Ⓧ, Ⓨ, Ⓧ, Ⓧ, Ⓨ, Left Thumb Stick.

MARGE'S OUTFITS AND TROPHIES (HAIR PRODUCTS)

At the main menu, press Ⓨ, Ⓧ, Ⓨ, Ⓨ, Ⓧ, Right Thumb Stick.

SKATE

EXCLUSIVE BEST BUY CLOTHES

At the Main Menu, press Up, Down, Left, Right, Ⓧ, Right Bumper, Ⓨ, Left Bumper. You can get the clothes at Reg's or Slappy's Skate Shop. Find it under Skate.

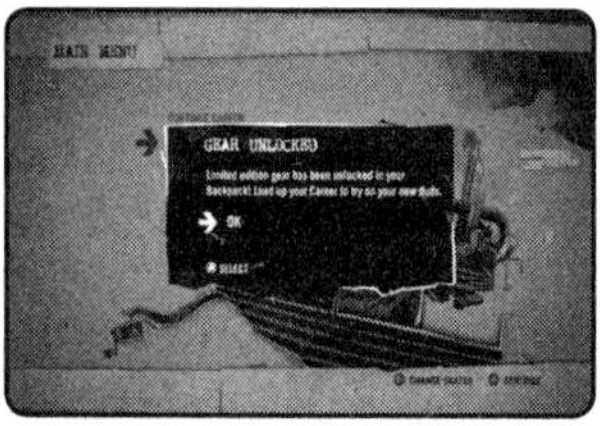

DEM BONES CHARACTER

Break each bone in your body at least 3 times.

SPIDER-MAN: FRIEND OR FOE

NEW GREEN GOBLIN AS A SIDEKICK

While standing in the Helicarrier between levels, press Left, Down, Right, Right, Down, Left.

SANDMAN AS A SIDEKICK

While standing in the Helicarrier between levels, press Right, Right, Right, Up, Down, Left.

VENOM AS A SIDEKICK

While standing in the Helicarrier between levels, press Left, Left, Right, Up, Down, Down.

5000 TECH TOKENS

While standing in the Helicarrier between levels, press Up, Up, Down, Down, Left, Right.

STAR WARS: THE FORCE UNLEASHED

CHEAT CODES

Pause the game and select Input Code. Here you can enter the following codes. Activating any of the following cheat codes will disable some unlockables, and you will be unable to save your progress.

CHEAT	CODE
All Force Powers at Max Power	KATARN
All Force Push Ranks	EXARKUN
All Saber Throw Ranks	ADEGAN
All Repulse Ranks	DATHOMIR

CHEAT	CODE
All Saber Crystals	HURRIKANE
All Talents	JOCASTA
Deadly Saber	LIGHTSABER

COMBOS

Pause the game and select Input Code. Here you can enter the following codes. Activating any of the following cheat codes will disable some unlockables, and you will be unable to save your progress.

COMBO	CODE
All Combos	MOLDYCROW
Aerial Ambush	VENTRESS
Aerial Assault	EETHKOTH
Aerial Blast	YADDLE
Impale	BRUTALSTAB
Lightning Bomb	MASSASSI
Lightning Grenade	RAGNOS

COMBO	CODE
Saber Slam	PLOKOON
Saber Sling	KITFISTO
Sith Saber Flurry	LUMIYA
Sith Slash	DARAGON
Sith Throw	SAZEN
New Combo	FREEDON
New Combo	MARAJADE

ALL DATABANK ENTRIES

Pause the game and select Input Code. Enter OSSUS.

MIRRORED LEVEL

Pause the game and select Input Code. Enter MINDTRICK. Re-enter the code to return level to normal.

SITH MASTER DIFFICULTY

Pause the game and select Input Code. Enter SITHSPAWN.

COSTUMES

Pause the game and select Input Code. Here you can enter the following codes.

COSTUME	CODE
All Costumes	SOHNDANN
Bail Organa	VICEROY
Ceremonial Jedi Robes	DANTOOINE
Drunken Kota	HARDBOILED

COSTUME	CODE
Emperor	MASTERMIND
Incinerator Trooper	PHOENIX
Jedi Adventure Robe	HOLOCRON
Kashyyyk Trooper	TK421GREEN

COSTUME	CODE
Kota	MANDALORE
Master Kento	WOOKIEE
Proxy	PROTOTYPE
Scout Trooper	FERRAL
Shadow Trooper	BLACKHOLE

COSTUME	CODE
Sith Stalker Armor	KORRIBAN
Snowtrooper	SNOWMAN
Stormtrooper	TK421WHITE
Stormtrooper Commander	TK421BLUE

STUNTMAN IGNITION

3 PROPS IN STUNT CREATOR MODE

Select Cheats from Extras and enter COOLPROP.

ALL ITEMS UNLOCKED FOR CONSTRUCTION MODE

Select Cheats from Extras and enter NOBLEMAN.

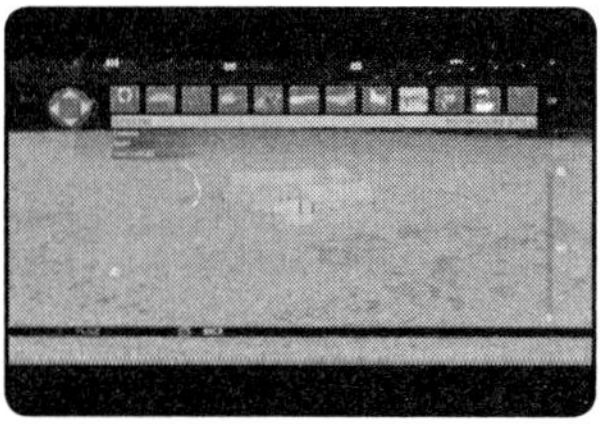

MVX SPARTAN

Select Cheats from Extras and enter fastride.

ALL CHEATS

Select Cheats from Extras and enter Wearefrozen. This unlocks the following cheats: Slo-mo Cool, Thrill Cam, Vision Switcher, Nitro Addiction, Freaky Fast, and Ice Wheels.

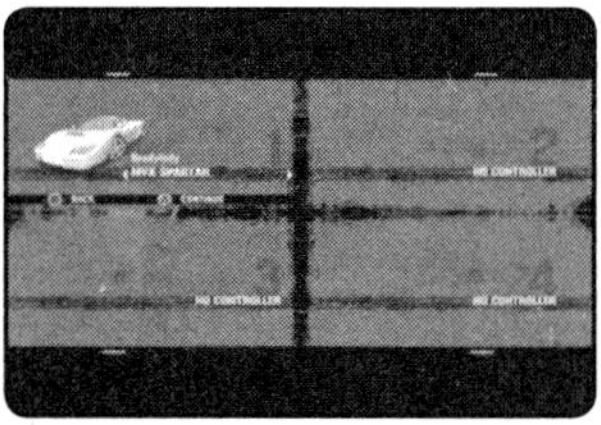

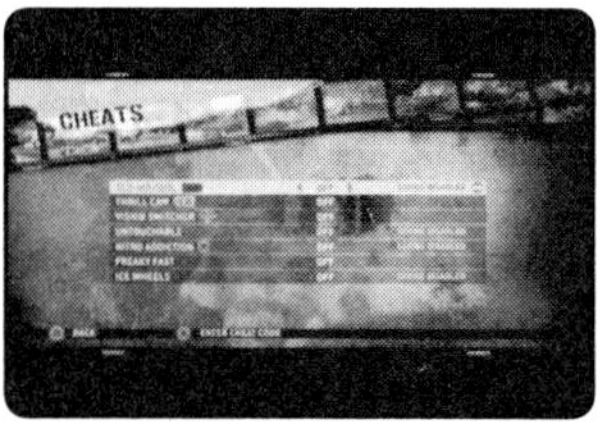

ALL CHEATS

Select Cheats from Extras and enter Kungfoopete.

ICE WHEELS CHEAT

Select Cheats from Extras and enter IceAge.

NITRO ADDICTION CHEAT

Select Cheats from Extras and enter TheDuke.

VISION SWITCHER CHEAT

Select Cheats from Extras and enter GFXMODES.

SUPER CONTRA

UNLIMITED LIVES AND SUPER MACHINEGUN

At the Main menu, select Arcade Game, and then press Up, Up, Down, Down, Left, Right, Left, Right, Ⓑ, Ⓐ. Achievements and the Leaderboard are disabled with this code.

SUPERMAN RETURNS: THE VIDEOGAME

GOD MODE

Pause the game, select Options and press Up, Up, Down, Down, Left, Right, Left, Right, Y, X.

INFINITE CITY HEALTH

Pause the game, select Options and press Y, Right, Y, Right, Up, Left, Right, Y.

ALL POWER-UPS

Pause the game, select Options and press Left, Y, Right, X, Down, Y, Up, Down, X, Y, X.

ALL UNLOCKABLES

Pause the game, select Options and press Left, Up, Right, Down, Y, X, Y Up, Right, X.

FREE ROAM AS BIZARRO

Pause the game, select Options and press Up, Right, Down, Right, Up, Left, Down, Right, Up.

SUPER PUZZLE FIGHTER II TURBO HD REMIX

PLAY AS AKUMA

At the Character Select screen, highlight Hsien-Ko and press Down.

PLAY AS DAN

At the Character Select screen, highlight Donovan and press Down.

PLAY AS DEVILOT

At the Character Select screen, highlight Morrigan and press Down.

PLAY AS ANITA

At the Character Select screen, hold Left Bumper + Right Bumper and choose Donovan.

PLAY AS HSIEN-KO'S TALISMAN

At the Character Select screen, hold Left Bumper + Right Bumper and choose Hsien-Ko.

PLAY AS MORRIGAN AS A BAT

At the Character Select screen, hold Left Bumper + Right Bumper and choose Morrigan.

SURF'S UP

ALL CHAMPIONSHIP LOCATIONS

Select Cheat Codes from the Extras menu and enter FREEVISIT.

ALL LEAF SLIDE STAGES

Select Cheat Codes from the Extras menu and enter GOINGDOWN.

ALL MULTIPLAYER LEVELS

Select Cheat Codes from the Extras menu and enter MULTIPASS.

ALL BOARDS

Select Cheat Codes from the Extras menu and enter MYPRECIOUS.

ASTRAL BOARD

Select Cheat Codes from the Extras menu and enter ASTRAL.

MONSOON BOARD

Select Cheat Codes from the Extras menu and enter MONSOON.

TINE SHOCKWAVE BOARD

Select Cheat Codes from the Extras menu and enter TINYSHOCKWAVE.

ALL CHARACTER CUSTOMIZATIONS

Select Cheat Codes from the Extras menu and enter TOPFASHION.

PLAY AS ARNOLD

Select Cheat Codes from the Extras menu and enter TINYBUTSTRONG.

PLAY AS ELLIOT

Select Cheat Codes from the Extras menu and enter SURPRISEGUEST.

PLAY AS GEEK

Select Cheat Codes from the Extras menu and enter SLOWANDSTEADY.

PLAY AS TANK EVANS

Select Cheat Codes from the Extras menu and enter IMTHEBEST.

PLAY AS TATSUHI KOBAYASHI

Select Cheat Codes from the Extras menu and enter KOBAYASHI.

PLAY AS ZEKE TOPANGA

Select Cheat Codes from the Extras menu and enter THELEGEND.

ALL VIDEOS AND SPEN GALLERY

Select Cheat Codes from the Extras menu and enter WATCHAMOVIE.

ART GALLERY

Select Cheat Codes from the Extras menu and enter NICEPLACE.

THRILLVILLE: OFF THE RAILS

$50,000

While in a park, press X, B, Y, X, B, Y, A.

500 THRILL POINTS

While in a park, press B, X, Y, B, X, Y, X.

ALL PARKS

While in a park, press X, B, Y, X, B, Y, X.

ALL RIDES IN CURRENT PARK

While in a park, press X, B, Y, X, B, Y, Y.

MISSION UNLOCK

While in a park, press X, B, Y, X, B, Y, B.

ALL MINI-GAMES IN PARTY PLAY

While in a park, press X, B, Y, X, B, Y, Right.

TIGER WOODS PGA TOUR 07

BIG HEAD MODE FOR CROWDS

Select Password and enter tengallonhat.

TIGER WOODS PGA TOUR 08

ALL COURSES

Select Password from EA Sports Extras and enter greensfees.

ALL GOLFERS

Select Password from EA Sports Extras and enter allstars.

WAYNE ROONEY

Select Password from EA Sports Extras and enter playfifa08.

INFINITE MONEY

Select Password from EA Sports Extras and enter cream.

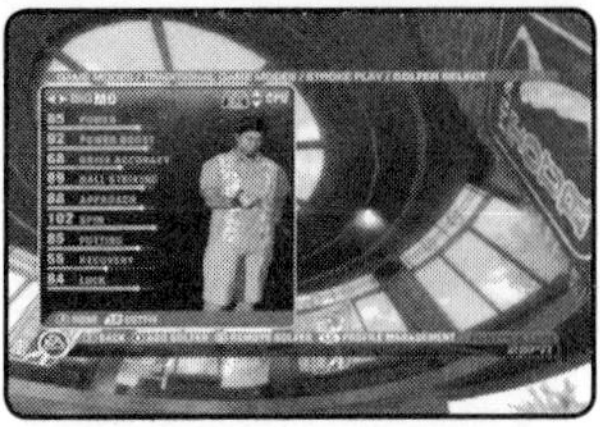

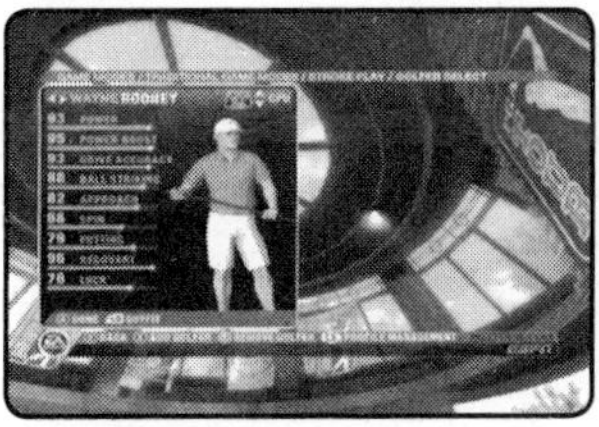

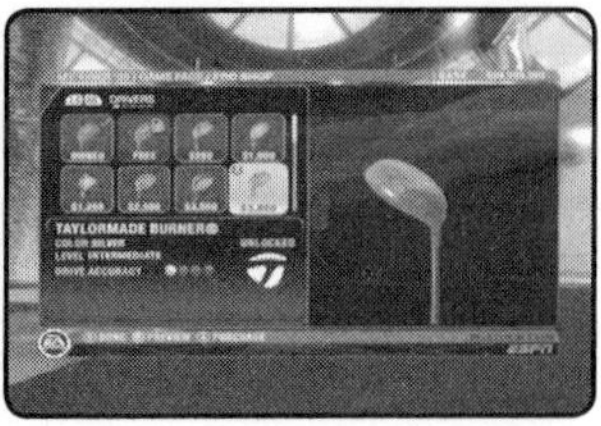

TIGER WOODS PGA TOUR 09

SPECTATORS BIG HEAD MODE

Select EA SPORTS Extras from My Tiger '09, choose Password and enter cephalus.

TMNT

CHALLENGE MAP 2

At the Main menu, hold the Left Bumper and press A, A, B, A.

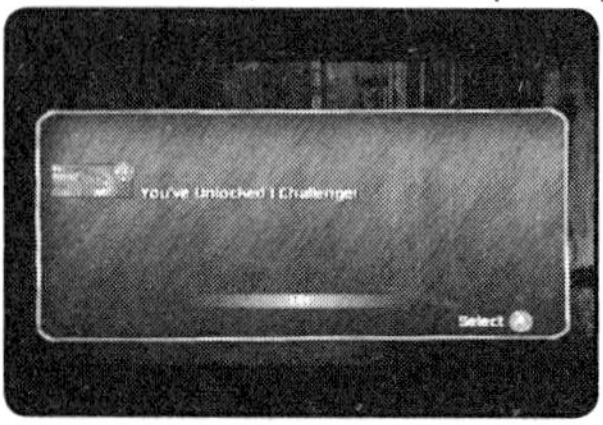

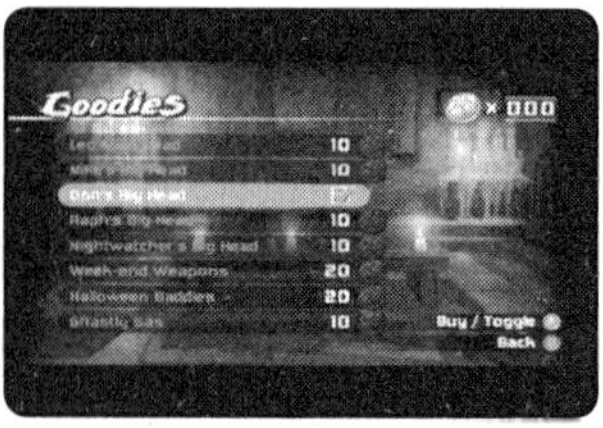

DON'S BIG HEAD GOODIE

At the Main menu, hold the Left Bumper and press B, Y, A, X.

TOMB RAIDER: LEGEND

The following codes must be unlocked in the game before using them.

BULLETPROOF

During a game, hold Left Trigger and press A, Right Trigger, Y, Right Trigger, X, Left Bumper.

DRAIN ENEMY HEALTH

During a game, hold Left Trigger and press X, B, A, Left Bumper, Right Trigger, Y.

INFINITE ASSAULT RIFLE AMMO

During a game, hold Left Bumper and press A, B, A, Left Trigger, X, Y.

INFINITE GRENADE LAUNCHER AMMO

During a game, hold Left Bumper and press Left Trigger, Y, Right Trigger, B, Left Trigger, X

INFINITE SHOTGUN AMMO

During a game, hold Left Bumper and press Right Trigger, B, X, Left Trigger, X, A.

INFINITE SMG AMMO

During a game, hold Left Bumper and press B, Y, Left Trigger, Right Trigger, A, B.

EXCALIBUR

During a game, hold Left Bumper and press Y, A, B, Right Trigger, Y, Left Trigger.

SOUL REAVER

During a game, hold Left Bumper and press A, Right Trigger, B, Right Trigger, Left Trigger, X.

ONE-SHOT KILL

During a game, hold Left Trigger and press Y, A, Y, X, Left Bumper, B.

TEXTURELESS MODE

During a game, hold Left Trigger and press Left Bumper, A, B, A, Y, Right Trigger.

TOM CLANCY'S GHOST RECON ADVANCED WARFIGHTER

ALL MISSIONS

At the Mission Select screen, hold Back + Left Trigger + Right Trigger and press Ⓨ, Right Bumper, Ⓨ, Right Bumper, Ⓧ.

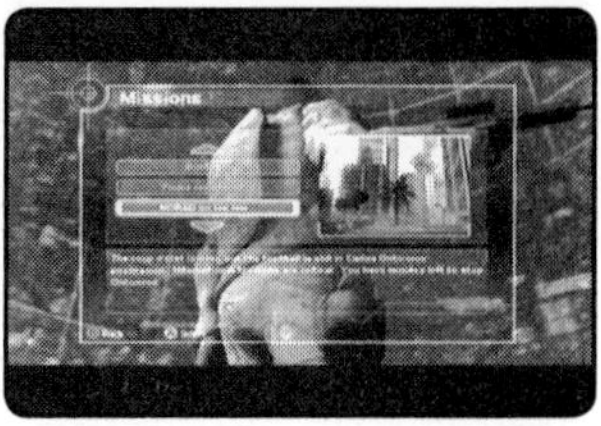

FULL HEALTH

Pause the game, hold Back + Left Trigger + Right Trigger and press Left Bumper, Left Bumper, Right Bumper, Ⓧ, Right Bumper, Ⓨ.

INVINCIBLE

Pause the game, hold Back + Left Trigger + Right Trigger and press Ⓨ, Ⓨ, Ⓧ, Right Bumper, Ⓧ, Left Bumper.

TEAM INVINCIBLE

Pause the game, hold Back + Left Trigger + Right Trigger and press Ⓧ, Ⓧ, Ⓨ, Right Bumper, Ⓨ, Left Bumper.

UNLIMITED AMMO

Pause the game, hold Back + Left Trigger + Right Trigger and press Right Bumper, Right Bumper, Left Bumper, Ⓧ, Left Bumper, Ⓨ.

TONY HAWK'S PROJECT 8

SPONSOR ITEMS

As you progress through Career mode and move up the rankings, you gain sponsors and each comes with its own Create-a-skater item.

RANK REQUIRED	CAS ITEM UNLOCKED
Rank 040	Adio Kenny V2 Shoes
Rank 050	Quiksilver Hoody 3
Rank 060	Birdhouse Tony Hawk Deck
Rank 080	Vans No Skool Gothic Shoes
Rank 100	Volcom Scallero Jacket
Rank 110	eS Square One Shoes
Rank 120	Almost Watch What You Say Deck
Rank 140	DVS Adage Shoe
Rank 150	Element Illuminate Deck
Rank 160	Etnies Sheckler White Lavender Shoes
Complete Skateshop Goal	Stereo Soundwave Deck

SKATERS

All of the skaters, except for Tony Hawk, must be unlocked by completing challenges in the Career Mode. They are useable in Free Skate and 2 Player modes.

SKATER	HOW THEY ARE UNLOCKED
Tony Hawk	Always UnlocOked
Lyn-z Adams Hawkins	Complete Pro Challenge
Bob Burquist	Complete Pro Challenge
Dustin Dollin	Complete Pro Challenge

SKATER	HOW THEY ARE UNLOCKED
Nyjah Huston	Complete Pro Challenge
Bam Margera	Complete Pro Challenge
Rodney Mullen	Complete Pro Challenge
Paul Rodriguez	Complete Pro Challenge
Ryan Sheckler	Complete Pro Challenge
Daewon Song	Complete Pro Challenge
Mike Vallely	Complete Pro Challenge
Stevie Willams	Complete Pro Challenge
Travis Barker	Complete Pro Challenge
Kevin Staab	Complete Pro Challenge
Zombie	Complete Pro Challenge
Christaian Hosoi	Rank #1
Jason Lee	Complete Final Tony Hawk Goal
Photographer	Unlock Shops
Security Guard	Unlock School
Bum	Unlock Car Factory
Beaver Mascot	Unlock High School
Real Estate Agent	Unlock Downtown
Filmer	Unlock High School
Skate Jam Kid	Rank #4
Dad	Rank #1
Colonel	All Gaps
Nerd	Complete School Spirit Goal

CHEAT CODES

Select Cheat Codes from the Options and enter the following codes. In game you can access some codes from the Options menu.

CHEAT CODE	RESULTS
plus44	Unlocks Travis Barker
hohohosoi	Unlocks Christian Hosoi
notmono	Unlocks Jason Lee
mixitup	Unlocks Kevin Staab
strangefellows	Unlocks Dad & Skater Jam Kid
themedia	Unlocks Photog Girl & Filmer
militarymen	Unlocks Colonel & Security Guard
jammypack	Unlocks Always Special
balancegalore	Unlocks Perfect Rail
frontandback	Unlocks Perect Manual
shellshock	Unlocks Unlimited Focus
shescaresme	Unlocks Big Realtor
birdhouse	Unlocks Inkblot deck
allthebest	Full Stats
needaride	All Decks unlocked and free, except for inkblot deck and gamestop deck
yougotitall	All specials unlocked and in player's special list and set as owned in skate shop
wearelosers	Unlocks Nerd and a Bum
manineedadate	Unlocks Beaver Mascot
suckstobedead	Unlocks Officer Dick
HATEDANDPROUD	Unlocks the Vans unlockable item

TONY HAWK'S PROVING GROUND

Select Cheat Codes from the Options and enter the following cheats. Some codes need to be enabled by selecting Cheats from the Options during a game.

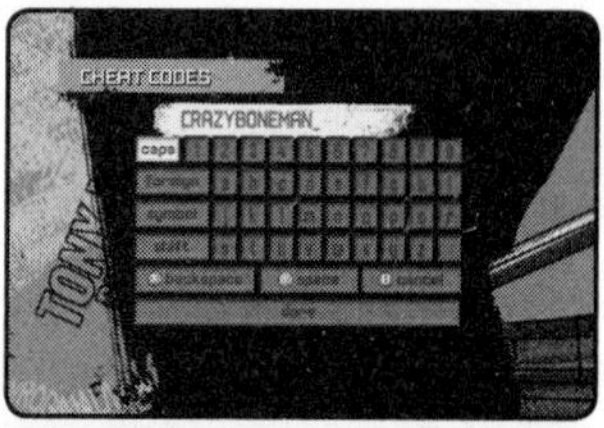

UNLOCK	CHEAT
Unlocks Boneman	CRAZYBONEMAN
Unlocks Bosco	MOREMILK
Unlocks Cam	NOTACAMERA
Unlocks Cooper	THECOOP
Unlocks Eddie X	SKETCHY
Unlocks El Patinador	PILEDRIVER
Unlocks Eric	FLYAWAY
Unlocks Mad Dog	RABBIES
Unlocks MCA	INTERGALACTIC
Unlocks Mel	NOTADUDE
Unlocks Rube	LOOKSSMELLY
Unlocks Spence	DAPPER
Unlocks Shayne	MOVERS
Unlocks TV Producer	SHAKER
Unlock FDR	THEPREZPARK
Unlock Lansdowne	THELOCALPARK
Unlock Air & Space Museum	THEINDOORPARK
Unlocks all Fun Items	OVERTHETOP
Unlocks all CAS items	GIVEMESTUFF
Unlocks all Decks	LETSGOSKATE
Unlock all Game Movies	WATCHTHIS
Unlock all Lounge Bling Items	SWEETSTUFF
Unlock all Lounge Themes	LAIDBACKLOUNGE
Unlock all Rigger Pieces	IMGONNABUILD
Unlock all Video Editor Effects	TRIPPY
Unlock all Video Editor Overlays	PUTEMONTOP
All specials unlocked and in player's special list	LOTSOFTRICKS
Full Stats	BEEFEDUP
Give player +50 skill points	NEEDSHELP

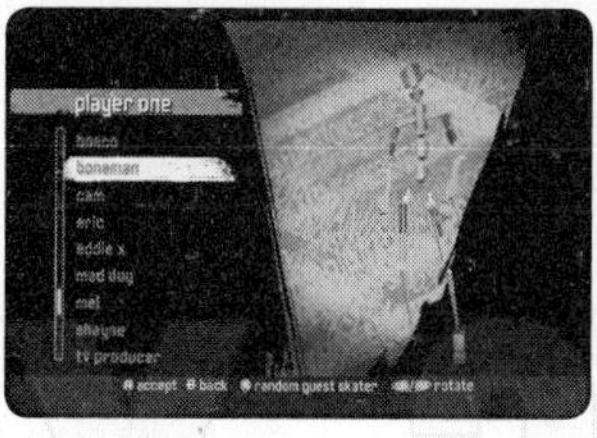

The following cheats lock you out of the Leaderboards:

UNLOCK	CHEAT
Unlocks Perfect Manual	STILLAINTFALLIN
Unlocks Perfect Rail	AINTFALLIN
Unlock Super Check	BOOYAH
Unlocks Unlimited Focus	MYOPIC
Unlock Unlimited Slash Grind	SUPERSLASHIN
Unlocks 100% branch completion in NTT	FOREVERNAILED
No Bails	ANDAINTFALLIN

You can not use the Video Editor with the following cheats:

UNLOCK	CHEAT
Invisible Man	THEMISSING
Mini Skater	TINYTATER
No Board	MAGICMAN

TRANSFORMERS: THE GAME

The following cheats disable saving and achievements:

INFINITE HEALTH

At the Main menu, press Left, Left, Up, Left, Right, Down, Right.

INFINITE AMMO

At the Main menu, press Up, Down, Left, Right, Up, Up, Down.

NO MILITARY OR POLICE

At the Main menu, press Right, Left, Right, Left, Right, Left, Right.

ALL MISSIONS

At the Main menu, press Down, Up, Left, Right, Right, Right, Up, Down.

BONUS CYBERTRON MISSIONS

At the Main menu, press Right, Up, Up, Down, Right, Left, Left.

GENERATION 1 SKIN: JAZZ

At the Main menu, press Left, Up, Down, Down, Left, Up, Right.

GENERATION 1 SKIN: MEGATRON

At the Main menu, press Down, Left, Left, Down, Right, Right, Up.

GENERATION 1 SKIN: OPTIMUS PRIME

At the Main menu, press Down, Right, Left, Up, Down, Down, Left.

GENERATION 1 SKIN: ROBOVISION OPTIMUS PRIME

At the Main menu, press Down, Down, Up, Up, Right, Right, Right.

GENERATION 1 SKIN: STARSCREAM

At the Main menu, press Right, Down, Left, Left, Down, Up, Up.

UNDERTOW

GAMER PIC 1 - SCUBA DIVER

Total 100 kills.

GAMER PIC 2 - ATLANTIS MAN

Total 10,000 kills.

VIRTUA TENNIS 3

KING & DUKE

At the Main menu, press Up, Up, Down, Down, Left, Right, Left, **LB**, **RB**.

ALL GEAR

At the Main menu, press Left, Right, Ⓑ, Left, Right, Ⓑ, Up, Down.

ALL COURTS

At the Main menu, press Up, Up, Down, Down, Left, Right, Left, Right.

WIN ONE MATCH TO WIN TOURNAMENT

At the Main menu, press Ⓑ, Left, Ⓑ, Right, Ⓑ, Up, Ⓑ, Down.

VIVA PINATA

NEW ITEMS IN PET STORE

Select New Garden and enter chewnicorn as the name.

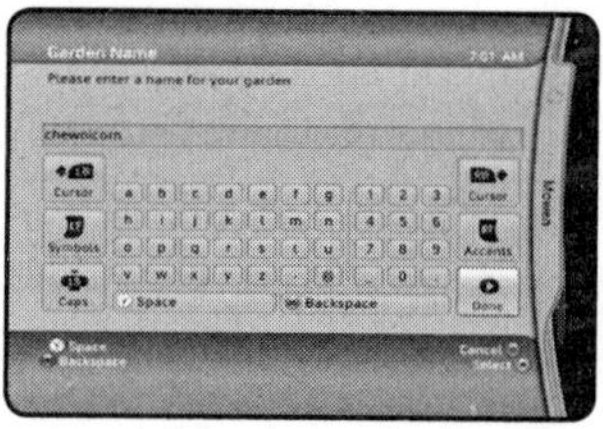

NEW ITEMS IN PET STORE

Select New Garden and enter bullseye as the name.

NEW ITEMS IN PET STORE

Select New Garden and enter goobaa as the name.

NEW ITEMS IN PET STORE

Select New Garden and enter kittyfloss as the name.

VIVA PINATA: PARTY ANIMALS

CLASSIC GAMER AWARD ACHIEVEMENT

At the START screen, press Up, Up, Down, Down, Left, Right, Left, Right, Ⓑ, Ⓐ. This earns you 10 points toward your Gamerscore.

VIVA PINATA: TROUBLE IN PARADISE

CREDITS

Select Play Garden and name your garden Piñata People. This unlocks the ability to view the credits on the main menu.

WALL-E

The following cheats will disable saving. The five possible characters starting with Wall-E and going down are: Wall-E, Auto, EVE, M-O, GEL-Ⓐ Steward.

ALL BONUS FEATURES UNLOCKED

Select Cheats from the Bonus Features menu and enter Wall-E, Auto, EVE, GEL-Ⓐ Steward.

ALL GAME CONTENT UNLOCKED

Select Cheats from the Bonus Features menu and enter M-O, Auto, GEL-Ⓐ Steward, EVE.

ALL SINGLE-PLAYER LEVELS UNLOCKED

Select Cheats from the Bonus Features menu and enter Auto, GEL-Ⓐ Steward, M-O, Wall-E.

ALL MULTIPLAYER MAPS UNLOCKED

Select Cheats from the Bonus Features menu and enter EVE, M-O, Wall-E, Auto.

ALL HOLIDAY COSTUMES UNLOCKED

Select Cheats from the Bonus Features menu and enter Auto, Auto, GEL-Ⓐ Steward, GEL-Ⓐ Steward.

ALL MULTIPLAYER COSTUMES UNLOCKED

Select Cheats from the Bonus Features menu and enter GEL-Ⓐ Steward, Wall-E, M-O, Auto.

UNLIMITED HEALTH UNLOCKED

Select Cheats from the Bonus Features menu and enter Wall-E, M-O, Auto, M-O.

WALL-E: MAKE ANY CUBE AT ANY TIME

Select Cheats from the Bonus Features menu and enter Auto, M-O, Auto, M-O.

WALL-EVE: MAKE ANY CUBE AT ANY TIME

Select Cheats from the Bonus Features menu and enter M-O, GEL-Ⓐ Steward, EVE, EVE.

WALL-E WITH A LASER GUN AT ANY TIME

Select Cheats from the Bonus Features menu and enter Wall-E, EVE, EVE, Wall-E.

WALL-EVE WITH A LASER GUN AT ANY TIME

Select Cheats from the Bonus Features menu and enter GEL-Ⓐ Steward, EVE, M-O, Wall-E.

WALL-E: PERMANENT SUPER LASER UPGRADE

Select Cheats from the Bonus Features menu and enter Wall-E, Auto, EVE, M-O.

EVE: PERMANENT SUPER LASER UPGRADE

Select Cheats from the Bonus Features menu and enter EVE, Wall-E, Wall-E, Auto.

CREDITS

Select Cheats from the Bonus Features menu and enter Auto, Wall-E, GEL-Ⓐ Steward, M-O.

WWE SMACKDOWN! VS. RAW 2008

HBK AND HHH'S DX OUTFIT

Select Cheat Codes from the Options and enter DXCostume69K2.

KELLY KELLY'S ALTERNATE OUTFIT

Select Cheat Codes from the Options and enter KellyKG12R.

BRET HART

Complete the March 31, 1996 Hall of Fame challenge by defeating Bret Hart with Shawn Michaels in a One-On-One 30-Minute Iron Man Match on Legend difficulty. Purchase from WWE Shop for $210,000.

MICK FOLEY

Complete the June 28, 1998 Hall of Fame challenge by defeating Mick Foley with The Undertaker in a H*** In a Cell Match on Legend difficulty. Purchase from WWE Shop for $210,000.

MR. MCMAHON

Win or successfully defend a championship (WWE or World Heavyweight) at WrestleMania in WWE 24/7 GM Mode. Purchase from WWE Shop for $110,000.

THE ROCK

Complete the April 1, 2001 Hall of Fame challenge by defeating The Rock with Steve Austin in a Single Match on Legend Difficulty. Purchase from WWE Shop for $210,000.

STEVE AUSTIN

Complete the March 23, 1997 Hall of Fame challenge by defeating Steve Austin with Bret Hart in a Submission Match on Legend Difficulty. Purchase from WWE Shop for $210,000.

TERRY FUNK

Complete the April 13, 1997 Hall of Fame challenge by defeating Tommy Dreamer, Sabu and Sandman with any Superstar in an ECW Extreme Rules 4-Way Match on Legend difficulty. Purchase from WWE Shop for $210,000.

MR. MCMAHON BALD

Must unlock Mr. McMahon as a playable character first. Purchase from WWE Shop for $60,000.

PLAYSTATION® 2

CONTENTS

ALIEN HOMINID

ALL LEVELS, MINI-GAMES, & HATS

Select Player 1 Setup or Player 2 Setup and change the name to ROYGBIV.

HATS FOR 2-PLAYER GAME

Go to the Options and rename your alien one of the following:

Abe	cletus	grrl
april	dandy	princess
behemoth	Goodman	superfly

AVATAR: THE LAST AIRBENDER-THE BURNING EARTH

1 HIT DISHONOR

At the Main menu, press **L1** and select Code Entry. Enter 28260.

ALL BONUS GAME

At the Main menu, press **L1** and select Code Entry. Enter 99801.

ALL GALLERY ITEMS

At the Main menu, press **L1** and select Code Entry. Enter 85061.

DOUBLE DAMAGE

At the Main menu, press **L1** and select Code Entry. Enter 90210.

INFINITE HEALTH

At the Main menu, press **L1** and select Code Entry. Enter 65049.

MAX LEVEL

At the Main menu, press **L1** and select Code Entry. Enter 89121.

UNLIMITED SPECIAL ATTACKS

At the Main menu, press **L1** and select Code Entry. Enter 66206.

AVATAR - THE LAST AIRBENDER: INTO THE INFERNO

ALL CHAPTERS
Select Game Secrets at Ember Islands and enter 52993833.

MAX COINS
Select Game Secrets at Ember Islands and enter 66639224.

ALL ITEMS AVAILABLE AT SHOP
Select Game Secrets at Ember Islands and enter 34737253.

ALL CONCEPT ART
Select Game Secrets at Ember Islands and enter 27858343.

BEN 10: ALIEN FORCE THE GAME

LEVEL LORD
Enter Gwen, Kevin, Big Chill, Gwen as a code.

INVINCIBILITY
Enter Kevin, Big Chill, Swampfire, Kevin as a code.

ALL COMBOS
Enter Swampfire, Gwen, Kevin, Ben as a code.

INFINITE ALIENS
Enter Ben, Swampfire, Gwen, Big Chill as a code.

BEN 10: PROTECTOR OF EARTH

INVINCIBILITY
Select a game from the Continue option. Go to the Map Selection screen, press Start and choose Extras. Select Enter Secret Code and enter XLR8, Heatblast, Wildvine, Fourarms.

ALL COMBOS
Select a game from the Continue option. Go to the Map Selection screen, press Start and choose Extras. Select Enter Secret Code and enter Cannonblot, Heatblast, Fourarms, Heatblast.

ALL LOCATIONS
Select a game from the Continue option. Go to the Map Selection screen, press Start and choose Extras. Select Enter Secret Code and enter Heatblast, XLR8, XLR8, Cannonblot.

DNA FORCE SKINS
Select a game from the Continue option. Go to the Map Selection screen, press Start and choose Extras. Select Enter Secret Code and enter Wildvine, Fourarms, Heatblast, Cannonbolt.

DARK HEROES SKINS
Select a game from the Continue option. Go to the Map Selection screen, press Start and choose Extras. Select Enter Secret Code and enter Cannonbolt, Cannonbolt, Fourarms, Heatblast.

ALL ALIEN FORMS
Select a game from the Continue option. Go to the Map Selection screen, press Start and choose Extras. Select Enter Secret Code and enter Wildvine, Fourarms, Heatblast, Wildvine.

MASTER CONTROL
Select a game from the Continue option. Go to the Map Selection screen, press Start and choose Extras. Select Enter Secret Code and enter Cannonbolt, Heatblast, Wildvine, Fourarms.

BRATZ: FOREVER DIAMONDZ

1000 BLINGZ

While in the Bratz Office, use the Cheat computer to enter SIZZLN.

2000 BLINGZ

While in the Bratz Office, use the Cheat computer to enter FLAUNT.

PET TREATS

While in the Bratz Office, use the Cheat computer to enter TREATZ.

GIFT SET A

While in the Bratz Office, use the Cheat computer to enter STYLIN.

GIFT SET B

While in the Bratz Office, use the Cheat computer to enter SKATIN.

GIFT SET C

While in the Bratz Office, use the Cheat computer to enter JEWELZ.

GIFT SET E

While in the Bratz Office, use the Cheat computer to enter DIMNDZ.

BRATZ: THE MOVIE

FEELIN' PRETTY CLOTHING LINE

In the Bratz office at the laptop computer, enter PRETTY.

HIGH SCHOOL CLOTHING LINE

In the Bratz office at the laptop computer, enter SCHOOL.

PASSION 4 FASHION CLOTHING LINE

In the Bratz office at the laptop computer, enter ANGELZ.

SWEETZ CLOTHING LINE

In the Bratz office at the laptop computer, enter SWEETZ.

CAPCOM CLASSICS COLLECTION VOL. 2

UNLOCK EVERYTHING

At the Title screen, press Left, Right, Up, Down, **L1**, **R1**, **L1**, **R1**. This code unlocks Cheats, Tips, Art, and Sound Tests.

CARS

UNLOCK EVERYTHING

Select Cheat Codes from the Options and enter IF900HP.

ALL CHARACTERS

Select Cheat Codes from the Options and enter YAYCARS.

ALL CHARACTER SKINS

Select Cheat Codes from the Options and enter R4MONE.

ALL MINI-GAMES AND COURSES

Select Cheat Codes from the Options and enter MATTL66.

MATER'S COUNTDOWN CLEAN-UP MINI-GAME AND MATER'S SPEEDY CIRCUIT

Select Cheat Codes from the Options and enter TRGTEXC.

FAST START

Select Cheat Codes from the Options and enter IMSPEED.

INFINITE BOOST

Select Cheat Codes from the Options and enter VROOOOM.

ART

Select Cheat Codes from the Options and enter CONC3PT.

VIDEOS

Select Cheat Codes from the Options and enter WATCHIT.

CARS MATER-NATIONAL

ALL ARCADE RACES, MINI-GAMES, AND WORLDS

Select Codes/Cheats from the options and enter PLAYALL.

ALL CARS

Select Codes/Cheats from the options and enter MATTEL07.

ALTERNATE LIGHTNING MCQUEEN COLORS

Select Codes/Cheats from the options and enter NCEDUDZ.

ALL COLORS FOR OTHERS

Select Codes/Cheats from the options and enter PAINTIT.

UNLIMITED TURBO

Select Codes/Cheats from the options and enter ZZOOOOM.

EXTREME ACCELERATION

Select Codes/Cheats from the options and enter 0TO200X.

EXPERT MODE

Select Codes/Cheats from the options and enter VRYFAST.

ALL BONUS ART

Select Codes/Cheats from the options and enter BUYTALL.

CRASH OF THE TITANS

BIG HEAD CRASH

Pause the game, hold **R1**, and press Square, Square, Triangle, X. Re-enter the code to disable.

SHADOW CRASH

Pause the game, hold **R1**, and press Triangle, Square, Triangle, Square. Re-enter the code to disable.

THE DA VINCI CODE

GOD MODE

Select Codes from the Options and enter VITRUVIAN MAN.

EXTRA HEALTH

Select Codes from the Options and enter SACRED FEMININE.

MISSION SELECT

Select Codes from the Options and enter CLOS LUCE 1519.

ONE-HIT FIST KILL

Select Codes from the Options and enter PHILLIPS EXETER.

ONE-HIT WEAPON KILL

Select Codes from the Options and enter ROYAL HOLLOWAY.

ALL VISUAL DATABASE

Select Codes from the Options and enter APOCRYPHA.

ALL VISUAL DATABASE AND CONCEPT ART

Select Codes from the Options and enter ET IN ARCADIA EGO.

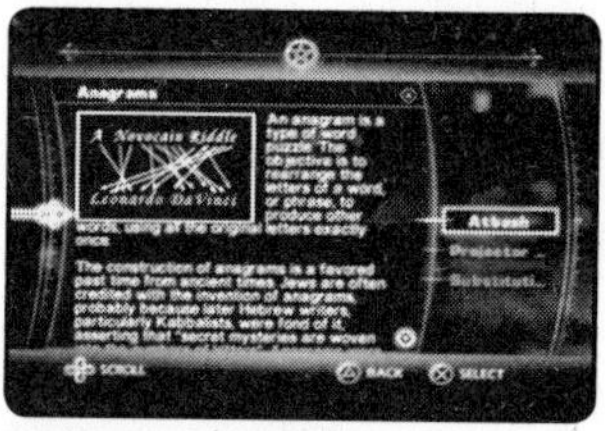

DISNEY PRINCESS: ENCHANTED JOURNEY

BELLE'S KINGDOM

Select Secrets and enter GASTON.

GOLDEN SET

Select Secrets and enter BLUEBIRD.

FLOWER WAND

Select Secrets and enter SLEEPY.

HEART WAND

Select Secrets and enter BASHFUL.

SHELL WAND

Select Secrets and enter RAJAH.

SHIELD WAND

Select Secrets and enter CHIP.

STAR WAND

Select Secrets and enter SNEEZY.

ERAGON

FURY MODE

Pause the game, hold **L1** + **L2** + **R1** + **R2** and press Square, Square, Circle, Circle.

FLATOUT 2

ALL CARS AND 1,000,000 CREDITS

Select Enter Code from the Extras and enter GIEVEPIX.

1,000,000 CREDITS

Select Enter Code from the Extras and enter GIVECASH.

PIMPSTER CAR

Select Enter Code from the Extras and enter RUTTO.

FLATMOBILE CAR

Select Enter Code from the Extras and enter WOTKINS.

MOB CAR

Select Enter Code from the Extras and enter BIGTRUCK.

SCHOOL BUS

Select Enter Code from the Extras and enter GIEVCARPLZ.

ROCKET CAR

Select Enter Code from the Extras and enter KALJAKOPPA.

TRUCK

Select Enter Code from the Extras and enter ELPUEBLO.

THE GRIM ADVENTURES OF BILLY & MANDY

CONCEPT ART

At the Main menu, hold ● and press Up, Up, Down, Down, Left, Right, Left, Right. Release ●.

ICE AGE 2: THE MELTDOWN

INFINITE PEBBLES

Pause the game and press Down, Down, Left, Up, Up, Right, Up, Down.

INFINITE ENERGY

Pause the game and press Down, Left, Right, Down, Down, Right, Left, Down.

INFINITE HEALTH

Pause the game and press Up, Right, Down, Up, Left, Down, Right, Left.

IRON MAN

ARMOR SELECTION

Iron Man's different armor suits are unlocked by completing certain missions. Refer to the following tables for when each is unlocked. After selecting a mission to play, you can pick the armor you wish to use.

COMPLETE MISSION	SUIT UNLOCKED
1: Escape	Mark I
2: First Flight	Mark II
3: Fight Back	Mark III
6: Flying Fortress	Comic Tin Can
9: Home Front	Classic
13: Showdown	Silver Centurion

CONCEPT ART

Concept Art is unlocked after finding certain numbers of Weapon Crates.

CONCEPT ART UNLOCKED	NUMBER OF WEAPON CRATES FOUND
Environments Set 1	6
Environments Set 2	12
Iron Man	18
Environments Set 3	24
Enemies	30
Environments Set 4	36
Villains	42
Vehicles	48
Covers	50

JUICED 2: HOT IMPORT NIGHTS

ASCARI KZ1

Select Cheats and Codes from the DNA Lab menu and enter KNOX. Defeat the challenge to earn the car.

NISSAN SKYLINE R34 GT-R

Select Cheats and Codes from the DNA Lab menu and enter JWRS. Defeat the challenge to earn the car.

KUNG FU PANDA

INVULNERABILITY

Select Cheats from the Extras menu and enter Down, Down, Right, Up, Left.

INFINITE CHI

Select Cheats from the Extras menu and enter Down, Right, Left, Up, Down.

BIG HEAD MODE

Select Cheats from the Extras menu and enter Down, Up, Left, Right, Right.

ALL MULTIPLAYER CHARACTERS

Select Cheats from the Extras menu and enter Left, Down, Left, Right, Down.

DRAGON WARRIOR OUTFIT IN MULTIPLAYER

Select Cheats from the Extras menu and enter Left, Down, Right, Left, Up.

THE LEGEND OF SPYRO: THE ETERNAL NIGHT

INFINITE MAGIC

Pause the game and press Up, Up, Down, Down, Left, Right, Left, Right, L1, R1, L1, R1.

LEGO BATMAN

BATCAVE CODES

Using the computer in the Batcave, select Enter Code and enter the following codes.

CHARACTERS

CHARACTER	CODE
Alfred	ZAQ637
Batgirl	JKR331
Bruce Wayne	BDJ327
Catwoman (Classic)	M1AAWW
Clown Goon	HJK327
Commissioner Gordon	DDP967
Fishmonger	HGY748
Freeze Girl	XVK541
Joker Goon	UTF782
Joker Henchman	YUN924
Mad Hatter	JCA283
Man-Bat	NYU942
Military Policeman	MKL382
Nightwing	MVY759
Penguin Goon	NKA238

CHARACTER	CODE
Penguin Henchman	BJH782
Penguin Minion	KJP748
Poison Ivy Goon	GTB899
Police Marksman	HKG984
Police Officer	JRY983
Riddler Goon	CRY928
Riddler Henchman	XEU824
S.W.A.T.	HTF114
Sailor	NAV592
Scientist	JFL786
Security Guard	PLB946
The Joker (Tropical)	CCB199
Yeti	NJL412
Zoo Sweeper	DWR243

VEHICLES

VEHICLE	CODE
Bat-Tank	KNTT4B
Bruce Wayne's Private Jet	LEA664
Catwoman's Motorcycle	HPL826
Garbage Truck	DUS483
Goon Helicopter	GCH328
Harbor Helicopter	CHP735
Harley Quinn's Hammer Truck	RDT637
Mad Hatter's Glider	HS000W
Mad Hatter's Steamboat	M4DM4N
Mr. Freeze's Iceberg	ICYICE
The Joker's Van	JUK657

VEHICLE	CODE
Mr. Freeze's Kart	BCT229
Penguin Goon Submarine	BTN248
Police Bike	LJP234
Police Boat	PLC999
Police Car	KJL832
Police Helicopter	CWR732
Police Van	MAC788
Police Watercraft	VJD328
Riddler's Jet	HAHAHA
Robin's Submarine	TTF453
Two-Face's Armored Truck	EFE933

CHEATS

CHEAT	CODE
Always Score Multiply	9LRGNB
Fast Batarangs	JRBDCB
Fast Walk	ZOLM6N
Flame Batarang	D8NYWH
Freeze Batarang	XPN4NG
Extra Hearts	ML3KHP
Fast Build	EVG26J
Immune to Freeze	JXUDY6
Invincibility	WYD5CP
Minikit Detector	ZXGH9J

CHEAT	CODE
More Batarang Targets	XWP645
Piece Detector	KHJ554
Power Brick Detector	MMN786
Regenerate Hearts	HJH7HJ
Score x2	N4NR3E
Score x4	CX9MAT
Score x6	MLVNF2
Score x8	WCCDB9
Score x10	18HW07

LEGO STAR WARS II: THE ORIGINAL TRILOGY

BEACH TROOPER

At Mos Eisley Canteena, select Enter Code and enter UCK868. You still need to select Characters and purchase this character for 20,000 studs.

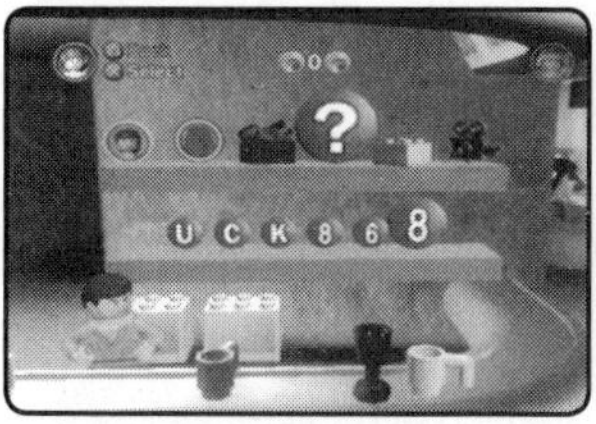

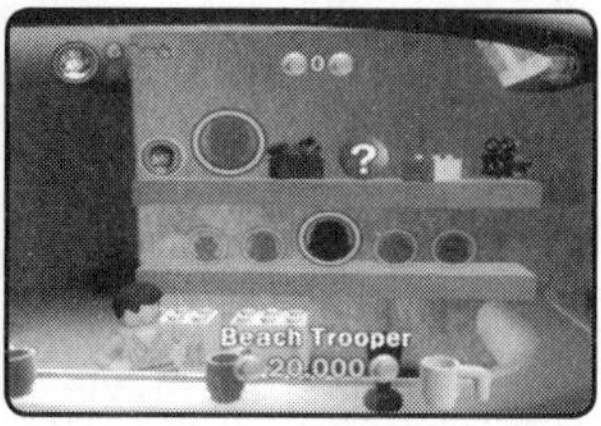

BEN KENOBI (GHOST)

At Mos Eisley Canteena, select Enter Code and enter BEN917. You still need to select Characters and purchase this character for 1,100,000 studs.

BESPIN GUARD

At Mos Eisley Canteena, select Enter Code and enter VHY832. You still need to select Characters and purchase this character for 15,000 studs.

BIB FORTUNA

At Mos Eisley Canteena, select Enter Code and enter WTY721. You still need to select Characters and purchase this character for 16,000 studs.

BOBA FETT

At Mos Eisley Canteena, select Enter Code and enter HLP221. You still need to select Characters and purchase this character for 175,000 studs.

DEATH STAR TROOPER

At Mos Eisley Canteena, select Enter Code and enter BNC332. You still need to select Characters and purchase this character for 19,000 studs.

EWOK

At Mos Eisley Canteena, select Enter Code and enter TTT289. You still need to select Characters and purchase this character for 34,000 studs.

GAMORREAN GUARD

At Mos Eisley Canteena, select Enter Code and enter YZF999. You still need to select Characters and purchase this character for 40,000 studs.

GONK DROID

At Mos Eisley Canteena, select Enter Code and enter NFX582. You still need to select Characters and purchase this character for 1,550 studs.

GRAND MOFF TARKIN

At Mos Eisley Canteena, select Enter Code and enter SMG219. You still need to select Characters and purchase this character for 38,000 studs.

GREEDO

At Mos Eisley Canteena, select Enter Code and enter NAH118. You still need to select Characters and purchase this character for 60,000 studs.

HAN SOLO (HOOD)

At Mos Eisley Canteena, select Enter Code and enter YWM840. You still need to select Characters and purchase this character for 20,000 studs.

IG-88

At Mos Eisley Canteena, select Enter Code and enter NXL973. You still need to select Characters and purchase this character for 30,000 studs.

IMPERIAL GUARD

At Mos Eisley Canteena, select Enter Code and enter MMM111. You still need to select Characters and purchase this character for 45,000 studs.

IMPERIAL OFFICER

At Mos Eisley Canteena, select Enter Code and enter BBV889. You still need to select Characters and purchase this character for 28,000 studs.

IMPERIAL SHUTTLE PILOT

At Mos Eisley Canteena, select Enter Code and enter VAP664. You still need to select Characters and purchase this character for 29,000 studs.

IMPERIAL SPY

At Mos Eisley Canteena, select Enter Code and enter CVT125. You still need to select Characters and purchase this character for 13,500 studs.

JAWA

At Mos Eisley Canteena, select Enter Code and enter JAW499. You still need to select Characters and purchase this character for 24,000 studs.

LOBOT

At Mos Eisley Canteena, select Enter Code and enter UUB319. You still need to select Characters and purchase this character for 11,000 studs.

PALACE GUARD

At Mos Eisley Canteena, select Enter Code and enter SGE549. You still need to select Characters and purchase this character for 14,000 studs.

REBEL PILOT

At Mos Eisley Canteena, select Enter Code and enter CYG336. You still need to select Characters and purchase this character for 15,000 studs.

REBEL TROOPER (HOTH)

At Mos Eisley Canteena, select Enter Code and enter EKU849. You still need to select Characters and purchase this character for 16,000 studs.

SANDTROOPER

At Mos Eisley Canteena, select Enter Code and enter YDV451. You still need to select Characters and purchase this character for 14,000 studs.

SKIFF GUARD

At Mos Eisley Canteena, select Enter Code and enter GBU888. You still need to select Characters and purchase this character for 12,000 studs.

SNOWTROOPER

At Mos Eisley Canteena, select Enter Code and enter NYU989. You still need to select Characters and purchase this character for 16,000 studs.

STROMTROOPER

At Mos Eisley Canteena, select Enter Code and enter PTR345. You still need to select Characters and purchase this character for 10,000 studs.

THE EMPEROR

At Mos Eisley Canteena, select Enter Code and enter HHY382. You still need to select Characters and purchase this character for 275,000 studs.

TIE FIGHTER

At Mos Eisley Canteena, select Enter Code and enter HDY739. You still need to select Characters and purchase this character for 60,000 studs.

TIE FIGHTER PILOT

At Mos Eisley Canteena, select Enter Code and enter NNZ316. You still need to select Characters and purchase this character for 21,000 studs.

TIE INTERCEPTOR

At Mos Eisley Canteena, select Enter Code and enter QYA828. You still need to select Characters and purchase this character for 40,000 studs.

TUSKEN RAIDER

At Mos Eisley Canteena, select Enter Code and enter PEJ821. You still need to select Characters and purchase this character for 23,000 studs.

UGNAUGHT

At Mos Eisley Canteena, select Enter Code and enter UGN694. You still need to select Characters and purchase this character for 36,000 studs.

LOONEY TUNES: ACME ARSENAL

UNLIMITED AMMUNITION

At the cheats menu, enter Down, Left, Up, Right, Down, Left, Up, Right, Down.

MADDEN NFL 07

MADDEN CARDS

Select Madden Cards from My Madden, then select Madden Codes and enter the following:

CARD	PASSWORD
#199 Gold Lame Duck Cheat	5LAWO0
#200 Gold Mistake Free Cheat	XL7SP1
#210 Gold QB on Target Cheat	WROA0R
#220 Super Bowl XLI Gold	RLA9R7
#221 Super Bowl XLII Gold	WRLUF8
#222 Super Bowl XLIII Gold	NIEV4A
#223 Super Bowl XLIV Gold	M5AB7L
#224 Aloha Stadium Gold	YI8P8U
#225 1958 Colts Gold	B57QLU
#226 1966 Packers Gold	1PL1FL
#227 1968 Jets Gold	MIE6WO
#228 1970 Browns Gold	CL2TOE
#229 1972 Dolphins Gold	NOEB7U
#230 1974 Steelers Gold	YOOFLA
#231 1976 Raiders Gold	MOA11I
#232 1977 Broncos Gold	C8UM7U
#233 1978 Dolphins Gold	VIU007
#234 1980 Raiders Gold	NLAPH3
#235 1981 Chargers Gold	COAGI4
#236 1982 Redskins Gold	WL8BRI
#237 1983 Raiders Gold	H0EW71
#238 1984 Dolphins Gold	M1AM1E
#239 1985 Bears Gold	QOET08
#240 1986 Giants Gold	ZI8S2L
#241 1988 49ers Gold	SP2A8H
#242 1990 Eagles Gold	2L4TRO

CARD	PASSWORD
#243 1991 Lions Gold	J1ETRI
#244 1992 Cowboys Gold	W9UVI9
#245 1993 Bills Gold	DLA3I7
#246 1994 49ers Gold	DR7EST
#247 1996 Packers Gold	F8LUST
#248 1998 Broncos Gold	FIES95
#249 1999 Rams Gold	S9OUSW
#250 Bears Pump Up the Crowd	B1OUPH
#251 Bengals Cheerleader	DRL2SW
#252 Bills Cheerleader	1PLUYO
#253 Broncos Cheerleader	3ROUJO
#254 Browns Pump Up the Crowd	T1UTOA
#255 Buccaneers Cheerleader	S9EWRI
#256 Cardinals Cheerleader	57IEPI
#257 Chargers Cheerleader	F7UHL8
#258 Chiefs Cheerleader	PRI5SL
#259 Colts Cheerleader	1R5AMI
#260 Cowboys Cheerleader	Z2ACHL
#261 Dolphins Cheerleader	C5AHLE
#262 Eagles Cheerleader	PO7DRO
#263 Falcons Cheerleader	37USPO
#264 49ers Cheerleader	KLOCRL
#265 Giants Pump Up the Crowd	C4USPI
#266 Jaguars Cheerleader	MIEH7E
#267 Jets Pump Up the Crowd	COLUXI
#268 Lions Pump Up the Crowd	3LABLU

CARD	PASSWORD
#269 Packers Pump Up the Crowd	4H07V0
#270 Panthers Cheerleader	F2IASP

CARD	PASSWORD
#282 All AFC Team Gold	PRO9PH
#283 All NFC Team Gold	RLATH7

MAJOR LEAGUE BASEBALL 2K7

MICKEY MANTLE ON THE FREE AGENTS LIST

Select Enter Cheat Code from the My 2K7 menu and enter themick.

MICKEY PINCH HITS

Select Enter Cheat Code from the My 2K7 menu and enter phmantle.

UNLOCK EVERYTHING

Select Enter Cheat Code from the My 2K7 menu and enter Derek Jeter. This does not unlock the Topps cheats.

MIGHTY MICK CHEAT

Select Enter Cheat Code from the My 2K7 menu and enter mightymick.

TRIPLE CROWN CHEAT

Select Enter Cheat Code from the My 2K7 menu and enter triplecrown.

BIG BLAST CHEAT

Select Enter Cheat Code from the My 2K7 menu and enter m4murder.

MAJOR LEAGUE BASEBALL 2K8

BIG HEAD MODE

Select Enter Cheat Code from the My 2K8 menu and enter Black Sox. This unlocks the Smart Choice cheat. Go to My Cheats to toggle the cheat on and off.

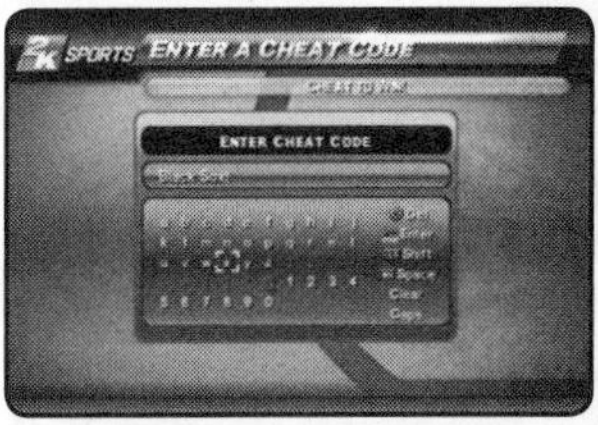

MARVEL ULTIMATE ALLIANCE

UNLOCK ALL SKINS

At the Team Menu, press Up, Down, Left, Right, Left, Right, Start.

UNLOCKS ALL HERO POWERS

At the Team Menu, press Left, Right, Up, Down, Up, Down, Start.

UNLOCK ALL HEROES

At the Team Menu, press Up, Up, Down, Down, Left, Left, Left, Start.

UNLOCK DAREDEVIL

At the Team Menu, press Left, Left, Right, Right, Up, Down, Up, Down, Start.

UNLOCK SILVER SURFER

At the Team Menu, press Down, Left, Left, Up, Right, Up, Down, Left, Start.

GOD MODE

During gameplay, press Up, Down, Up, Down, Up, Left, Down, Right, Start.

TOUCH OF DEATH

During gameplay, press Left, Right, Down, Down, Right, Left, Start.

SUPER SPEED

During gameplay, press Up, Left, Up, Right, Down, Right, Start.

FILL MOMENTUM

During gameplay, press Left, Right, Right, Left, Up, Down, Down, Up, Start.

UNLOCK ALL COMICS

At the Review menu, press Left, Right, Right, Left, Up, Up, Right, Start.

UNLOCK ALL CONCEPT ART

At the Review menu, press Down, Down, Down, Right, Right, Left, Down, Start.

UNLOCK ALL MOVIES

At the Review menu, press Up, Left, Left, Up, Right, Right, Up, Start.

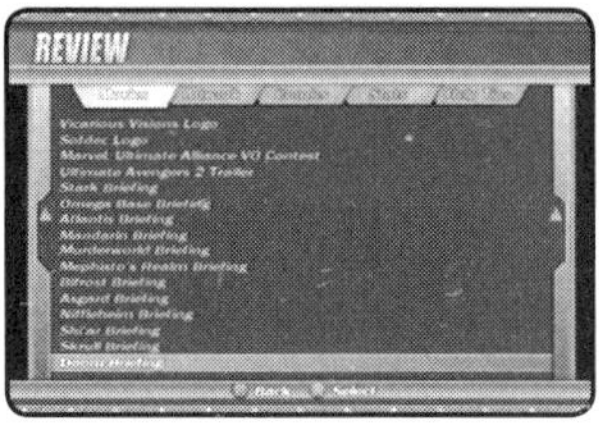

UNLOCK ALL LOAD SCREENS

At the Review menu, press Up, Down, Right, Left, Up, Up Down, Start.

UNLOCK ALL COURSES

At the Comic Missions menu, press Up, Right, Left, Down, Up, Right, Left, Down, Start.

MLB 07: THE SHOW

CLASSIC STADIUMS

At the Main menu, press Down, Up, Right, Down, Up, Left, Down, Up.

GOLDEN/SLIVER ERA PLAYERS

At the Main menu, press Left, Up, Right, Down, Down, Left, Up, Down.

MLB 08: THE SHOW

ALL CLASSIC STADIUMS

At the main menu, press Down, Right, Circle, Square, Left, Triangle, Up, L1. The controller will vibrate if entered correctly.

ALL GOLDEN & SILVER ERA PLAYERS IN EXHIBITION

At the main menu, press L1, L2, Square, Square, Triangle, Circle, Down. The controller will vibrate if entered correctly.

MLB POWER PROS

VIEW MLB PLAYERS AT CREATED PLAYERS MENU

Select View or Delete Custom Players/Password Display from the My Data menu. Press Up, Up, Down, Down, Left, Right, Left Right, L1, R1.

ALVIN LOCKHART'S BATTING STANCE AND PITCHING FORM

At the main menu, press Right, Left, Up, Down, Down, Right, Right, Up, Up, Left, Down, Left. These will be available at the shop.

MVP 07 NCAA BASEBALL

ALL CHALLENGE ITEMS

In Dynasty Mode, create a player with the name David Hamel.

MX VS. ATV UNTAMED

EVERYTHING

Select Cheat Codes from the options menu and enter YOUGOTIT.

1,000,000 STORE POINTS

Select Cheat Codes from the options menu and enter MANYZEROS.

50CC BIKE CLASS

Select Cheat Codes from the options menu and enter LITTLEGUY.

ALL BIKES

Select Cheat Codes from the options menu and enter ONRAILS.

ALL CHALLENGES

Select Cheat Codes from the options menu and enter MORESTUFF.

ALL FREESTYLE TRACKS

Select Cheat Codes from the options menu and enter ALLSTYLE.

ALL GEAR

Select Cheat Codes from the options menu and enter WELLDRESSED.

ALL MACHINES

Select Cheat Codes from the options menu and enter MCREWHEELS.

ALL RIDERS

Select Cheat Codes from the options menu and enter WHOSTHAT.

ALL TRACKS

Select Cheat Codes from the options menu and enter FREETICKET.

MONSTER TRUCK

Select Cheat Codes from the options menu and enter PWNAGE.

NARUTO: ULTIMATE NINJA 2

In Naruto's house, select Input Password. This is where you can enter an element, then three signs. Enter the following here:

1,000 RYO

Water, Hare, Monkey, Monkey
Water, Ram, Horse, Dog
Water, Horse, Horse, Horse
Water, Rat, Rooster, Boar
Water, Rat, Monkey, Rooster
Fire, Rat, Dragon, Dog

5,000 RYO

Water, Tiger, Dragon, Tiger
Water, Snake, Rooster, Horse

10,000 RYO

Fire, Tiger, Tiger, Rooster
Fire, Tiger, Dragon, Hare

NASCAR 07

$10,000,000

In Fight to the Top mode, enter your name as GiveMe More.

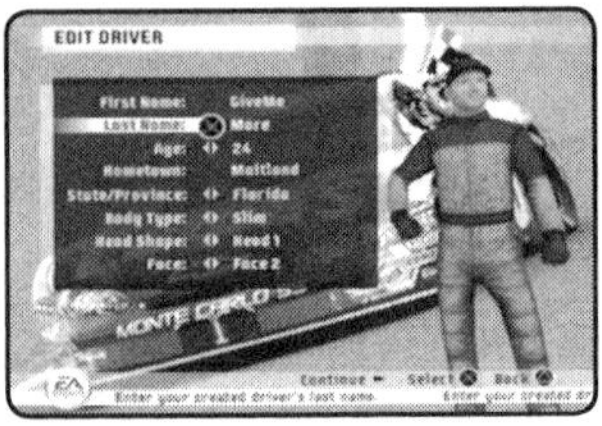

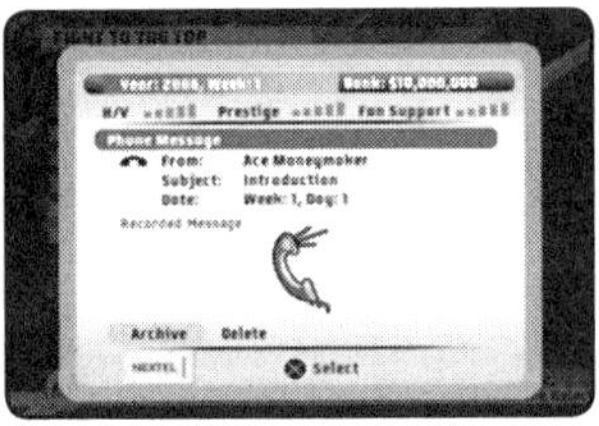

10,000,000 FANS

In Fight to the Top mode, enter your name as AllBow ToMe.

PRESTIGE LEVEL 10 WITH 2,000,000 POINTS

In Fight to the Top mode, enter your name as Outta MyWay.

100% TEAM PRESTIGE

In Fight to the Top mode, enter your name as MoMoney BlingBling.

ALL CHASE PLATES

In Fight to the Top mode, enter your name as ItsAll ForMe.

OLD SPICE TRACKS AND CARS.

In Fight to the Top mode, enter your name as KeepCool SmellGreat.

WALMART TRACK AND CARS

In Fight to the Top mode, enter your name as Walmart EveryDay.

NASCAR 08

ALL CHASE MODE CARS

Select Cheat Codes from the Options menu and enter checkered flag.

EA SPORTS CAR

Select Cheat Codes from the Options menu and enter ea sports car.

FANTASY DRIVERS

Select Cheat Codes from the Options menu and enter race the pack.

WALMART CAR AND TRACK

Select Cheat Codes from the Options menu and enter walmart everyday.

NASCAR 09

WALMART TRACK AND THE WALMART CAR

In Chase for the Sprint Cup, enter the driver's name as WalMart EveryDay.

NBA 07

2006 CHARLOTTE BOBCATS ALTERNATE JERSEY

Select NBA.com from the Trophy Room. Press ◉ to bring up the Enter Code screen. Enter JKL846ETK5.

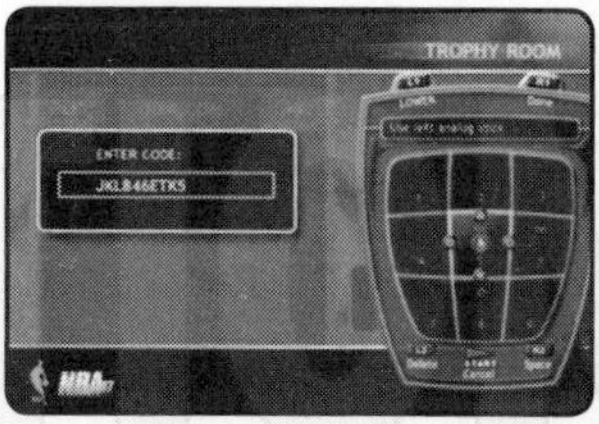

2006 NOK HORNETS ALTERNATE JERSEY

Select NBA.com from the Trophy Room. Press ● to bring up the Enter Code screen. Enter EL2E3T8H58.

2006 NEW JERSEY NETS ALTERNATE JERSEY

Select NBA.com from the Trophy Room. Press ● to bring up the Enter Code screen. Enter NB79D965D2.

2006 UTAH JAZZ ALTERNATE JERSEY

Select NBA.com from the Trophy Room. Press ● to bring up the Enter Code screen. Enter 228GG7585G.

2006 WASH WIZARDS ALTERNATE JERSEY

Select NBA.com from the Trophy Room. Press ● to bring up the Enter Code screen. Enter PL5285F37F.

2007 EASTERN ALL-STARS

Select NBA.com from the Trophy Room. Press ● to bring up the Enter Code screen. Enter 5F89RE3H8G.

2007 WESTERN ALL-STARS

Select NBA.com from the Trophy Room. Press ● to bring up the Enter Code screen. Enter 2H5E89EH8C.

NBA 09 THE INSIDE

ALL-STAR 09 EAST

Select Trophy Room from the Options. Press L1, then ●, and enter SHPNV2K699.

ALL-STAR 09 WEST

Select Trophy Room from the Options. Press L1, then ●, and enter K8AV6YMLNF.

ALL TROPHIES

Select Trophy Room from the Options. Press L1, then ●, and enter K@ZZ@@M!.

LA LAKERS LATIN NIGHTS

Select Trophy Room from the Options. Press L1, then ●, and enter NMTWCTC84S.

MIAMI HEAT LATIN NIGHTS

Select Trophy Room from the Options. Press L1, then ●, and enter WCTGSA8SPD.

PHOENIX SUNS LATIN NIGHTS

Select Trophy Room from the Options. Press L1, then ●, and enter LKUTSENFJH.

SAN ANTONIO LATIN NIGHTS

Select Trophy Room from the Options. Press L1, then ●, and enter JFHSY73MYD.

NBA 2K7

ABA BALL

Select Codes from the Features menu and enter payrespect.

ALL-STAR BALL

Select Codes from the Features menu and enter ply8mia.

MAX DURABILITY

Select Codes from the Features menu and enter ironman.

UNLIMITED STAMINA

Select Codes from the Features menu and enter norest.

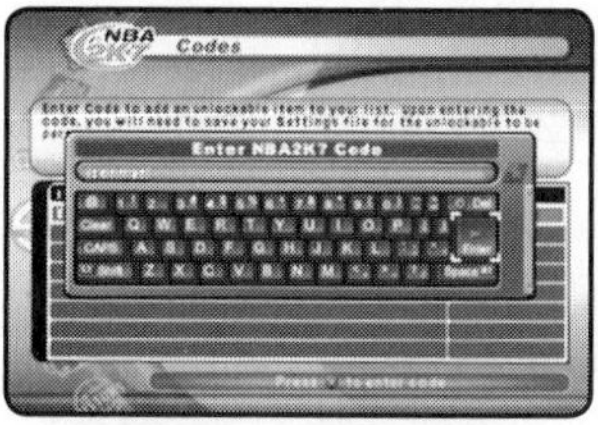

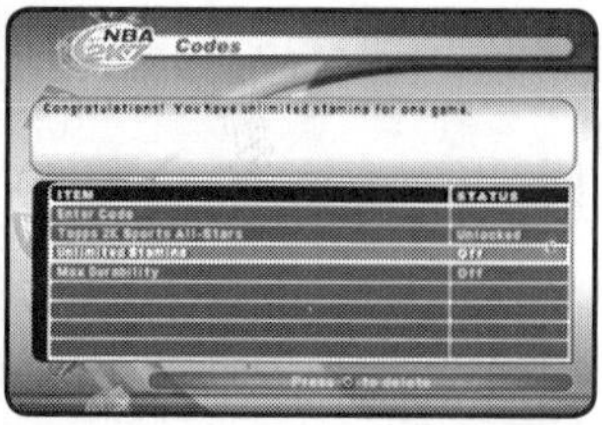

+10 DEFENSIVE AWARENESS

Select Codes from the Features menu and enter getstops.

+10 OFFENSIVE AWARENESS

Select Codes from the Features menu and enter inthezone.

2007 ALL-STAR UNIFORMS

Select Codes from the Features menu and enter syt6cii.

BOBCATS ALTERNATE

Select Codes from the Features menu and enter bcb8sta.

JAZZ ALTERNATE

Select Codes from the Features menu and enter zjb3lau.

NETS ALTERNATE

Select Codes from the Features menu and enter nrd4esj.

WIZARDS ALTERNATE

Select Codes from the Features menu and enter zw9idla.

ST. PATRICK'S DAY UNIFORMS

Select Codes from the Features menu and enter tpk7sgn.

VALENTINE'S DAY UNIFORMS

Select Codes from the Features menu and enter vdr5lya.

INTERNATIONAL ALL-STARS

Select Codes from the Features menu and enter tns9roi.

NBA 2K TEAM

Select Codes from the Features menu and enter bestsim.

SUPERSTARS

Select Codes from the Features menu and enter rta1spe

TOPPS 2K SPORTS ALL-STARS

Select Codes from the Features menu and enter topps2ksports.

NBA 2K8

2K SPORTS TEAM

Select Codes from the Features menu and enter 2ksports.

NBA DEVELOPMENT TEAM

Select Codes from the Features menu and enter nba2k.

VISUAL CONCEPTS TEAM

Select Codes from the Features menu and enter vcteam.

ABA BALL

Select Codes from the Features menu and enter payrespect.

NBA LIVE 07

ADIDAS ARTILLERY II BLACK & THE RBK ANSWER 9 VIDEO

Select NBA Codes from My NBA Live and enter 99B6356HAN.

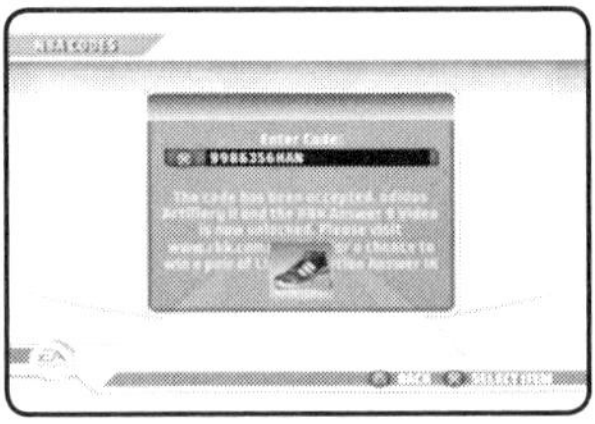

ADIDAS ARTILLERY II

Select NBA Codes and enter NTGNFUE87H.

ADIDAS BTB LOW AND THE MESSAGE FROM ALLEN IVERSON VIDEO

Select NBA Codes and enter 7FB3KS9JQ0.

ADIDAS C-BILLUPS

Select NBA Codes and enter BV6877HB9N.

ADIDAS C-BILLUPS BLACK

Select NBA Codes and enter 85NVLDMWS5.

ADIDAS CAMPUS LT

Select NBA Codes and enter CLT2983NC8.

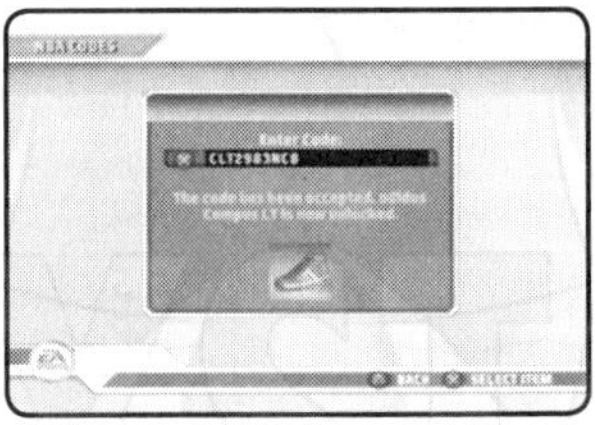

ADIDAS CRAZY 8

Select NBA Codes and enter CC98KKL814.

ADIDAS EQUIPMENT BBALL

Select NBA Codes and enter 220IUJKMDR.

ADIDAS GARNETT BOUNCE

Select NBA Codes and enter HYIOUHCAAN.

ADIDAS GARNETT BOUNCE BLACK

Select NBA Codes and enter KDZ2MQL17W.

ADIDAS GIL-ZERO
Select NBA Codes and enter 23DN1PPOG4.

ADIDAS GIL-ZERO BLACK
Select NBA Codes and enter QQQ3JCUYQ7.

ADIDAS GIL-ZERO MID
Select NBA Codes and enter 1GSJC8JWRL.

ADIDAS GIL-ZERO MID BLACK
Select NBA Codes and enter 369V6RVU3G.

ADIDAS STEALTH
Select NBA Codes and enter FE454DFJCC.

ADIDAS T-MAC 6
Select NBA Codes and enter MCJK843NNC.

ADIDAS T-MAC 6 WHITE
Select NBA Codes and enter 84GF7EJG8V.

AIR JORDAN V
Select NBA Codes and enter PNBBX1EVT5.

AIR JORDAN V
Select NBA Codes and enter VIR13PC451.

AIR JORDAN V
Select NBA Codes and enter IB7G8NN91Z.

JORDAN MELO M3
Select NBA Codes and enter JUL38TC485.

CHARLOTTE BOBCATS 2006-2007 ALTERNATE JERSEY
Select NBA Codes and enter WEDX671H7S.

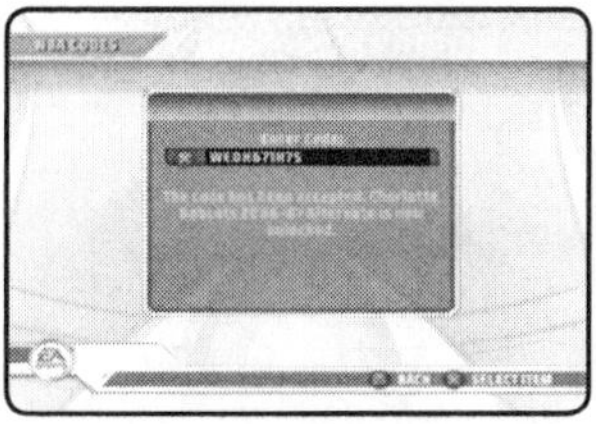

UTAH JAZZ 2006-2007 ALTERNATE JERSEY
Select NBA Codes and enter VCBI89FK83.

NEW JERSEY NETS 2006-2007 ALTERNATE JERSEY
Select NBA Codes and enter D4SAA98U5H.

WASHINGTON WIZARDS 2006-2007 ALTERNATE JERSEY
Select NBA Codes and enter QV93NLKXQC.

EASTERN ALL-STARS 2006-2007 ROAD JERSEY
Select NBA Codes and enter WOCNW4KL7L.

EASTERN ALL-STARS 2006-2007 HOME JERSEY
Select NBA Codes and enter 5654ND43N6.

WESTERN ALL-STARS 2006-2007 ROAD JERSEY
Select NBA Codes and enter XX93BVL20U.

WESTERN ALL-STARS 2006-2007 HOME JERSEY
Select NBA Codes and enter 993NSKL199.

NBA LIVE 08

ADIDAS GIL II ZERO SHOE CODES
Select NBA Codes from My NBA Live and enter the following:

SHOES	CODE
Agent Zero	ADGILLIT6BE
Black President	ADGILLIT7BF
Cuba	ADGILLIT4BC
CustOmize Shoe	ADGILLIT5BD
GilWood	ADGILLIT1B9
TS Lightswitch Away	ADGILLIT0B8
TS Lightswitch Home	ADGILLIT2BA

NCAA FOOTBALL 07

#16 BAYLOR
Select Pennant Collection from My NCAA. Press Select and enter Sic Em.

#16 NIKE SPEED TD
Select Pennant Collection from My NCAA. Press Select and enter Light Speed.

#63 ILLINOIS
Select Pennant Collection from My NCAA. Press Select and enter Oskee Wow.

#160 TEXAS TECH
Select Pennant Collection from My NCAA. Press Select and enter Fight.

#200 FIRST AND FIFTEEN
Select Pennant Collection from My NCAA. Press Select and enter Thanks.

#201 BLINK
Select Pennant Collection from My NCAA. Press Select and enter For.

#202 BOING
Select Pennant Collection from My NCAA. Press Select and enter Registering.

#204 BUTTER FINGERS
Select Pennant Collection from My NCAA. Press Select and enter With EA.

#205 CROSSED THE LINE
Select Pennant Collection from My NCAA. Press Select and enter Tiburon.

#206 CUFFED
Select Pennant Collection from My NCAA. Press Select and enter EA Sports.

#207 EXTRA CREDIT
Select Pennant Collection from My NCAA. Press Select and enter Touchdown.

#208 HELIUM
Select Pennant Collection from My NCAA. Press Select and enter In The Zone.

#209 HURRICANE
Select Pennant Collection from My NCAA. Press Select and enter Turnover.

#210 INSTANT FREPLAY
Select Pennant Collection from My NCAA. Press Select and enter Impact.

#211 JUMBALAYA
Select Pennant Collection from My NCAA. Press Select and enter Heisman.

#212 MOLASSES
Select Pennant Collection from My NCAA. Press Select and enter Game Time.

#213 NIKE FREE
Select Pennant Collection from My NCAA. Press Select and enter Break Free.

#214 NIKE MAGNIGRIP
Select Pennant Collection from My NCAA. Press Select and enter Hand Picked.

#215 NIKE PRO
Select Pennant Collection from My NCAA. Press Select and enter No Sweat.

#219 QB DUD
Select Pennant Collection from My NCAA. Press Select and enter Elite 11.

#221 STEEL TOE
Select Pennant Collection from My NCAA. Press Select and enter Gridiron.

#222 STIFFED
Select Pennant Collection from My NCAA. Press Select and enter NCAA.

#223 SUPER DIVE
Select Pennant Collection from My NCAA. Press Select and enter Upset.

#224 TAKE YOUR TIME
Select Pennant Collection from My NCAA. Press Select and enter Football.

#225 THREAD & NEEDLE
Select Pennant Collection from My NCAA. Press Select and enter 06.

#226 TOUGH AS NAILS
Select Pennant Collection from My NCAA. Press Select and enter Offense.

#227 TRIP
Select Pennant Collection from My NCAA. Press Select and enter Defense.

#228 WHAT A HIT
Select Pennant Collection from My NCAA. Press Select and enter Blitz.

#229 KICKER HEX
Select Pennant Collection from My NCAA. Press Select and enter Sideline.

#273 2004 ALL-AMERICANS
Select Pennant Collection from My NCAA. Press Select and enter Fumble.

#274 ALL-ALABAMA
Select Pennant Collection from My NCAA. Press Select and enter Roll Tide.

#276 ALL-ARKANSAS
Select Pennant Collection from My NCAA. Press Select and enter Woopigsooie.

#277 ALL-AUBURN
Select Pennant Collection from My NCAA. Press Select and enter War Eagle.

#278 ALL-CLEMSON
Select Pennant Collection from My NCAA. Press Select and enter Death Valley.

#279 ALL-COLORADO
Select Pennant Collection from My NCAA. Press Select and enter Glory.

#280 ALL-FLORIDA
Select Pennant Collection from My NCAA. Press Select and enter Great To Be.

#281 ALL-FSU
Select Pennant Collection from My NCAA. Press Select and enter Uprising.

#282 ALL-GEORGIA
Select Pennant Collection from My NCAA. Press Select and enter Hunker Down.

#283 ALL-IOWA
Select Pennant Collection from My NCAA. Press Select and enter On Iowa.

#284 ALL-KANSAS STATE
Select Pennant Collection from My NCAA. Press Select and enter Victory.

#285 ALL-LSU
Select Pennant Collection from My NCAA. Press Select and enter Geaux Tigers.

#286 ALL-MIAMI
Select Pennant Collection from My NCAA. Press Select and enter Raising Cane.

#287 ALL-MICHIGAN
Select Pennant Collection from My NCAA. Press Select and enter Go Blue.

#288 ALL-MISSISSIPPI STATE
Select Pennant Collection from My NCAA. Press Select and enter Hail State.

#289 ALL-NEBRASKA
Select Pennant Collection from My NCAA. Press Select and enter Go Big Red.

#290 ALL-NORTH CAROLINA
Select Pennant Collection from My NCAA. Press Select and enter Rah Rah.

#291 ALL-NOTRE DAME
Select Pennant Collection from My NCAA. Press Select and enter Golden Domer.

#292 ALL-OHIO STATE
Select Pennant Collection from My NCAA. Press Select and enter Killer Nuts.

#293 ALL-OKLAHOMA
Select Pennant Collection from My NCAA. Press Select and enter Boomer.

#294 ALL-OKLAHOMA STATE
Select Pennant Collection from My NCAA. Press Select and enter Go Pokes.

#295 ALL-OREGON
Select Pennant Collection from My NCAA. Press Select and enter Quack Attack.

#296 ALL-PENN STATE
Select Pennant Collection from My NCAA. Press Select and enter We Are.

#297 ALL-PITTSBURGH
Select Pennant Collection from My NCAA. Press Select and enter Lets Go Pitt.

#298 ALL-PURDUE
Select Pennant Collection from My NCAA. Press Select and enter Boiler Up.

#299 ALL-SYRACUSE
Select Pennant Collection from My NCAA. Press Select and enter Orange Crush.

#300 ALL-TENNESSEE
Select Pennant Collection from My NCAA. Press Select and enter Big Orange.

#301 ALL-TEXAS
Select Pennant Collection from My NCAA. Press Select and enter Hook Em.

#302 ALL-TEXAS A&M
Select Pennant Collection from My NCAA. Press Select and enter Gig Em.

#303 ALL-UCLA
Select Pennant Collection from My NCAA. Press Select and enter MIGHTY.

#304 ALL-USC
Select Pennant Collection from My NCAA. Press Select and enter Fight On.

#305 ALL-VIRGINIA
Select Pennant Collection from My NCAA. Press Select and enter Wahoos.

#306 ALL-VIRGINIA TECH
Select Pennant Collection from My NCAA. Press Select and enter Tech Triumph.

#307 ALL-WASHINGTON
Select Pennant Collection from My NCAA. Press Select and enter Bow Down.

#308 ALL-WISCONSIN
Select Pennant Collection from My NCAA. Press Select and enter U Rah Rah.

#311 ARK MASCOT
Select Pennant Collection from My NCAA. Press Select and enter Bear Down.

#329 GT MASCOT
Select Pennant Collection from My NCAA. Press Select and enter RamblinWreck.

#333 ISU MASCOT
Select Pennant Collection from My NCAA. Press Select and enter Red And Gold.

#335 KU MASCOT
Select Pennant Collection from My NCAA. Press Select and enter Rock Chalk.

#341 MINN MASCOT
Select Pennant Collection from My NCAA. Press Select and enter Rah Rah Rah.

#344 MIZZOU MASCOT
Select Pennant Collection from My NCAA. Press Select and enter Mizzou Rah.

#346 MSU MASCOT
Select Pennant Collection from My NCAA. Press Select and enter Go Green.

#349 NCSU MASCOT
Select Pennant Collection from My NCAA. Press Select and enter Go Pack.

#352 NU MASCOT
Select Pennant Collection from My NCAA. Press Select and enter Go Cats.

#360 S CAR MASCOT
Select Pennant Collection from My NCAA. Press Select and enter Go Carolina.

#371 UK MASCOT

Select Pennant Collection from My NCAA. Press Select and enter On On UK.

#382 WAKE FOREST

Select Pennant Collection from My NCAA. Press Select and enter Go Deacs Go.

#385 WSU MASCOT

Select Pennant Collection from My NCAA. Press Select and enter All Hail.

#386 WVU MASCOT

Select Pennant Collection from My NCAA. Press Select and enter Hail WV.

NCAA FOOTBALL 08

PENNANT CODES

Go to My Shrine and select Pennants. Press Select and enter the following:

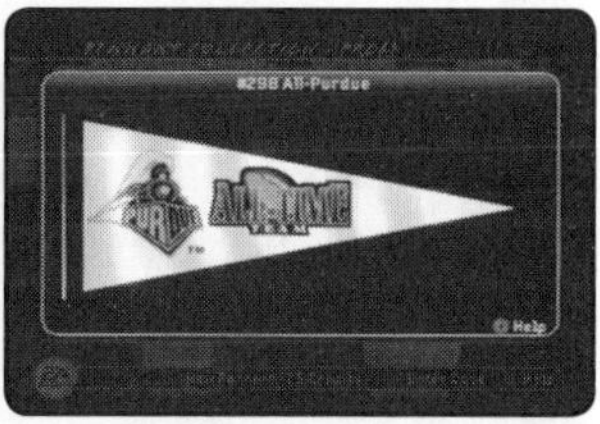

PENNANT	CODE
#200 1st & 15 Cheat	Thanks
#201 Blink Cheat	For
#202 Boing Cheat	Registering
#204 Butter Fingers Cheat	With EA
#205 Crossed The Line Cheat	Tiburon
#206 Cuffed Cheat	EA Sports
#207 Extra Credit Cheat	Touchdown
#208 Helium Cheat	In The Zone
#209 Hurricane Cheat	Turnover
#210 Instant FrePlay Cheat	Impact
#211 Jumbalaya Cheat	Heisman
#212 Molasses Cheat	Game Time
#213 Nike Free Cheat	Break Free
#214 Nike Magnigrip Cheat	Hand Picked
#215 Nike Pro Cheat	No Sweat
#219 QB Dud Cheat	Elite 11
#221 Steel Toe Cheat	Gridiron
#222 Stiffed Cheat	NCAA
#223 Super Dive Cheat	Upset
#226 Tough As Nail Cheat	Offense
#228 What A Hit Cheat	Blitz
#229 Kicker Hex Cheat	Sideline
#273 2004 All-American Team	Fumble
#274 All-Alabama Team	Roll Tide
#276 All-Arkansas Team	Woopigsooie
#277 All-Auburn Team	War Eagle

PENNANT	CODE
#278 All-Clemson Team	Death Valley
#279 All-Colorado Team	Glory
#281 All-FSU Team	Uprising
#282 All-Georgia Team	Hunker Down
#283 All-Iowa Team	On Iowa
#285 All-LSU Team	Geaux Tigers
#287 All-Michigan Team	Go Blue
#288 All-Mississippi State Team	Hail State
#289 All-Nebraska Team	Go Big Red
#291 All-Notre Dame Team	Golden Domer
#292 All-Ohio State Team	Killer Nuts
#293 All-Oklahoma Team	Boomer
#294 All-Oklahoma State Team	Go Pokes
#296 All-Penn State Team	We Are
#298 All-Purdue Team	Boiler Up
#300 All-Tennessee Team	Big Orange
#301 All-Texas Team	Hook Em
#302 All-Texas A&M Team	Gig Em
#303 All-UCLA Team	Mighty
#304 All-USC Team	Fight On
#305 All-Virginia Team	Wahoos
#307 All-Washington Team	Bow Down
#308 All-Wisconsin Team	U Rah Rah
#344 MSU Mascot Team	Mizzou Rah
#385 Wyo Mascot	All Hail
#386 Zips Mascot	Hail WV

NEED FOR SPEED CARBON

CASTROL CASH

At the Main menu, press Down, Up, Left, Down, Right, Up, ■, ▲. This gives you 10,000 extra cash.

INFINITE CREW CHARGE

At the Main menu, press Down, Up, Up, Right, Left, Left, Right, ■.

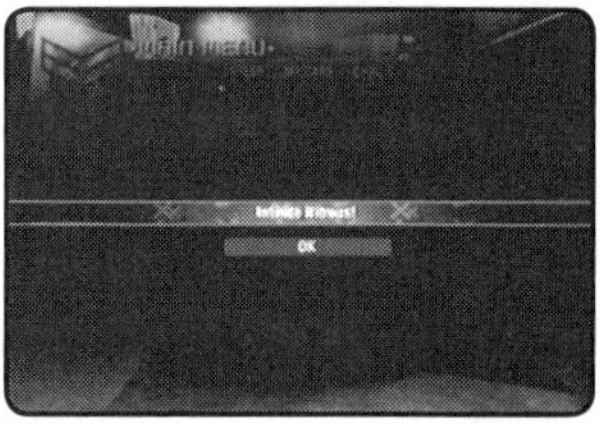

INFINITE NITROUS

At the Main menu, press Left, Up, Left, Down, Left, Down, Right, ■.

INFINITE SPEEDBREAKER

At the Main menu, press Down, Right, Right, Left, Right, Up, Down, ■.

NEED FOR SPEED CARBON LOGO VINYLS

At the Main menu, press Right, Up, Down, Up, Down, Left, Right, ■.

NEED FOR SPEED CARBON SPECIAL LOGO VINYLS

At the Main menu, press Up, Up, Down, Down, Down, Down, Up, ■.

NEED FOR SPEED PROSTREET

$2,000

Select Career and then choose Code Entry. Enter 1MA9X99.

$4,000

Select Career and then choose Code Entry. Enter W2IOLL01.

$8,000

Select Career and then choose Code Entry. Enter L1IS97A1.

$10,000

Select Career and then choose Code Entry. Enter 1MI9K7E1.

$10,000

Select Career and then choose Code Entry. Enter CASHMONEY.

$10,000

Select Career and then choose Code Entry. Enter REGGAME.

AUDI TT

Select Career and then choose Code Entry. Enter ITSABOUTYOU.

CHEVELLE SS

Select Career and then choose Code Entry. Enter HORSEPOWER.

COKE ZERO GOLF GTI

Select Career and then choose Code Entry. Enter COKEZERO.

DODGE VIPER

Select Career and then choose Code Entry. Enter WORLDSLONGESTLASTING.

MITSUBISHI LANCER EVOLUTION

Select Career and then choose Code Entry. Enter MITSUBISHIGOFAR.

UNLOCK ALL BONUSES

Select Career and then choose Code Entry. Enter UNLOCKALLTHINGS.

5 REPAIR MARKERS

Select Career and then choose Code Entry. Enter SAFETYNET.

ENERGIZER VINYL

Select Career and then choose Code Entry. Enter ENERGIZERLITHIUM.

CASTROL SYNTEC VINYL

Select Career and then choose Code Entry. Enter CASTROLSYNTEC. This also gives you $10,000.

NHL 08

ALL RBK EDGE JERSEYS

At the RBK Edge Code option, enter h3oyxpwksf8ibcgt.

NICKTOONS: ATTACK OF THE TOYBOTS

DAMAGE BOOST

Select Cheats from the Extras menu. Choose Enter Cheat Code and enter 456645.

INVULNERABILITY

Select Cheats from the Extras menu. Choose Enter Cheat Code and enter 313456.

UNLOCK EXO-HUGGLES 9000

Select Cheats from the Extras menu. Choose Enter Cheat Code and enter 691427.

UNLOCK MR. HUGGLES

Select Cheats from the Extras menu. Choose Enter Cheat Code and enter 654168.

UNLIMITED LOBBER GOO

Select Cheats from the Extras menu. Choose Enter Cheat Code and enter 118147.

UNLIMITED SCATTER GOO

Select Cheats from the Extras menu. Choose Enter Cheat Code and enter 971238.

UNLIMITED SPLITTER GOO

Select Cheats from the Extras menu. Choose Enter Cheat Code and enter 854511.

OVER THE HEDGE

COMPLETE LEVELS

Pause the game, hold **L1** + **R1** and press Triangle, Circle, Triangle, Circle, Circle, Square.

ALL MINI-GAMES

Pause the game, hold **L1** + **R1** and press Triangle, Circle, Triangle, Triangle, Square, Square.

ALL MOVES

Pause the game, hold **L1** + **R1** and press Triangle, Circle, Triangle, Square, Square, Circle.

EXTRA DAMAGE

Pause the game, hold **L1** + **R1** and press Triangle, Circle, Triangle, Circle, Triangle, Square.

MORE HP FROM FOOD

Pause the game, hold **L1** + **R1** and press Triangle, Circle, Triangle, Circle, Square, Triangle.

ALWAYS POWER PROJECTILE

Pause the game, hold **L1** + **R1** and press Triangle, Circle, Triangle, Circle, Square, Circle.

BONUS COMIC 14

Pause the game, hold **L1** + **R1** and press Triangle, Circle, Square, Square, Circle, Triangle.

BONUS COMIC 15

Pause the game, hold **L1** + **R1** and press Triangle, Triangle, Square, Circle, Square, Circle.

RATATOUILLE

Select Gusteau's Shop from the Extras menu. Choose Secrets, select the appropriate code number, and then enter the code. Once the code is entered, select the cheat you want to activate it.

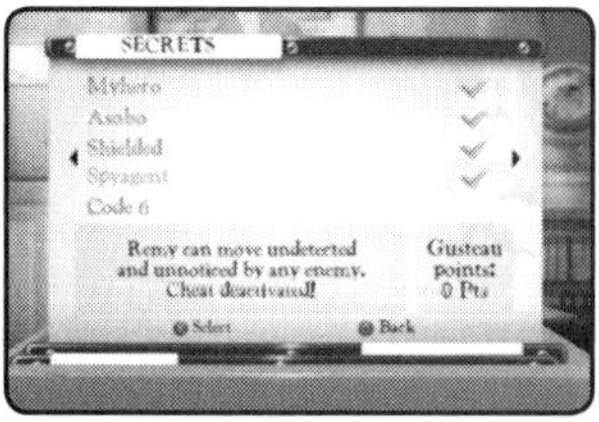

CODE NUMBER	CODE	EFFECT
1	Pieceocake	Very Easy difficulty mode
2	Myhero	No impact and no damage from enemies
3	Asobo	Plays the Asobo logo
4	Shielded	No damage from enemies
5	Spyagent	Move undetected by any enemy
6	Ilikeonions	Release air every time Remy jumps
7	Hardfeelings	Head butt when attacking instead of tailswipe
8	Slumberparty	Multiplayer mode
9	Gusteauart	All Concept Art
10	Gusteauship	All four championship modes
11	Mattelme	All single player and multiplayer mini-games
12	Gusteauvid	All Videos
13	Gusteaures	All Bonus Artworks
14	Gusteaudream	All Dream Worlds in Gusteau's Shop
15	Gusteauslide	All Slides in Gusteau's Shop
16	Gusteaulevel	All single player mini-games
17	Gusteaucombo	All items in Gusteau's Shop
18	Gusteaupot	5,000 Gusteau points
19	Gusteaujack	10,000 Gusteau points
20	Gusteauomni	50,000 Gusteau points

SHREK THE THIRD

10,000 GOLD COINS

At the gift shop, press Up, Up, Down, Up, Right, Left.

THE SIMPSONS GAME

UNLIMITED POWER FOR ALL CHARACTERS

At the Extras menu, press Circle, Left, Right, Circle, Square, L1.

ALL CLICHÉS.

At the Extras menu, press Left, Square, Right, Circle, Right, L1.

ALL MOVIES

At the Extras menu, press Square, Left, Square, Right, Circle, R1.

SEGA SUPERSTARS TENNIS

UNLOCK CHARACTERS

Complete the following missions to unlock the corresponding character.

CHARACTER	MISSION TO COMPLETE
Alex Kidd	Mission 1 of Alex Kidd's World
Amy Rose	Mission 2 of Sonic the Hedgehog's World
Gilius	Mission 1 of Golden Axe's World
Gum	Mission 12 of Jet Grind Radio's World
Meemee	Mission 8 of Super Monkey Ball's World
Pudding	Mission 1 of Space Channel 5's World
Reala	Mission 2 of NiGHTs' World
Shadow The Hedgehog	Mission 14 of Sonic the Hedgehog's World

THE SIMS 2: CASTAWAY

CHEAT GNOME

During a game, press **R1**, **L1**, Down, Square, **R2**. You can now use this Gnome to get the following:

MAX ALL MOTIVES

During a game, press **R2**, Up, X, Square, **L1**.

MAX CURRENT INVENTORY

During a game, press Left, Right, Square, **R2**, Square.

MAX RELATIONSHIPS

During a game, press **L1**, Up, **R2**, Left, Triangle.

ALL RESOURCES

During a game, press Square, Triangle, Down, X, Left.

ALL CRAFTING PLANS

During a game, press X, Triangle, **L2**, Square, **R1**.

ADD 1 TO SKILL

During a game, press Triangle, **L1**, **L1**, Left, Triangle.

EXCLUSIVE VEST AND TANKTOP

Pause the game and go to Fashion and Grooming. Press Square, R2, R2, Triangle, Down.

THE SIMS 2: PETS

CHEAT GNOME

During a game, press **L1**, **L1**, **R1**, ⊗, ⊗, Up.

GIVE SIM PET POINTS

After activating the Cheat Gnome, press △, ○, ⊗, □, **L1**, **R1** during a game. Select the Gnome to access the cheat.

ADVANCE 6 HOURS

After activating the Cheat Gnome, press Up, Left, Down, Right, **R1** during a game. Select the Gnome to access the cheat.

GIVE SIM SIMOLEONS

After activating the Cheat Gnome, enter the Advance 6 Hours cheat. Access the Gnome and exit. Enter the cheat again. Now, Give Sim Simoleons should be available from the Gnome.

CAT AND DOG CODES

When creating a family, press □ to Enter Unlock Code. Enter the following for new fur patterns.

FUR PATTERN/CAT OR DOG	UNLOCK CODE
Bandit Mask Cats	EEGJ2YRQZZAIZ9QHA64
Bandit Mask Dogs	EEGJ2YRQZQARQ9QHA64
Black Dot Cats	EEGJ2YRZQQ1IQ9QHA64
Black Dot Dogs	EEGJ2YRQZZ1IQ9QHA64
Black Smiley Cats	EEGJ2YRQQZ1RQ9QHA64
Black Smiley Dogs	EEGJ2YRZQQARQ9QHA64
Blue Bones Cats	EEGJ2YRQZZARQ9QHA64
Blue Bones Dogs	EEGJ2YRZZZ1IZ9QHA64
Blue Camouflage Cats	EEGJ2YRZZQ1IQ9QHA64
Blue Camouflage Dogs	EEGJ2YRZZZ1RQ9QHA64
Blue Cats	EEGJ2YRQZZAIQ9QHA64
Blue Dogs	EEGJ2YRQQQ1IZ9QHA64
Blue Star Cats	EEGJ2YRQQZ1IZ9QHA64

FUR PATTERN/CAT OR DOG	UNLOCK CODE
Blue Star Dogs	EEGJ2YRQZQ1IQ9QHA64
Deep Red Cats	EEGJ2YRQQQAIQ9QHA64
Deep Red Dogs	EEGJ2YRQZQ1RQ9QHA64
Goofy Cats	EEGJ2YRQZQ1IZ9QHA64
Goofy Dogs	EEGJ2YRZZZARQ9QHA64
Green Cats	EEGJ2YRZQQAIZ9QHA64
Green Dogs	EEGJ2YRQZQAIQ9QHA64
Green Flower Cats	EEGJ2YRZQZAIQ9QHA64
Green Flower Dogs	EEGJ2YRQZZ1RQ9QHA64
Light Green Cats	EEGJ2YRZZQ1RQ9QHA64
Light Green Dogs	EEGJ2YRZQQ1RQ9QHA64
Navy Hearts Cats	EEGJ2YRZQZ1IQ9QHA64
Navy Hearts Dogs	EEGJ2YRQQZ1IQ9QHA64
Neon Green Cats	EEGJ2YRZZQAIQ9QHA64
Neon Green Dogs	EEGJ2YRZQQAIQ9QHA64
Neon Yellow Cats	EEGJ2YRZZQARQ9QHA64
Neon Yellow Dogs	EEGJ2YRQQQAIZ9QHA64
Orange Diagonal Cats	EEGJ2YRQQZAIQ9QHA64
Orange Diagonal Dogs	EEGJ2YRZQZ1IZ9QHA64
Panda Cats	EEGJ2YRQZQAIZ9QHA64
Pink Cats	EEGJ2YRQZZ1IZ9QHA64
Pink Dogs	EEGJ2YRZQZ1RQ9QHA64
Pink Vertical Strip Cats	EEGJ2YRQQQARQ9QHA64
Pink Vertical Strip Dogs	EEGJ2YRZZZAIQ9QHA64
Purple Cats	EEGJ2YRQQZARQ9QHA64
Purple Dogs	EEGJ2YRQQZAIZ9QHA64
Star Cats	EEGJ2YRZQZARQ9QHA64
Star Dogs	EEGJ2YRZQZAIZ9QHA64
White Paws Cats	EEGJ2YRQQQ1RQ9QHA64
White Paws Dogs	EEGJ2YRZQQ1IZ9QHA64
White Zebra Stripe Cats	EEGJ2YRZZQ1IZ9QHA64
White Zebra Stripe Dogs	EEGJ2YRZZZ1IQ9QHA64
Zebra Stripes Dogs	EEGJ2YRZZQAIZ9QHA64

SLY 3: HONOR AMONG THIEVES

TOONAMI PLANE

While flying the regular plane, pause the game and press **R1**, **R1**, Right, Down, Down, Right.

RESTART EPISODES

Pause the game during the Episode and enter the following codes to restart that Episode. You must first complete that part of the Episode to use the code.

EPISODE	CODE
Episode 1, Day 1	Left, R2, Right, L1, R2, L1
Episode 1, Day 2	Down, L2, Up, Left, R2, L2
Episode 2, Day 1	Right, L2, Left, Up, Right, Down
Episode 2, Day 2	Down, Up, R1, Up, R2, L2
Episode 3, Day 1	R2, R1, L1, Left, L1, Down
Episode 3, Day 2	L2, R1, R2, L2, L1, Up
Episode 4, Day 1	Left, Right, L1, R2, Right, R2
Episode 4, Day 2	L1, Left, L2, Left, Up, L1
Episode 5, Day 1	Left, R2, Right, Up, L1, R2
Episode 5, Day 2	R2, R1, L1, R1, R2, R1
Operation Laptop Retrieval	L2, Left, R1, L2, L1, Down
Operation Moon Crash	L2, Up, Left, L1, L2, L1

EPISODE	CODE
Operation Reverse Double Cross	Right, Left, Up, Left, R2, Left
Operation Tar Be-Gone	Down, L2, R1, L2, R1, Right
Operation Turbo Dominant Eagle	Down, Right, Left, L2, R1, Right
Operation Wedding Crasher	L2, R2, Right, Down, L1, R2

SPIDER-MAN: FRIEND OR FOE

NEW GREEN GOBLIN AS A SIDEKICK

While standing in the Helicarrier between levels, press Left, Down, Right, Right, Down, Left.

SANDMAN AS A SIDEKICK

While standing in the Helicarrier between levels, press Right, Right, Right, Up, Down, Left.

VENOM AS A SIDEKICK

While standing in the Helicarrier between levels, press Left, Left, Right, Up, Down, Down.

5000 TECH TOKENS

While standing in the Helicarrier between levels, press Up, Up, Down, Down, Left, Right.

THE SPIDERWICK CHRONICLES

INVULNERABILITY

During the game, hold L1 + R1 and press Triangle, Triangle, Triangle, Triangle, X, X, Triangle, Triangle.

HEAL

During the game, hold L1 + R1 and press Triangle, Square, X, Circle, Triangle, Square, X, Circle.

COMBAT LOADOUT

During the game, hold L1 + R1 and press Triangle, Triangle, X, X, Square, Circle, Square, Circle.

INFINITE AMMO

During the game, hold L1 + R1 and press Square, Square, Square, Circle, X, X, X, Triangle.

FIELD GUIDE UNLOCKED

During the game, hold L1 + R1 and press Circle, Circle, Circle, Square, Triangle, Triangle, Triangle, X.

SPRITE A

During the game, hold L2 + R2 and press Triangle, X, Circle, Square, X, Triangle, Square, Circle.

SPRITE B

During the game, hold L2 + R2 and press X, X, Triangle, Square, Square, Circle, Triangle, X.

SPRITE C

During the game, hold L2 + R2 and press Circle, Triangle, Square, X, Circle, Triangle, Square, X.

SPONGEBOB SQUAREPANTS FEATURING NICKTOONS: GLOBS OF DOOM

When entering the following codes, the order of the characters going down is: SpongeBob SquarePants, Nicolai Technus, Danny Phantom, Dib, Zim, Tlaloc, Tak, Beautiful Gorgeous, Jimmy Neutron, Plankton. These names are shortened to the first name in the following.

ATTRACT COINS

Using the Upgrade Machine on the bottom level of the lair, select "Input cheat codes here". Enter Tlaloc, Plankton, Danny, Plankton, Tak. Coins are attracted to you making them much easier to collect.

DON'T LOSE COINS

Using the Upgrade Machine on the bottom level of the lair, select "Input cheat codes here". Enter Plankton, Jimmy, Beautiful, Jimmy, Plankton. You don't lose coins when you get knocked out.

GOO HAS NO EFFECT

Using the Upgrade Machine on the bottom level of the lair, select "Input cheat codes here". Enter Danny, Danny, Danny, Nicolai, Nicolai. Goo does not slow you down.

MORE GADGET COMBO TIME

Using the Upgrade Machine on the bottom level of the lair, select "Input cheat codes here". Enter SpongeBob, Beautiful, Danny, Plankton, Nicolai. You have more time to perform gadget combos.

STAR WARS: THE FORCE UNLEASHED

CHEATS

Once you have accessed the Rogue Shadow, select Enter Code from the Extras menu. Now you can enter the following codes:

CHEAT	CODE
Invincibility	CORTOSIS
Unlimited Force	VERGENCE
1,000,000 Force Points	SPEEDER
All Force Powers	TYRANUS
Max Force Power Level	KATARN
Max Combo Level	COUNTDOOKU
Stronger Lightsaber	LIGHTSABER

COSTUMES

Once you have accessed the Rogue Shadow, select Enter Code from the Extras menu. Now you can enter the following codes:

COSTUME	CODE
All Costumes	GRANDMOFF
501st Legion	LEGION
Aayla Secura	AAYLA
Admiral Ackbar	ITSATWAP
Anakin Skywalker	CHOSENONE
Asajj Ventress	ACOLYTE
Ceremonial Jedi Robes	DANTOOINE
Chop'aa Notimo	NOTIMO
Classic stormtrooper	TK421
Count Dooku	SERENNO
Darth Desolous	PAUAN
Darth Maul	ZABRAK
Darth Phobos	HIDDENFEAR
Darth Vader	SITHLORD
Drexl Roosh	DREXLROOSH
Emperor Palpatine	PALPATINE
General Rahm Kota	MANDALORE
Han Solo	NERFHERDER
Heavy trooper	SHOCKTROOP
Juno Eclipse	ECLIPSE
Kento's Robe	WOOKIEE
Kleef	KLEEF
Lando Calrissian	SCOUNDREL
Luke Skywalker	T16WOMPRAT
Luke Skywalker (Yavin)	YELLOWJCKT
Mace Windu	JEDIMASTER
Mara Jade	MARAJADE
Maris Brook	MARISBROOD
Navy commando	STORMTROOP
Obi Wan Kenobi	BENKENOBI
Proxy	HOLOGRAM
Qui Gon Jinn	MAVERICK
Shaak Ti	TOGRUTA
Shadow trooper	INTHEDARK
Sith Robes	HOLOCRON
Sith Stalker Armor	KORRIBAN
Twi'lek	SECURA

STREET FIGHTER ALPHA ANTHOLOGY

STREET FIGHTER ALPHA

PLAY AS DAN

At the Character Select screen in Arcade Mode, hold the Start button and place the cursor on the Random Select space then input one of the following commands within 1 second:

LP LK MK HK HP MP

HP HK MK LK LP MP

LK LP MP HP HK MK

HK HP MP LP LK HK

PLAY AS M.BISON

At the Character Select screen, hold the Start button, place the cursor on the random select box, and input:

1P side: Down, Down, Back, Back, Down, Back, Back + LP + HP

2P side: Down, Down, Forward, Forward, Down, Forward, Forward + LP + HP

PLAY AS AKUMA

At the Character Select screen, hold the Start button, place the cursor on the random select box, and input:

1P side: Down, Down, Down, Back, Back, Back + LP + HP

2P side: Down, Down, Down, Forward, Forward, Forward + LP + HP

AKUMA MODE

Select your character in Arcade mode, then press and hold Start + MP + MK as the Character Selection screen ends.

RYU AND KEN VS. M.BISON

On both the 1p and 2p side in Arcade mode, press and hold Start, then:

1P side: place the cursor on Ryu and input Up, Up, release Start, Up, Up + LP

2P side: place the cursor on Ken and input Up, Up, release Start, Up, Up + HP

LAST BOSS MODE

Select Arcade mode while holding ■, ⊗, and **R1**.

DRAMATIC BATTLE MODE

Select Dramatic Battle mode while holding ■, ⊗, and **R2**.

RANDOM BATTLE MODE

Select Versus mode while holding ■, ⊗, and **R2**.

STREET FIGHTER ALPHA 2

PLAY AS ORIGINAL CHUN-LI

Highlight Chun-Li on the Character Select screen, hold the Start button for 3 seconds, then select Chun-Li normally.

PLAY AS SHIN AKUMA

Highlight Akuma on the Character Select screen, hold the Start button for 3 seconds, then select Akuma normally.

PLAY AS EVIL RYU

Highlight Ryu on the Character Select screen, hold the Start button, input Forward, Up, Down, Back, then select Ryu normally.

PLAY AS EX DHALSIM

Highlight Dhalsim on the Character Select screen, hold the Start button, input Back, Down, Forward, Up, then select Dhalsim normally.

PLAY AS EX ZANGIEF

Highlight Zangief on the Character Select screen, hold the Start button, input Down, Back, Back, Back, Back, Up, Up, Forward, Forward, Forward, Forward, Down, then select Zangief normally.

LAST BOSS MODE

Select Arcade mode while holding the ■, ●, and **R1** buttons.

DRAMATIC BATTLE MODE

Select Dramatic Battle mode while holding the ■ + ✖ + **R2**.

SELECT SPECIAL ROUTE IN SURVIVAL MODE

Select Survival Battle while holding the **R1** or **R2**.

RANDOM BATTLE MODE

Select Versus mode while holding the ■ + ✖ + **R2**.

STREET FIGHTER ALPHA 2 GOLD

PLAY AS EX RYU

Highlight Ryu and press the Start button once before selecting normally.

PLAY AS EVIL RYU

Highlight Ryu and press the Start button twice before selecting normally.

PLAY AS ORIGINAL CHUN-LI

Highlight Chun-Li and press the Start button once before selecting normally.

PLAY AS EX CHUN-LI

Highlight Chun-Li and press the Start button twice before selecting normally.

PLAY AS EX KEN

Highlight Ken and press the Start button once before selecting normally.

PLAY AS EX DHALSIM

Highlight Dhalsim and press the Start button once before selecting normally.

PLAY AS EX ZANGIEF

Highlight Zangief and press the Start button once before selecting normally.

PLAY AS EX SAGAT

Highlight Sagat and press the Start button once before selecting normally.

PLAY AS EX M.BISON

Highlight M.Bison and press the Start button once before selecting normally.

PLAY USING SAKURA'S ALTERNATE COLORS

Highlight Sakura and press the Start button five times before selecting normally.

PLAY AS SHIN AKUMA

Highlight Akuma and press the Start button five times before selecting normally.

PLAY AS CAMMY

Highlight M.Bison and press the Start button twice before selecting normally.

LAST BOSS MODE

Select Arcade mode while holding ■ + ● + **R1**.

SELECT SPECIAL ROUTE IN SURVIVAL MODE

Select Survival Battle while holding the **R1** or **R2**.

DRAMATIC BATTLE MODE

Select Dramatic Battle mode while holding ■ + ✖ + **R2**.

RANDOM BATTLE MODE

Select Versus mode while holding ■ + ✖ + **R2**.

STREET FIGHTER ALPHA 3

PLAY AS BALROG

Highlight Karin for one second, then move the cursor to the random select box and hold Start before selecting normally.

PLAY AS JULI

Highlight Karin for one second, then move the cursor to the random select box and press Up, or Down, while selecting normally.

PLAY AS JUNI

Highlight Karin for one second, then move the cursor to the random select box and press Back, or Forward, while selecting normally.

CLASSICAL MODE

Press and hold HP + HK while starting game.

SPIRITED MODE

Press and hold MP + MK while starting game.

SAIKYO MODE

Press and hold LP + LK while starting game.

SHADALOO MODE

Press and hold LK + MK + HK while starting game.

SELECT SPECIAL ROUTE IN SURVIVAL MODE

Select Survival mode while holding **R1** or **R2**.

DRAMATIC BATTLE MODE

Select Dramatic Battle mode while holding ■ + ✖ + **R2**.

RANDOM BATTLE MODE

Select Versus mode while holding ■ + ✖ + **R2**.

STUNTMAN IGNITION

3 PROPS IN STUNT CREATOR MODE

Select Cheats from Extras and enter COOLPROP.

ALL ITEMS UNLOCKED FOR CONSTRUCTION MODE

Select Cheats from Extras and enter NOBLEMAN.

MVX SPARTAN

Select Cheats from Extras and enter fastride.

ALL CHEATS

Select Cheats from Extras and enter Wearefrozen. This unlocks the following cheats: Slo-mo Cool, Thrill Cam, Vision Switcher, Nitro Addiction, Freaky Fast, and Ice Wheels.

ALL CHEATS

Select Cheats from Extras and enter Kungfoopete.

ICE WHEELS CHEAT

Select Cheats from Extras and enter IceAge.

NITRO ADDICTION CHEAT

Select Cheats from Extras and enter TheDuke.

VISION SWITCHER CHEAT

Select Cheats from Extras and enter GFXMODES.

SUPERMAN RETURNS

GOD MODE

Pause the game, select Options and press Up, Up, Down, Down, Left, Right, Left, Right, ●, ■.

INFINITE CITY HEALTH

Pause the game, select Options and press ●, Right, ●, Right, Up, Left, Right, ●.

ALL POWER-UPS

Pause the game, select Options and press Left, ●, Right, ■, Down, ●, Up, Down, ■, ●, ■.

ALL UNLOCKABLES

Pause the game, select Options and press Left, Up, Right, Down, ●, ■, ●, Up, Right, ■.

FREE ROAM AS BIZARRO

Pause the game, select Options and press Up, Right, Down, Right, Up, Left, Down, Right, Up.

TAITO LEGENDS

EXTRA GAMES

At the Title screen, press **L1**, **R1**, **R2**, **L2**, Select, Start.

TAK: THE GREAT JUJU CHALLENGE

BONUS SOUND EFFECTS

In Juju's Potions, select Universal Card and enter 20, 17, 5 for Bugs, Crystals and Fruits respectively.

BONUS SOUND EFFECTS 2

In Juju's Potions, select Universal Card and enter 50, 84, 92 for Bugs, Crystals and Fruits respectively.

BONUS MUSIC TRACK 1

In Juju's Potions, select Universal Card and enter 67, 8, 20 for Bugs, Crystals and Fruits respectively.

BONUS MUSIC TRACK 2

In Juju's Potions, select Universal Card and enter 6, 18, 3 for Bugs, Crystals and Fruits respectively.

MAGIC PARTICLES

In Juju's Potions, select Universal Card and enter 24, 40, 11 for Bugs, Crystals and Fruits respectively.

MORE MAGIC PARTICLES

In Juju's Potions, select Universal Card and enter 48, 57, 57 for Bugs, Crystals and Fruits respectively.

VIEW JUJU CONCEPT ART

In Juju's Potions, select Universal Card and enter Art 33, 22, 28 for Bugs, Crystals and Fruits respectively.

VIEW VEHICLE ART

In Juju's Potions, select Universal Card and enter 11, 55, 44 for Bugs, Crystals and Fruits respectively.

VIEW WORLD ART

In Juju's Potions, select Universal Card and enter 83, 49, 34 for Bugs, Crystals and Fruits respectively.

TAK AND THE GUARDIANS OF GROSS

INVULNERABILITY

Select Cheat Codes from the Extras menu and enter KRUNKIN.

INFINITE NOVA

Select Cheat Codes from the Extras menu and enter CAKEDAY.

WEAK ENEMIES

Select Cheat Codes from the Extras menu and enter CODMODE.

ALL LEVELS

Select Cheat Codes from the Extras menu and enter GUDGEON.

ALL MINI GAMES

Select Cheat Codes from the Extras menu and enter CURLING.

ALL AWARDS

Select Cheat Codes from the Extras menu and enter SNEAKER.

ALL CONCEPT ART

Select Cheat Codes from the Extras menu and enter FRIVERS.

RAINBOW TRAIL

Select Cheat Codes from the Extras menu and enter UNICORN.

THRILLVILLE: OFF THE RAILS

ALL PARKS

While in a park, press Square, Circle, Triangle, Square, Circle, Triangle, Square.

ALL RIDES IN PARK

While in a park, press Square, Circle, Triangle, Square, Circle, Triangle, Triangle.

$50,000

While in a park, press Square, Circle, Triangle, Square, Circle, Triangle, X.

MISSION COMPLETE

While in a park, press Square, Circle, Triangle, Square, Circle, Triangle, Circle.

TIGER WOODS PGA TOUR 08

ALL GOLFERS

Select Passwords from the Options and enter GAMEFACE.

BRIDGESTONE ITEMS

Select Passwords from the Options and enter SHOJIRO.

COBRA ITEMS

Select Passwords from the Options and enter SNAKEKING.

GRAFALLOY ITEMS

Select Passwords from the Options and enter JUSTSHAFTS.

MACGREGOR ITEMS

Select Passwords from the Options and enter MACTEC.

MIZUNO ITEMS

Select Passwords from the Options and enter RIHACHINRIZO.

NIKE ITEMS

Select Passwords from the Options and enter JUSTDOIT.

OAKLEY ITEMS

Select Passwords from the Options and enter JANNARD.

PING ITEMS

Select Passwords from the Options and enter SOLHEIM.

PRECEPT ITEMS

Select Passwords from the Options and enter GUYSAREGOOD.

TAYLORMADE ITEMS

Select Passwords from the Options and enter MRADAMS.

TIGER WOODS PGA TOUR 09

$1,000,000

Select Passwords from the Extras menu and enter JACKPOT.

MAX SKILL POINTS

Select Passwords from the Extras menu and enter IAMRUBBISH.

ALL CLOTHING & EQUIPMENT

Select Passwords from the Extras menu and enter SHOP2DROP.

ALL PGA TOUR EVENTS

Select Passwords from the Extras menu and enter BEATIT.

ALL COVER STORIES

Select Passwords from the Extras menu and enter HEADLINER.

TIM BURTON'S THE NIGHTMARE BEFORE CHRISTMAS: OOGIE'S REVENGE

ALL LEVELS

At the Title screen, press **L1**, **L2**, **L1**, **L2**, **L3**, **R1**, **R2**, **R1**, **R2**, **R3**.

INVINCIBILITY

During a game, press Right, Left, **L3**, **R3**, Left, Right, **R3**, **L3**.

OPEN PUMKIN JACK AND SANTA JACK COUSTUMES

During a game, press Down, Up, Right, Left, **L3**, **R3**.

TOKYO XTREME RACER DRIFT 2

START WITH EXTRA CP

Enter the following as your name to get the corresponding amount of CP to start the game.

CP	NAME
1,700,000	Ikentani
1,950,000	Wataru
2,840,000	Toshiya
2,850,000	Fujiwara
2,880,000	Tomoyuki
2,900,000	Richard
2,900,000	Ryosuke
2,910,000	Nakazato

CP	NAME
2,910,000	Hachiroku
2,960,000	Takeshi
2,960,000	Bunta
2,960,000	Takahashi
2,960,000	Tsuchiya
2,980,000	DRIFT
2,990,000	Takumi

TONY HAWK'S PROVING GROUND

CHEAT CODES

Select Cheat Codes from the Options and enter the following cheats. Some codes need to be enabled by selecting Cheats from the Options during a game.

UNLOCK	CHEAT
Unlocks Bosco	MOREMILK
Unlocks Cam	NOTACAMERA
Unlocks Cooper	THECOOP
Unlocks Eddie X	SKETCHY
Unlocks El Patinador	PILEDRIVER
Unlocks Eric	FLYAWAY
Unlocks Judy Nails	LOVEROCKNROLL
Unlocks Mad Dog	RABBIES
Unlocks MCA	INTERGALACTIC
Unlocks Mel	NOTADUDE
Unlocks Rube	LOOKSSMELLY
Unlocks Spence	DAPPER
Unlocks Shayne	MOVERS
Unlocks TV Producer	SHAKER
Unlock FDR	THEPREZPARK
Unlock Lansdowne	THELOCALPARK
Unlock Air & Space Museum	THEINDOORPARK
Unlocks all Fun Items	OVERTHETOP
Unlock all Game Movies	WATCHTHIS
Unlock all Rigger Pieces	IMGONNABUILD
All specials unlocked and in player's special list	LOTSOFTRICKS
Full Stats	BEEFEDUP

UNLOCK	CHEAT
Give player +50 skill points	NEEDSHELP
Unlocks Perfect Manual	STILLAINTFALLIN
Unlocks Perfect Rail	AINTFALLIN
Unlocks Unlimited Focus	MYOPIC
Invisible Man	THEMISSING
Mini Skater	TINYTATER

TRANSFORMERS: THE GAME

INFINITE HEALTH

At the Main menu, press Left, Left, Up, Left, Right, Down, Right.

INFINITE AMMO

At the Main menu, press Up, Down, Left, Right, Up, Up, Down.

NO MILITARY OR POLICE

At the Main menu, press Right, Left, Right, Left, Right, Left, Right.

ALL MISSIONS

At the Main menu, press Down, Up, Left, Right, Right, Right, Up, Down.

BONUS CYBERTRON MISSIONS

At the Main menu, press Right, Up, Up, Down, Right, Left, Left.

GENERATION 1 SKIN: JAZZ

At the Main menu, press Left, Up, Down, Down, Left, Up, Right.

GENERATION 1 SKIN: MEGATRON

At the Main menu, press Down, Left, Left, Down, Right, Right, Up.

GENERATION 1 SKIN: OPTIMUS PRIME

At the Main menu, press Down, Right, Left, Up, Down, Down, Left.

GENERATION 1 SKIN: ROBOVISION OPTIMUS PRIME

At the Main menu, press Down, Down, Up, Up, Right, Right, Right.

GENERATION 1 SKIN: STARSCREAM

At the Main menu, press Right, Down, Left, Left, Down, Up, Up.

ULTIMATE SPIDER-MAN

ALL CHARACTERS

Pause the game and select Controller Setup from the Options. Press Right, Down, Right, Down, Left, Up, Left, Right.

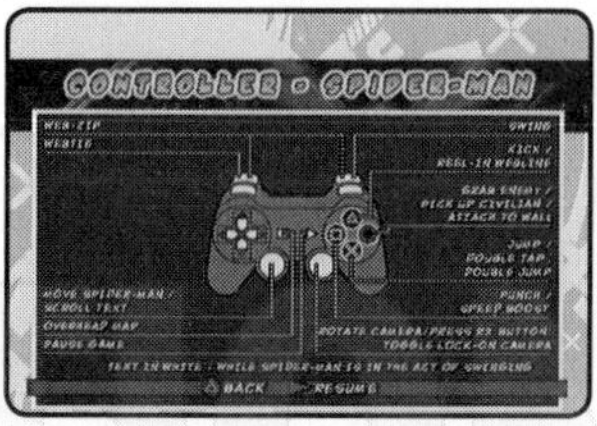

ALL COVERS

Pause the game and select Controller Setup from the Options. Press Left, Left, Right, Left, Up, Left, Left, Down.

ALL CONCEPT ART

Pause the game and select Controller Setup from the Options. Press Down, Down, Down, Up, Down, Up, Left, Left.

ALL LANDMARKS

Pause the game and select Controller Setup from the Options. Press Up, Right, Down, Left, Down, Up, Right, Left.

WWE SMACKDOWN! VS. RAW 2008

HBK AND HHH'S DX OUTFIT

Select Cheat Codes from the Options and enter DXCostume69K2.

KELLY KELLY'S ALTERNATE OUTFIT

Select Cheat Codes from the Options and enter KellyKG12R.

X-MEN: THE OFFICIAL GAME

DANGER ROOM ICEMAN

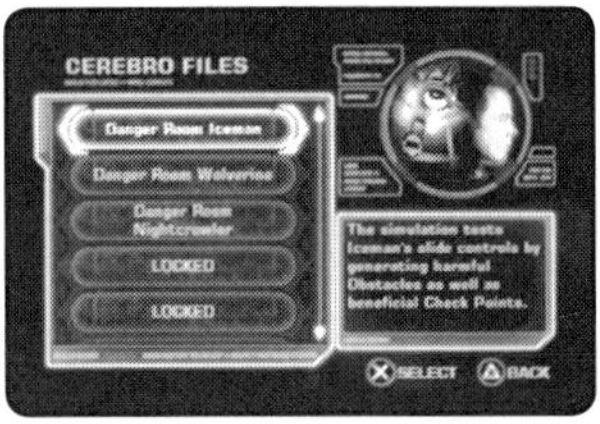

At the Cerebro Files menu, press Right, Right, Left, Left, Down, Up, Down, Up, Start.

DANGER ROOM NIGHTCRAWLER

At the Cerebro Files menu, press Up, Up, Down, Down, Left, Right, Left, Right, Start.

DANGER ROOM WOLVERINE

At the Cerebro Files menu, press Down, Down, Up, Up, Right, Left, Right, Left, Start.

CHEAT CODE EXPLOSION

FOR HANDHELDS

FLIP THIS BOOK OVER FOR HOME CONSOLES

- PlayStation® 3
- Nintendo Wii™
- Xbox 360™
- PlayStation® 2

LOOK FOR CODEY

When you see Codey's face, you've found the newest and coolest codes!

CHEAT CODE EXPLOSION

EXCLUSIVE SCHOLASTIC EDITION

DK/BradyGames, a division of Penguin Group (USA) Inc.
800 East 96th Street, 3rd Floor
Indianapolis, IN 46240

ISBN: 978-0-7440-1075-6

Printing Code: The rightmost double-digit number is the year of the book's printing; the rightmost single-digit number is the number of the book's printing. For example, 08-1 shows that the first printing of the book occurred in 2008.

11 10 09 08 4 3 2 1

Printed in the USA.

CREDITS

Title Manager
Tim Fitzpatrick

Cheat Code and Screenshot Editor
Michael Owen

Book Designer
Doug Wilkins

Production Designer
Wil Cruz

BRADYGAMES STAFF

Publisher
David Waybright

Editor-In-Chief
H. Leigh Davis

Licensing Director
Mike Degler

Marketing Director
Debby Neubauer

International Translations
Brian Saliba

NINTENDO DS™

TABLE OF CONTENTS

ADVANCE WARS: DAYS OF RUIN

UNLOCK COS

Complete the following missions to unlock the corresponding CO.

COMPLETE MISSION	CO UNLOCKED
12	Tasha
13	Gage
14	Forthsythe
20	Waylon
21	Greyfield
24	Penny
25	Tabitha
26	Caulder

ADVANCE WARS: DUAL STRIKE

ADVANCE WARS MAP

Select Map from the Design Room menu and immediately press and hold L + R. You will get a map that spells out Advance Wars.

By having old versions of advance wars inserted in your DS at the same time as Dual Strike, you can unlock new buyables at the the Battle Maps Shop!

ADVANCE WARPAPER

Insert Advance Wars in the GBA slot of your Nintendo DS. Start Advance Wars: Dual Strike. Select Battle Maps and purchase Advance Warpaper. Select Display from the Design Room and choose Classic 1.

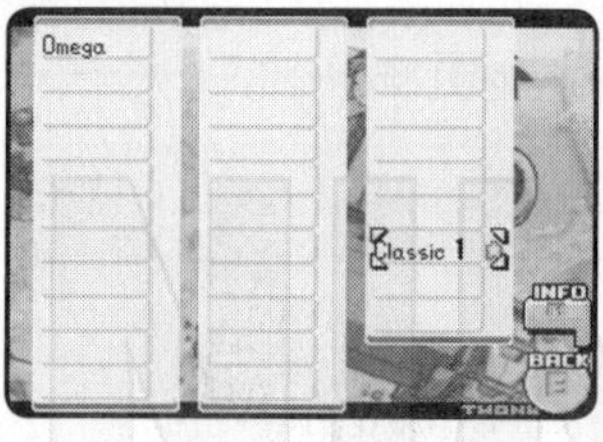

HACHI'S LAND

Insert Advance Wars in the GBA slot of your Nintendo DS. Start Advance Wars: Dual Strike. Select Battle Maps and purchase Hachi's Land for 1.

NELL'S LAND

Insert Advance Wars in the GBA slot of your Nintendo DS. Start Advance Wars: Dual Strike. Select Battle Maps and purchase Nell's Land for 1.

ADVANCE WARPAPER 2

Insert Advance Wars 2: Black Hole Rising in the GBA slot of your Nintendo DS. Start Advance Wars: Dual Strike. Select Battle Maps and purchase Advance Warpaper 2. Select Display from the Design Room and choose Classic 2.

LASH'S LAND

Insert Advance Wars 2: Black Hole Rising in the GBA slot of your Nintendo DS. Start Advance Wars: Dual Strike. Select Battle Maps and purchase Lash's Land for 1.

STRUM'S LAND

Insert Advance Wars 2: Black Hole Rising in the GBA slot of your Nintendo DS. Start Advance Wars: Dual Strike. Select Battle Maps and purchase Strum's Land for 1.

ANIMANIACS: LIGHTS, CAMERA, ACTION!

SKIP LEVEL

Pause the game and press L, L, R, R, Down, Down.

DISABLE TIME

Pause the game and press L, R, Left, Left, Up, Up.

KINGSIZE PICKUPS

Pause the game and press Right, Right, Right, Left, Left, Left, R, L.

PASSWORDS

LEVEL	PASSWORD
1	Wakko, Wakko, Wakko, Wakko, Wakko
2	Dot, Yakko, Brain, Wakko, Pinky
3	Yakko, Dot, Wakko, Wakko, Brain
4	Pinky, Yakko, Yakko, Dot, Brain
5	Pinky, Pinky, Yakko, Wakko, Wakko
6	Brain, Dot, Brain, Pinky, Yakko
7	Brain, Pinky, Wakko, Pinky, Brain
8	Brain Pinky, Pinky, Wakko, Wakko

LEVEL	PASSWORD
9	Dot, Dot, Yakko, Pinky, Wakko
10	Brain, Dot, Brain, Yakko, Wakko
11	Akko, Yakko, Pinky, Dot, Dot
12	Pinky, Pinky, Brain, Dot, Wakko
13	Yakko, Wakko, Pinky, Wakko, Brain
14	Pinky, Wakko, Brain, Wakko, Yakko
15	Dot, Pinky, Wakko, Wakko, Yakko

ASPHALT URBAN GT

MONEY FOR NOTHING

Buy the Chevrolet 2005 Corvette C6 for $45,000. Then, go to your garage and sell it for $45,500.

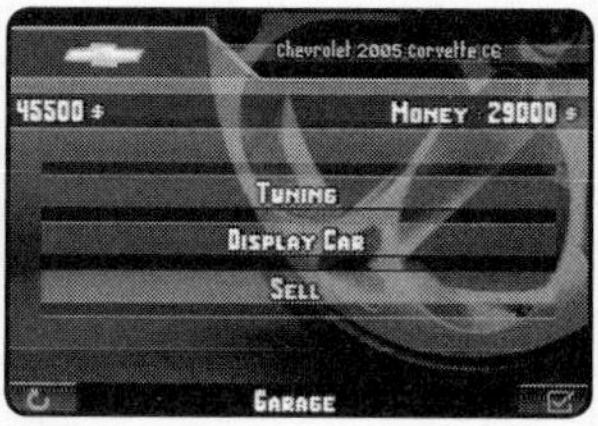

BEN 10: PROTECTOR OF EARTH

GWEN 10 SKINS

At the level select, press Left, Right, Left, Right, L, R, Select.

GALACTIC ENFORCER SKINS

At the level select, press A, B, X, Y, L, R, Select.

ULTRA BEN SKINS

At the level select, press Up, Right, Down, Left, A, B, Select.

BRAIN AGE: TRAIN YOUR BRAIN IN MINUTES A DAY

BRAIN AGE CHECK SELECTION MENU

At the Daily Training Menu, hold Select while choosing Brain Age Check.

TOP 3 LISTS

At the Daily Training Menu, hold Select while choosing Graph.

BRAIN VOYAGE

ALL GOLD MEDALS

At the World Map, press A, B, Up, L, L, Y.

INFINITE COINS

At the World Tour Mode, press L, Up, X, Up, R, Y.

BUBBLE BOBBLE REVOLUTION

BONUS LEVELS IN CLASSIC MODE

At the Classic mode Title screen, press L, R, L, R, L, R, Right, Select. Touch the door at Level 20.

POWER UP! MODE IN CLASSIC VERSION

At the Classic mode Title screen, press Select, R, L, Left, Right, R, Select, Right.

SUPER BUBBLE BOBBLE IN CLASSIC VERSION

You must first defeat the boss with two players. At the Classic mode Title screen, press Left, R, Left, Select, Left, L, Left, Select.

BUILD-A-BEAR WORKSHOP

At the Select a Slot screen, press Up, Up, Down, Down, Left, Right, Left, Right, B, A. Now you can enter the following codes:

ALL LEVELS

At the level select, hold L + R.

ALL ACTIVITIES

At the workshop screen, press R.

ALL MOVES

At the garden screen, press L.

BUST-A-MOVE DS

DARK WORLD

First you must complete the game. At the Title screen, press A Left Right A.

SOUND TEST

At the Main menu, press Select, A, B, Left, Right, A, Select, Right.

CODE LYOKO

CODELYOKO.COM SECRET FILES

Enter the following as Secret Codes on the My Secret Album page of www.codelyoko.com:

SECRET FILE	CODE
Dark Enemies Wallpaper	9L8Q
Desert Sketch	6G7T
Fight Video	4M9P
FMV Ending	5R5K
Forest Sketch	8C3X
Ice Sketch	2F6U
Mountain Sketch	7E5V
Overbike	3Q4L

SECRET FILE	CODE
Overboard	8P3M
Overwing	8N2N
Scorpion Video	9H8S
Scorpion Wallpaper	3D4W
Sector 5 Sketch	5J9R
Ulrich	9A9Z
Yumi	4B2Y

DRAGLADE

CHARACTERS

CHARACTER	TO UNLOCK
Asuka	Defeat Daichi's story
Gyamon	Defeat Guy's story
Koki	Defeat Hibito's story
Shura	Defeat Kairu's story

HIDDEN QUEST: SHADOW OF DARKNESS

Defeat Story Mode with all of the main characters. This unlocks the hidden quest in Synethesia.

ZEKE

Complete all of the quests including Shadow of Darkness to unlock Zeke in wireless battle.

DRAGON QUEST HEROES: ROCKET SLIME

KNIGHTRO TANK IN MULTIPLAYER

While in the church, press Y, L, L, Y, R, R, Y, Up, Down, Select.

THE NEMESIS TANK IN MULTIPLAYER

While in the church, press Y, R, R, up, L, L, Y, Down, Down, Down, Y, Select.

DRAGON QUEST MONSTERS: JOKER

CAPTAIN CROW

As you travel between the islands on the sea scooters, you are occasionally attacked by pirates. Discover the route on which the pirates are located at the bulletin board in any scoutpost den. When you face them between Infant Isle and Celeste Isle, Captain Crow makes an appearance. Defeat him and he forces himself into your team.

SOLITAIRE'S CHALLENGE

After completing the main game, load your game again for a new endeavor. The hero is in Solitaire's office, where she proposes a new nonstop challenge known as Solitaire's Challenge.

METAL KING SLIME

Acquire 100 different skills for your library and talk to the woman in Solitaire's office.

METAL KAISER SLIME

Acquire 150 different skills for your library and talk to the woman in Solitaire's office.

LEOPOLD

Acquire all of the skills for your library and talk to the woman in Solitaire's office.

LIQUID METAL SLIME

Collect 100 monsters in your library and talk to the man in Solitaire's office.

GRANDPA SLIME

Collect 200 monsters in your library and talk to the man in Solitaire's office.

EMPYREA

Collect all of the monsters in your library and talk to the man in Solitaire's office.

TRODE AND ROBBIN' HOOD

Complete both the skills and monster libraries and talk to both the man and woman in Solitaire's office.

DRAWN TO LIFE

HEAL ALL DAMAGE

During a game, press Start, hold L and press Y, X, Y, X, Y, X, A.

INVINCIBLITY

During a game, press Start, hold L and press A, X, B, B, Y.

ALIEN TEMPLATES

During a game, press Start, hold L and press X, Y, B, A, A.

ANIMAL TEMPLATES

During a game, press Start, hold L and press B, B, A, A, X.

ROBOT TEMPLATES

During a game, press Start, hold L and press Y, X, Y, X, A.

SPORTS TEMPLATES

During a game, press Start, hold L and press Y, A, B, A, X.

DRAWN TO LIFE: SPONGEBOB SQUAREPANTS EDITION

9,999,999 COINS

Select Cheat Entry and enter Down, Down, B, B, Down, Left, Up, Right, A.

FINAL FANTASY FABLES: CHOCOBO TALES

OMEGA—WAVE CANNON CARD

Select Send from the Main menu and then choose Download Pop-Up Card. Press L, L, Up, B, B, Left.

GODZILLA UNLEASHED: DOUBLE SMASH

ANGUIRUS

Defeat Hedorah Terrorizes San Francisco.

DESTOROYAH

Defeat Monster Island, The Final Battle.

FIRE RODAN

Defeat Biollante Attacks Paris.

KING GHIDORAH

Defeat Mecha King Ghidorah Ravages Bangkok.

GRID

UNLOCK ALL

Select Cheat Codes from the Options and enter 233558.

INVULNERABILITY

Select Cheat Codes from the Options and enter 161650.

DRIFT MASTER

Select Cheat Codes from the Options and enter 789520.

PERFECT GRIP

Select Cheat Codes from the Options and enter 831782.

HIGH ROLLER

Select Cheat Codes from the Options and enter 401134.

GHOST CAR

Select Cheat Codes from the Options and enter 657346.

TOY CARS

Select Cheat Codes from the Options and enter 592014.

MM MODE

Select Cheat Codes from the Options and enter 800813.

IZUNA: LEGEND OF THE UNEMPLOYED NINJA

PATH OF TRAILS BONUS DUNGEON

After completing the game, touch the crystal from the beginning.

JAKE HUNTER: DETECTIVE CHRONICLES

PASSWORDS

Select Password from the main menu and enter the following:

UNLOCKABLE	PASSWORD
1 Password Info	AAAA
2 Visuals	LEET
3 Visuals	GONG
4 Visuals	CARS
5 Movies	ROSE
6 Jukebox	BIKE
7 Hints	HINT

JAM SESSIONS

BONUS SONGS

At the Free Play menu, press Up, Up, Down, Down, Left, Right, Left, Right. This unlocks I'm Gonna Miss Her by Brad Paisley, Needles and Pins by Tom Petty, and Wild Thing by Jimi Hendrix.

KIRBY: CANVAS CURSE

JUMP GAME

Defeat the game with all five characters. Select the game file to get Jump Game next to the options on the Main menu.

KONAMI CLASSICS SERIES: ARCADE HITS

GRADIUS

ALL POWER-UPS EXCEPT SPEED

At the Gradius title screen, press Up, Up, Down, Down, Left, Right, Left, Right, B, A. After starting a game, press Start to get every power-up except Speed. This code can be entered only once.

LEGO BATMAN

You should hear a confirmation sound after the following codes are entered.

ALL CHARACTERS

At the main menu, press X, Up, B, Down, Y, Left, Start, Right, R, R, L, R, R, Down, Down, Up, Y, Y, Start, Select.

ALL EPISODES AND FREE PLAY MODE

At the main menu, press Right, Up, R, L, X, Y, Right, Left, B, L, R, L, Down, Down, Up, Y, Y, X, X, B, B, Up, Up, L, R, Start, Select.

ALL EXTRAS

At the main menu, press Up, Down, L, R, L, R, L, Left, Right, X, X, Y, Y, B, B, L, Up, Down, L, R, L, R, Up, Up, Down, Start, Select.

1 MILLION STUDS

At the main menu, press X, Y, B, B, Y, X, L, L, R, R, Up, Down, Left, Right, Start, Select.

3 MILLION STUDS

At the main menu, press Up, Up, B, Down, Down, X, Left, Left, Y, L, R, L, R, B, Y, X, Start, Select.

LEGO INDIANA JONES: THE ORIGINAL ADVENTURES

You should hear a confirmation sound after the following codes are entered.

ALL CHARACTERS

At the title screen, press X, Up, B, Down, Y, Left, Start, Right, R, R, L, R, R, Down, Down, Up, Y, Y, Y, Start, Select.

ALL EPISODES AND FREE PLAY MODE

Right, Up, R, L, X, Y, Right, Left, B, L, R, L, Down, Down, Up, Y, Y, X, X, B, B, Up, Up, L, R, Start, Select.

ALL EXTRAS

Up, Down, L, R, L, R, L, Left, Right, X, X, Y, Y, B, B, L, Up, Down, L, R, L, R, Up, Up, Down, Start, Select.

1,000,000 STUDS

At the title screen, press X, Y, B, B, Y, X, L, L, R, R, Up, Down, Left, Right, Start, Select.

3,000,000 STUDS

At the title screen, press Up, Up, B, Down, Down, X, Left, Left, Y, L, R, L, R, B, Y, X, Start, Select.

LEGO STAR WARS II: THE ORIGINAL TRILOGY

10 STUDS

At the Mos Eisley cantina, enter 4PR28U.

OBI WAN GHOST

At the Mos Eisley cantina, enter BEN917.

LEGO STAR WARS: THE COMPLETE SAGA

3,000,000 STUDS

At the main menu, press Start, Start, Down, Down, Left, Left, Up, Up, Select. This cheat can only be used once.

DEBUG MENUS

At the main menu, press Up, Left, Down, Right, Up, Left, Down, Right, Up, Left, Down, Right, R, L, Start, Select.

BONUS TOUCH GAME 1

At the main menu, press Up, Up, Down, L, L, R, R.

LOCK'S QUEST

REPLACE CLOCKWORKS WITH KINGDOM FORCE
After completing the game, hold R and select your profile.

ENDING STORY
After completing the game, hold L and select your profile.

LUNAR KNIGHTS

SOUND DATA (BOKTAI)
With Boktai in the GBA slot, purchase this from the General Store in Acuna.

SOUND DATA (BOKTAI 2)
With Boktai 2 in the GBA slot, purchase this from the General Store in Acuna.

MARIO PARTY DS

BOSS BASH
Complete Story Mode.

EXPERT CPU DIFFICULTY LEVEL
Complete Story Mode.

MUSIC AND VOICE ROOM
Complete Story Mode.

SCORE SCUFFLE
Complete Story Mode.

TRIANGLE TWISTER PUZZLE MODE
Complete Story Mode.

METROID PRIME PINBALL

PHAZON MINES
Complete Omega Pirate in Multi Mission mode.

PHENDRANA DRIFTS
Complete Thardus in Multi Mission mode.

MY WORD COACH

WORD POPPERS MINIGAME
After reaching 200 word successes, at the options menu, press A, B, X, Y, A, B.

N+

ATARI BONUS LEVELS
Select Unlockables from the main menu, hold L + R and press A, B, A, B, A, A, B.

NAMCO MUSEUM DS

DIG-DUG 2 OLD VERSION

From the Dig Dug 2 menu, select Hardcore Options from the Settings. Change New Version to Old.

SECRET GAME: SUPER XEVIOUS

From the Xevious menu, select Hardcore Options from the Settings. Change the version to Super Xevious.

NARUTO: PATH OF THE NINJA

After defeating the game, talk to Knohamaru on the roof of the Ninja Academy. He allows you go get certain cheats by tapping four successive spots on the touch screen in order. There are 12 different spots on the screen. We have numbered them from left to right, top to bottom, as follows:

1	2	3	4
5	6	7	8
9	10	11	12

Enter the following codes by touching the four spots in the order listed.

UNLOCK	CODE
4th Hokage's Sword	4, 7, 11, 5
Fuji Fan	8, 11, 2, 5
Jiraiya	11, 3, 1, 6
Rajin's Sword	7, 6, 5, 11
Rasengan	9, 2, 12, 7

NARUTO: PATH OF THE NINJA 2

CHARACTER PASSWORDS

Talk to Konohamaru at the school to enter the following passwords. You must first complete the game for the passwords to work.

CHARACTER	PASSWORD
Gaara	D K F I A B J L
Gai	I K A G D E F L
Iruka	J G D L K A I B
Itachi Uchiha	G B E I D A L F
Jiraiya	E B J D A G F L
Kankuro	A L J K B E D G
Kyuubi Naruto	G J H L B F D E
Orochimaru	A H F B L E J G
Temari	H F I C L K B G
The Third Hokage	C G H A J B E L

MISSION PASSWORDS

Talk to Konohamaru at the school to enter the following passwords. You must first complete the game for the passwords to work.

MISSION	PASSWORD
An Extreme Battle!	H L B A K G C D
The Legendary Haze Ninja!	F G E H I D A L
The Legendary Sannin!	B C E G K F H L

NEED FOR SPEED CARBON: OWN THE CITY

INFINITE NITROUS

At the Main menu, press Up, Up, Down, Left, A, B, B, A.

NEW SUPER MARIO BROS.

PLAY AS LUIGI IN SINGLE PLAYER

At the Select a File screen, hold L + R while selecting a saved game.

SECRET CHALLENGE MODE

On the map, pause the game and press L, R, L, R, X, X, Y, Y.

THE NEW YORK TIMES CROSSWORDS

BLACK & WHITE

At the Main menu, press Up, Up, Down, Down, B, B, Y, Y.

NICKTOONS: ATTACK OF THE TOYBOTS

DANNY PHANTOM 2

Select Unlock Code from the Options and enter Tak, Jimmy, Zim, El Tigre.

SPONGEBOB 2

Select Unlock Code from the Options and enter Patrick, Jenny, Timmy, Tak.

NICKTOONS: BATTLE FOR VOLCANO ISLAND

FRUIT BECOMES TOYS IN FRUIT COLLECTING MINI-GAME

Select Unlock Codes from the Options and enter Spongebob, Danny, Timmy, Cosmo.

PAC-PIX

BUTTERFLY HIDDEN GESTURE

Select Sketchbook from the Gallery. Draw a figure eight. The drawing should fly upwards.

CHERRIES HIDDEN GESTURE

Select Sketchbook from the Gallery. Draw a pair of cherries starting with one of the circles.

POGO STICK HIDDEN GESTURE

Select Sketchbook from the Gallery. Draw a P and it will bounce off the screen.

RAIN CLOUD HIDDEN GESTURE

Select Sketchbook from the Gallery. Draw a cloud and it will turn blue and rain will fall from the drawing.

SNAKE HIDDEN GESTURE

Select Sketchbook from the Gallery. Draw an a squiggly line. It will turn green and slither away.

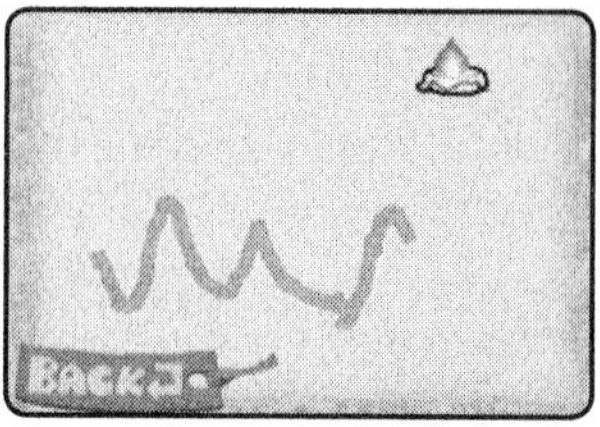

TREBLE CLEF HIDDEN GESTURE

Select Sketchbook from the Gallery. Draw a treble clef.

SHOOT ARROWS AT PAC-MAN

After you have earned the Arrow gesture in Chapter 4, select Sketchbook from the Gallery. Draw an arrow facing Pac-man.

PIRATES OF THE CARIBBEAN: DEAD MAN'S CHEST

10 GOLD

During a game, press Right, X, X, Right, Left.

INVINCIBILITY

During a game, press Up, Down, Left, Right (x5), Left, Right, Up, Down, Left, Right, Up (x5), Left.

UNLIMITED POWER

During a game, press Up, Up, Down, Down, Left, Right, Left, Right, L, R.

RESTORE HEALTH

During a game, press Y, Y, Select, Left, Right, Left, Right, Left.

RESTORE SAVVY

During a game, press X, X, Select, Up, Down, Up, Down, Up.

GHOST FORM MODE
During a game, press Y, X, Y, X, Y, X.

SEASICKNESS MODE
During a game, press X, X, Y, X, X, Y.

SILLY WEAPONS
During a game, press Y, Y, X, Y (x3).

AXE
During a game, press Left, L, L, Down, Down, Left, Up, Up, Down, Down.

BLUNDERBUSS
During a game, press Down, L, L, Down (x3).

CHICKEN
During a game, press Right, L, L, Up, Down, Down.

EXECUTIONER AXE
During a game, press Right, L, L, Up, Down, Up, Right, Right, Left(x2).

PIG
During a game, press Right, R, R, Down, Up, Up.

PISTOL
During a game, press Down, L, L, Down, Down, Right.

RIFLE
During a game, press Left, L, L, Up (x3).

FAST MUSIC
During a game, press Y, Select, Y (x4).

SLOW MUSIC
During a game, press Y, Select, X (x4).

DISABLE CHEATS
During a game, press X (x6).

PRINCESS NATASHA

ALL GADGETS
Select Codes from the Extras menu and enter OLEGSGIZMO.

EXTRA LEVELS
Select Codes from the Extras menu and enter SMASHROBOT.

INFINITE LIVES
Select Codes from the Extras menu and enter CRUSHLUBEK.

PUYO POP FEVER

ALL CHARACTERS AND CUTSCENES
Select Gallery from the Options. Highlight cutscene viewer, hold X and press Up, Down, Left, Right.

RACE DRIVER: CREATE & RACE

ALL CHALLENGES
Select Cheat Codes from Extras and enter 942785.

ALL CHAMPIONSHIPS
Select Cheat Codes from Extras and enter 761492.

ALL REWARDS
Select Cheat Codes from Extras and enter 112337.

FREE DRIVE
Select Cheat Codes from Extras and enter 171923.

NO DAMAGE
Select Cheat Codes from Extras and enter 505303.

EASY STEERING
Select Cheat Codes from Extras and enter 611334.

MINIATURE CARS
Select Cheat Codes from Extras and enter 374288.

MM VIEW
Select Cheat Codes from Extras and enter 467348.

RIDGE RACER DS

00-AGENT CAR
Finish more than ten races in multi-player.

CADDY CAR
Finish more than ten races in multi-player.

GALAGA '88 CAR
Finish more than ten races in multi-player.

MARIO RACING CAR
Finish more than ten races in multi-player.

POOKA CAR
Finish more than ten races in multi-player.

RED SHIRT RAGE CAR
Finish more than ten races in multi-player.

SHY GUY CAR
Finish more than ten races in multi-player.

GALAGA PAC JAM SONG
Unlock the Pooka car.

MUSHROOM KINGDOM II SONG
Unlock the DK Team Racing car.

SIMCITY CREATOR

99999999 MONEY
Enter MONEYBAGS as a password.

AMERICAN PROSPERITY AGE MAP
Enter NEWWORLD as a password.

ASIA AGE MAP
Enter SAMURAI as a password.

ASIA AGE BONUS MAP
Enter FEUDAL as a password.

DAWN OF CIVILIZATION MAP
Enter ANCIENT as a password.

GLOBAL WARMING MAP
Enter MODERN as a password.

GLOBAL WARMING BONUS MAP
Enter BEYOND as a password.

RENAISSANCE BONUS MAP
Enter HEREANDNOW as a password.

SIMCITY DS

LANDMARK BUILDINGS

Select Landmark Collection from the Museum menu. Choose Password and enter the following:

BUILDING	PASSWORD
Anglican Cathedral (UK)	kipling
Arc de Triomphe (France)	gaugin
Atomic Dome (Japan)	kawabata
Big Ben (UK)	orwell
Bowser Castle (Nintendo)	hanafuda
Brandenburg Gate (Germany)	gropius
Coit Tower	kerouac
Conciergerie (France)	rodin
Daibutsu (Japan)	mishima
Edo Castle (Japan)	shonagon
Eiffel Tower (France)	camus
Gateway Arch (USA)	twain
Grand Central Station (USA)	f.scott
Great Pyramids (Egypt)	mahfouz
Hagia Sofia (Turkey)	ataturk
Helsinki Cathedral (Finland)	kivi
Himeji Castle (Japan)	hokusai
Holstentor (Germany)	durer
Independence Hall (USA)	mlkingjr
Jefferson Memorial (USA)	thompson
Kokkai (Japan)	soseki
LA Landmark (USA)	hemingway
Lincoln Memorial (USA)	melville
Liver Building (UK)	dickens
Melbourne Cricket Ground (Australia)	damemelba
Metropolitan Cath. (UK)	austen
Moai (Chile)	allende
Mt. Fuji (Japan)	hiroshige
National Museum (Taiwan)	yuantlee
Neuschwanstein Castle (Germany)	beethoven
Notre Dame (France)	hugo
Palace of Fine Arts (USA)	bunche
Palacio Real (Spain)	cervantes
Paris Opera (France)	daumier
Parthenon (Greece)	callas
Pharos of Alexandria (Egypt)	zewail
Rama IX Royal Park (Thailand)	phu
Reichstag (Germany)	goethe
Sagrada Familia (Spain)	dali
Shuri Castle (Japan)	basho
Smithsonian Castle (USA)	pauling
Sphinx (Egypt)	haykal
St Paul's Cathedral (UK)	defoe
St. Basil's Cathedral (Russia)	tolstoy
St. Stephen's Cathedral (Austria)	mozart
Statue of Liberty (USA)	pollack
Stockholm Palace (Sweden)	bergman
Taj Mahal (India)	tagore
Tower of London (UK)	maugham
Trafalgar Square (UK)	joyce
United Nations (UN)	amnesty
United States Capitol (USA)	poe
Washington Monument	capote
Westminster Abbey (UK)	greene
White House (USA)	Steinbeck

THE SIMS 2

MONGOO MONKEY FOR THE CASINO

Start the game with Sims 2 in the GBA slot of your Nintendo DS.

SOUL BUBBLES

REVEAL ALL CALABASH LOCATIONS

Pause the game and press A, L, L, R, A, Down, A, R.

ALL LEVELS

At the World Select, press L, Up, X, Up, R, Y.

ALL GALLERY ITEMS

At the Gallery, press B, Up, B, B, L, Y.

CARD INPUT SYSTEM

When the Upsilon Cube is unearthed and shown to Aldous, the Card Input System feature becomes available. This will allow you to input data from Spectrobe Cards. These give you new Spectrobes and Custom Parts. If you get your hands on a Spectrobe Card and the system is unlocked, investigate the card input system in the spaceship's lower deck. Follow the instructions on the upper screen to match the four corner points of the card to the corners of the touch screen. Touch the screen through the seven holes in the card in the order indicated on the card. If the code you input is correct, you receive Spectrobes, custom Parts, minerals or Cubes.

You can input the same card a maximum of four times. This means that you can only obtain four of the same Spectrobes from a single card. You can only input cards once. And some cards cannot be input until you have reached a certain point in the game.

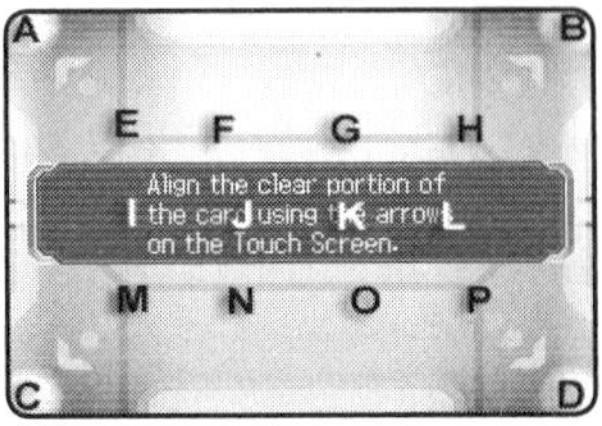

The following table gives you a seven character code which refers to the spots you touch in order. The first four characters have you touching the four corners and the final three are spots among the 12 in the middle. To get Cyclone Geo, Hammer Geo, Ice Geo, Plasma Geo, or Thunder Geo, you must first beat the game.

EFFECT	CODE
Aobasat Apex	BACD HEP
Cyclone Geo	CDAB LGM
Danaphant Tuska	ABDC ELI
Danilob	DABC GLO
Emerald Mineral	BACD FKN
Grilden Biblad	ABDC FIH
Grildragos Drafly	CDAB MHK
Gristar	BACD EJN
Hammer Geo	ABDC ELH
Harumitey Lazos	DABC ILM
Ice Geo	CDAB HEK
Inataflare Auger	ABDC IGH
Inkalade	ABDC GLP
Iota Cube	ABDC OHE
Komainu	CDAB HMJ
Kugaster Sonara	DABC LOE
Mossax Jetspa (Custom Color 1)	BACD JML
Naglub	ABDC EJM
Plasma Geo	BACD KLE
Rho Cube	BACD PNI
Ruby Mineral	CDAB FKO
Samukabu	ABDC OIL

EFFECT	CODE
Samurite Voltar	BACD LHM
Sapphire Mineral	ABDC FJO
Segulos Propos	CDAB KIH
Seguslice	CDAB GKP
Shakor Bristle	DABC MLK
Sigma Cube	CDAB PML
Tau Cube	DABC LIF
Thunder Geo	DABC MEL
Vilagrisp (Custom Part)	DABC EIN
Vilakroma	BACD NLM
Vilakroma (Custom Color 1)	CDAB LJI
Vilakroma (Custom Color 2)	DABC EGP
Windora	ABDC MGP
Windora (Custom Color 1)	DABC EHG
Windora (Custom Color 2)	CDAB JPM
Windora Ortex	BACD IPG
Windora Ortex (Custom Color 1)	ABDC MPH
Windora Ortex (Custom Color 2)	DABC MGH
Windora Sordina	CDAB PEO
Windora Sordina (Custom Color 1)	BACD MOH
Windora Sordina (Custom Color 2)	ABDC LEN
Wing Geo (must beat game	DABC MNP

SPIDER-MAN 2

ALL SPECIAL MOVES

Load the game with Spider-Man: Mysterio's Menace for Game Boy Advance in the Nintendo DS.

STAR TREK: TACTICAL ASSAULT

KLINGON CAMPAIGN

At the Main menu, press Up, Down, Left, Right, Select, Start, X.

UNLOCK MISSIONS

At the Main menu, press Up, Down, Left, Right, Select, Start, Start.

EXTRA CREW UPGRADES

At the Main menu, press Up, Down, Left, Right, Select, Start, Select.

ALL SHIPS IN SKIRMISH AND MULTIPLAYER

At the Main menu, press Up, Down, Left, Right, Select, Start, Y.

ANY SHIP IN MISSIONS

At the Main menu, press Up, Down, Left, Right, Select, Start, B.

STAR WARS EPISODE III: REVENGE OF THE SITH

MASTER DIFFICULTY

Defeat the game.

ANAKIN'S STARFIGHTER

Beat the Anakin bot in multiplayer.

DARTH VADER'S TIE FIGHTER

Defeat the Darth Vader bot in multiplayer.

GENERAL GREVIOUS'S STARFIGHTER

Defeat the General Grevious bot in multiplayer.

MILLENIUM FALCON

Defeat the Solo bot in multiplayer.

SLAVE I

Defeat the Fett bot in multiplayer.

X-WING

Defeat the Luke bot in multiplayer.

STAR WARS: THE FORCE UNLEASHED

INCREASED HEALTH

Select Unleashed Codes from the Extras menu and enter QSSPVENXO.

MAX OUT FORCE POWERS

Select Unleashed Codes from the Extras menu and enter CPLOOLKBF.

UNLIMITED FORCE ENERGY

Select Unleashed Codes from the Extras menu and enter TVENCVMJZ.

MORE POWERFUL LIGHTSABER

Select Unleashed Codes from the Extras menu and enter lightsaber.

UBER LIGHTSABER

Select Unleashed Codes from the Extras menu and enter MOMIROXIW.

ROM KOTA

Select Unleashed Codes from the Extras menu and enter mandalore.

CEREMONIAL JEDI ROBES

Select Unleashed Codes from the Extras menu and enter CURSEZRUX.

DAD'S ROBES

Select Unleashed Codes from the Extras menu and enter wookiee.

DARTH VADER'S COSTUME
Select Unleashed Codes from the Extras menu and enter HRMXRKVEN.

KENTO'S ROBE
Select Unleashed Codes from the Extras menu and enter KBVMSEVNM.

KOTA'S OUTFIT
Select Unleashed Codes from the Extras menu and enter EEDOPVENG.

SITH ROBE
Select Unleashed Codes from the Extras menu and enter ZWSFVENXA.

SITH ROBES
Select Unleashed Codes from the Extras menu and enter holocron.

SITH STALKER ARMOR
Select Unleashed Codes from the Extras menu and enter CPLZKMZTD.

TAMAGOTCHI CONNECTION: CORNER SHOP 3

DOUBLE LAYERED CAKE
Select Enter Code from the Special menu and enter R6194BJD6F.

TEENAGE MUTANT NINJA TURTLES 3: MUTANT NIGHTMARE

CRYSTALS ARE EASTER EGGS
Select Input Password from the Options and enter SRDSLLMS.

CRYSTALS ARE JACK-O-LANTERNS
Select Input Password from the Options and enter DRSSMRLD.

CRYSTALS ARE SANTAS
Select Input Password from the Options and enter LLDMSRMD.

LIFE ICONS ARE PIZZA
Select Input Password from the Options and enter DDRMLRDS.

COWABUNGA
At the Title screen, press U, U, D, D, L, R, L, R, B, A.

TIGER WOODS PGA TOUR 2005

EMERALD DRAGON
Earn $1,000,000.

GREEK ISLES
Earn $1,500,000.

PARADISE COVER
Earn $2,000,000.

EA SPORTS FAVORITES
Earn $5,000,000

MEAN8TEEN
Earn $10,000,000.

FANTASY SPECIALS
Earn $15,000,000.

LEGEND COMPILATION 1
Defeat Hogan in Legend Tour.

LEGEND COMPILATION 2
Defeat Gary Player in Legend Tour.

LEGEND COMPILATION 3
Defeat Ballesteros in Legend Tour.

LEGEND COMPILATION 4
Defeat Palmer in Legend Tour.

LEGEND COMPILATION 5
Defeat Nicklaus in Legend Tour.

THE HUSTLER'S DREAM 18
Defeat The Hustler in Legend Tour.

TIGER'S DREAM 18
Defeat Tiger Woods in Legend Tour.

TOM CLANCY'S SPLINTER CELL CHAOS THEORY

UNLIMITED AMMO/GADGETS

Defeat the game.

CHARACTER SKINS

Defeat the game.

TONY HAWK'S DOWNHILL JAM

ALWAYS SNOWSKATE

Select Buy Stuff from the Skateshop. Choose Enter Code and enter SNOWSK8T.

MIRRORED MAPS

Select Buy Stuff from the Skateshop. Choose Enter Code and enter MIRRORBALL.

ABOMINABLE SNOWMAN OUTFIT

Select Buy Stuff from the Skateshop. Choose Enter Code and enter BIGSNOWMAN.

ZOMBIE SKATER OUTFIT

Select Buy Stuff from the Skateshop. Choose Enter Code and enter ZOMBIEALIVE.

TRAUMA CENTER: UNDER THE KNIFE

X1: KYRIAKI MISSION

Defeat the game. Find the X Missions under Challenge Mode.

X2: DEFTERA MISSION

Defeat X1 : Kyriaki Mission. Find the X Missions under Challenge Mode.

X3: TRITI MISSION

Defeat X2 : Deftera Mission. Find the X Missions under Challenge Mode.

X4: TETARTI MISSION

Defeat X3 : Triti Mission. Find the X Missions under Challenge Mode.

X5: PEMPTI MISSION

Defeat X4 : Tetarti Mission. Find the X Missions under Challenge Mode.

X6: PARAKEVI MISSION

Defeat X5 : Pempti Mission. Find the X Missions under Challenge Mode.

X7: SAVATO MISSION

Defeat X6 : Parakevi Mission. Find the X Missions under Challenge Mode.

THE URBZ: SIMS IN THE CITY

CLUB XIZZLE

Once you gain access to Club Xizzle, enter with the password "bucket."

WORLD CHAMPIONSHIP POKER

UNLOCK CASINOS

At the Title screen, press Y, X, Y, B, L, R. Then press the following direction:

DIRECTION	CASINO
Left	Amazon
Right	Nebula
Down	Renaissance

YU-GI-OH! NIGHTMARE TROUBADOUR

CREDITS

Unlock the Password Machine by defeating the Expert Cup. Enter the Duel Shop and select the Slot maching. Enter 00000375.

SOUND TEST

Unlock the Password Machine by defeating the Expert Cup. Enter the Duel Shop and select the Slot maching. Enter 57300000.

YU-GI-OH! WORLD CHAMPIONSHIP 2008

CARD PASSWORDS

Enter the following in the password machine to receive the corresponding card. You must already have the card to use the password.

PASSWORD EFFECT

CARD	PASSWORD
7	67048711
7 Colored Fish	23771716
7 Completed	86198326
A Feint Plan	68170903
A Hero Emerges	21597117
Abyss Soldier	18318842
Acid Rain	21323861
Acid Trap Hole	41356845
Adhesive Explosive	53828196
Agido	16135253
Airknight Parshath	18036057
Aitsu	48202661
Alkana Knight Joker	06150044
Alligator's Sword	64428736
Alligator's Sword Dragon	03366982
Alpha the Magnet Warrior	99785935
Altar for Tribute	21070956
Amazon Archer	91869203
Amazoness Archers	67987611
Amazoness Blowpiper	73574678
Amazoness Chain Master	29654737
Amazoness Fighter	55821894
Amazoness Paladin	47480070
Amazoness Spellcaster	81325903
Amazoness Swords Woman	94004268
Amazoness Tiger	10979723
Amphibian Beast	67371383

CARD	PASSWORD
Amplifier	00303660
Anti-Spell	53112492
Aqua Madoor	85639257
Aqua Spirit	40916023
Archfiend of Gilfer	50287060
Armed Changer	90374791
Armed Ninja	09076207
Armored Glass	21070956
Armored Zombie	20277860
Array of Revealing Light	69296555
Arsenal Bug	42364374
Arsenal Robber	55348096
Assault on GHQ	62633180
Asura Priest	02134346
Attack and Receive	63689843
Autonomous Action Unit	71453557
Axe of Despair	40619825
Axe Raider	48305365
B. Skull Dragon	11901678
Baby Dragon	88819587
Back to Square One	47453433
Backfire	82705573
Bad Reaction to Simochi	40633297
Bait Doll	07165085
Ballista of Rampart Smashing	00242146
Banisher of the Light	61528025
Banner of Courage	10012614

CARD	PASSWORD
Bark of The Dark Ruler	41925941
Baron of the Fiend Sword	86325596
Barrel Behind the Door	78783370
Barrel Dragon	81480460
Battery Charger	61181383
Batteryman AA	63142001
Batteryman C	19733961
Batteryman D	55401221
Battle Ox	05053103
Battle Warrior	55550921
Beast Fangs	46009906
Beast Soul Swap	35149085
Beastking of the Swamps	99426834
Beautiful Headhuntress	16899564
Beckoning Light	16255442
Berfomet	77207191
Berserk Gorilla	39168895
Beta the Magnet Warrior	39256679
Bickuribox	25655502
Big Bang Shot	61127349
Big Eye	16768387
Big Shield Gardna	65240384
Birdface	45547649
Black Illusion Ritual	41426869
Black Luster Ritual	55761792
Black Luster Soldier	72989439
Black Magic Ritual	76792184
Black Pendant	65169794
Bladefly	28470714
Blast Held by a Tribute	89041555
Blast Magician	21051146
Blast Sphere	26302522
Blast with Chain	98239899
Blasting the Ruins	21466326
Blessings of the Nile	30653173
Blowback Dragon	25551951
Blue Medicine	20871001
Blue-Eyes Toon Dragon	53183600
Blue-Eyes Ultimate Dragon	23995346
Blue-Eyes White Dragon	80906030
Blue-Eyes White Dragon	80906030
Book of Taiyou	38699854
Bottomless Trap Hole	29401950
Bowganian	52090844
Bracchio-Raidus	16507828
Brain Control	87910978
Breaker the Magical Warrior	71413901
Breath of Light	20101223
Bright Castle	82878489
Burning Land	24294108
Burning Spear	18937875
Burst Return	27191436
Burst Stream of Destruction	17655904
Buster Rancher	84740193
Cannon Soldier	11384280
Cannonball Spear Shellfish	95614612

CARD	PASSWORD
Card Destruction	72892473
Card of Sanctity	04266498
Card Shuffle	12183332
Castle of Dark Illusions	00062121
Castle Walls	44209392
Catapult Turtle	95727991
Ceasefire	36468556
Celtic Guardian	91152256
Cemetery Bomb	51394546
Centrifugal Field	01801154
Cestus of Dagla	28106077
Chain Destruction	01248895
Chain Disappearance	57139487
Chain Energy	79323590
Chaos Command Magician	72630549
Chaos End	61044390
Chaos Greed	97439308
Chimera the Flying Mythical Beast	04796100
Chiron the Mage	16956455
Chorus of Sanctuary	81380218
Chthonian Alliance	46910446
Chthonian Blast	18271561
Chthonian Polymer	72287557
Clay Charge	22479888
Cocoon of Evolution	40240595
Coffin Seller	65830223
Cold Wave	60682203
Command Knight	10375182
Conscription	31000575
Continuous Destruction Punch	68057622
Contract with Exodia	33244944
Contract with the Dark Master	96420087
Convulsion of Nature	62966332
Copycat	26376390
Cosmo Queen	38999506
Covering Fire	74458486
Crass Clown	93889755
Crawling Dragon #2	38289717
Crimson Sunbird	46696593
Crush Card Virus	57728570
Curse of Anubis	66742250
Curse of Darkness	84970821
Curse of Dragon	28279543
Curse of the Masked Beast	94377247
Cursed Seal of the Forbidden Spell	58851034
Cyber Raider	39978267
Cyber Shield	63224564
Cyber-Tech Alligator	48766543
D.D. Borderline	60912752
D.D. Designator	33423043
D.D. Assailant	70074904
D.D. Dynamite	08628798
D.D. Trap Hole	05606466
D.D. Warrior	37043180
D.D. Warrior Lady	07572887
D. Tribe	02833249

CARD	PASSWORD
Dark Artist	72520073
Dark Deal	65824822
Dark Dust Spirit	89111398
Dark Elf	21417692
Dark Energy	04614116
Dark Factory of Mass Production	90928333
Dark Jeroid	90980792
Dark Magic Attack	02314238
Dark Magic Curtain	99789342
Dark Magician	46986414
Dark Magician Girl	38033121
Dark Magician of Chaos	40737112
Dark Master - Zorc	97642679
Dark Mimic LV1	74713516
Dark Mimic LV3	01102515
Dark Mirror Force	20522190
Dark Necrofear	31829185
Dark Paladin	98502113
Dark Rabbit	99261403
Dark Room of Nightmare	85562745
Dark Sage	92377303
Dark Snake Syndrome	47233801
Dark Spirit of the Silent	93599951
Dark World Lightning	93554166
Darkness Approaches	80168720
Dark-Piercing Light	45895206
Deck Devastation Virus	35027493
Decoy Dragon	02732323
Dedication through Light and Darkness	69542930
De-Fusion	95286165
Delta Attacker	39719977
Despair from the Dark	71200730
De-Spell	19159413
Destiny Board	94212438
Destruction Ring	21219755
Dian Keto the Cure Master	84257639
Dice Re-Roll	83241722
Different Dimension Capsule	11961740
Different Dimension Dragon	50939127
Different Dimension Gate	56460688
Diffusion Wave-Motion	87880531
Dimension Fusion	23557835
Dimension Wall	67095270
Dimensional Prison	70342110
Dimensionhole	22959079
Disappear	24623598
Disarmament	20727787
Divine Sword - Phoenix Blade	31423101
Divine Wrath	49010598
DNA Surgery	74701381
Doomcaliber Knight	78700060
Double Coston	44436472
Double Snare	03682106
Double Spell	24096228
Dragged Down into the Grave	16435235

CARD	PASSWORD
Dragon Capture Jar	50045299
Dragon Seeker	28563545
Dragon Treasure	01435851
Dragonic Attack	32437102
Dragon's Mirror	71490127
Draining Shield	43250041
Dramatic Rescue	80193355
Dream Clown	13215230
Drill Bug	88733579
Driving Snow	00473469
Drop Off	55773067
Dunames Dark Witch	12493482
Dust Barrier	31476755
Dust Tornado	60082867
Earth Chant	59820352
Earthbound Spirit's Invitation	65743242
Earthquake	82828051
Eatgaboon	42578427
Ectoplasmer	97342942
Ekibyo Drakmord	69954399
Electro-Whip	37820550
Elegant Egotist	90219263
Elemental Hero Avian	21844576
Elemental Hero Burstinatrix	58932615
Elemental Hero Clayman	84327329
Elemental Hero Flame Wingman	35809262
Elemental Hero Rampart Blaster	47737087
Elemental Hero Sparkman	20721928
Elemental Hero Thunder Giant	61204971
Embodiment of Apophis	28649820
Emergency Provisions	53046408
Enchanted Arrow	93260132
Enchanting Fitting Room	30531525
Enemy Controller	98045062
Energy Drain	56916805
Enervating Mist	26022485
Enraged Battle Ox	76909279
Eradicating Aerosol	94716515
Eternal Drought	56606928
Eternal Rest	95051344
Exarion Universe	63749102
Exchange	05556668
Exhausting Spell	95451366
Exodia Necross	12600382
Exodia the Forbidden One	33396948
Fairy Box	21598948
Fairy King Truesdale	45425051
Fairy Meteor Crush	97687912
Fairy's Hand Mirror	17653779
Fake Trap	03027001
Feather Shot	19394153
Feather Wind	71060915
Fengsheng Mirror	37406863
Feral Imp	41392891
Fiend Comedian	81172176
Fiend Skull Dragon	66235877

CARD	PASSWORD
Fiend's Hand Mirror	58607704
Fiend's Sanctuary	24874630
Final Countdown	95308449
Final Destiny	18591904
Firewing Pegasus	27054370
Fissure	66788016
Flame Cerebrus	60862676
Flame Manipulator	34460851
Flame Swordsman	40502030
Flying Kamakiri #1	84834865
Foolish Burial	81439173
Forced Ceasefire	97806240
Forest	87430998
Fortress Whale	62337487
Fortress Whale's Oath	77454922
Frozen Soul	57069605
Fulfillment of the Contract	48206762
Full Salvo	70865988
Fusilier Dragon, the Duel-Mode Beast	51632798
Fusion Gate	24094653
Fusion Sage	26902560
Fusion Sword Murasame Blade	37684215
Gaia Power	56594520
Gaia the Dragon Champion	66889139
Gaia the Fierce Knight	06368038
Gamma the Magnet Warrior	11549357
Garoozis	14977074
Garuda the Wind Spirit	12800777
Gazelle the King of Mythical Beasts	05818798
Gear Golem the Moving Fortress	30190809
Gearfried the Iron Knight	00423705
Gearfried the Swordmaster	57046845
Gemini Elf	69140098
Generation Shift	34460239
Germ Infection	24668830
Getsu Fuhma	21887179
Giant Flea	41762634
Giant Germ	95178994
Giant Rat	97017120
Giant Red Seasnake	58831685
Giant Soldier of Stone	13039848
Giant Trunade	42703248
Gigantes	47606319
Gilasaurus	45894482
Gilford the Legend	69933858
Gilford the Lightning	36354007
Gil Garth	38445524
Goblin Attack Force	78658564
Goblin Fan	04149689
Goblin King	18590133
Goblin Thief	45311864
Goblin's Secret Remedy	11868825
Goddess of Whim	67959180
Goddess with the Third Eye	53493204

CARD	PASSWORD
Gokibore	15367030
Gorgon's Eye	52648457
Graceful Dice	74137509
Gradius' Option	14291024
Granadora	13944422
Grand Tiki Elder	13676474
Gravedigger Ghoul	82542267
Gravekeeper's Assailant	25262697
Gravekeeper's Cannonholder	99877698
Gravekeeper's Chief	62473983
Gravekeeper's Commandant	17393207
Gravekeeper's Curse	50712728
Gravekeeper's Guard	37101832
Gravekeeper's Servant	16762927
Gravekeeper's Spear Soldier	63695531
Gravekeeper's Spy	24317029
Gravekeeper's Vassal	99690140
Gravekeeper's Watcher	26084285
Gravity Axe - Grarl	32022366
Gravity Bind	85742772
Great Moth	14141448
Greed	89405199
Green Baboon, Defender of the Forest	46668237
Greenkappa	61831093
Ground Collapse	90502999
Gust	73079365
Gust Fan	55321970
Gyaku-Gire Panda	09817927
Hammer Shot	26412047
Hand Collapse	74519184
Hannibal Necromancer	05640330
Harpie Lady	76812113
Harpie Lady 1	91932350
Harpie Lady 2	27927359
Harpie Lady 3	54415063
Harpie Lady Sisters	12206212
Harpies' Hunting Ground	75782277
Harpie's Pet Dragon	52040216
Headless Knight	5434080
Heart of Clear Water	64801562
Heart of the Underdog	35762283
Heavy Mech Support Platform	23265594
Heavy Slump	52417194
Heavy Storm	19613556
Helpoemer	76052811
Hercules Beetle	52584282
Hero Kid	32679370
Hero Signal	22020907
Hidden Book of Spell	21840375
Hieroglyph Lithograph	10248192
Hinotama	46130346
Hiro's Shadow Scout	81863068
Hitotsu-Me Giant	76184692
Horn Imp	69669405
Horn of Light	38552107

CARD	PASSWORD
Horn of the Unicorn	64047146
Hoshiningen	67629977
House of Adhesive Tape	15083728
Human-Wave Tactics	30353551
Illusionist Faceless Mage	28546905
Impenetrable Formation	96631852
Inferno	74823665
Inferno Fire Blast	52684508
Infinite Cards	94163677
Infinite Dismissal	54109233
Injection Fairy Lily	79575620
Insect Armor with Laser Cannon	03492538
Insect Barrier	23615409
Insect Imitation	96965364
Insect Queen	91512835
Inspection	16227556
Interdimensional Matter Transporter	36261276
Invigoration	98374133
Jack's Knight	90876561
Jade Insect Whistle	95214051
Jam Breeding Machine	21770260
Jam Defender	21558682
Jar of Greed	83968380
Jigen Bakudan	90020065
Jinzo	77585513
Jinzo #7	77585513
Jowgen the Spiritualist	41855169
Jowls of Dark Demise	05257687
Judge Man	30113682
Judgment of the Pharaoh	55948544
Just Desserts	24068492
Kabazauls	51934376
Kabazauls	51934376
Kanan the Swordsmistress	12829151
Killer Needle	88979991
Kinetic Soldier	79853073
King of the Skull Servants	36021814
King of the Swamp	79109599
King Tiger Wanghu	83986578
King's Knight	64788463
Koitsu	69456283
Krokodilus	76512652
Kryuel	82642348
Kunai with Chain	37390589
Kuriboh	40640057
Kycoo the Ghost Destroyer	88240808
Labyrinth of Nightmare	66526672
Labyrinth Tank	99551425
Larvae Moth	87756343
Laser Cannon Armor	77007920
Last Day of the Witch	90330453
Launcher Spider	87322377
Lava Battleguard	20394040
Lava Golem	00102380
Left Arm of the Forbidden One	07902349

CARD	PASSWORD
Left Leg of the Forbidden One	44519536
Legacy of Yata-Garasu	30461781
Legendary Sword	61854111
Level Conversion Lab	84397023
Level Limit - Area A	54976796
Level Limit - Area B	03136426
Level Modulation	61850482
Level Up!	25290459
Light of Judgment	44595286
Lighten the Load	37231841
Lightforce Sword	49587034
Lightning Vortex	69162969
Little Chimera	68658728
Luminous Soldier	57482479
Luminous Spark	81777047
Luster Dragon	11091375
Machine Duplication	63995093
Machine King	46700124
Mad Sword Beast	79870141
Mage Power	83746708
Magic Cylinder	62279055
Magic Drain	59344077
Magic Formula	67227834
Magic Jammer	77414722
Magical Arm Shield	96008713
Magical Dimension	28553439
Magical Explosion	32723153
Magical Hats	81210420
Magical Stone Excavation	98494543
Magical Thorn	53119267
Magician of Black Chaos	30208479
Magician of Faith	31560081
Magician's Circle	00050755
Magician's Unite	36045450
Magician's Valkyria	80304126
Maha Vailo	93013676
Maharaghi	40695128
Maiden of the Aqua	17214465
Major Riot	09074847
Malevolent Catastrophe	01224927
Malevolent Nuzzler	99597615
Malfunction	06137091
Malice Dispersion	13626450
Man-Eater Bug	54652250
Man-Eating Treasure Chest	13723605
Manga Ryu-Ran	38369349
Marauding Captain	02460565
Marie the Fallen One	57579381
Marshmallon	31305911
Marshmallon Glasses	66865880
Mask of Brutality	82432018
Mask of Darkness	28933734
Mask of Dispel	20765952
Mask of Restrict	29549364
Mask of the Accursed	56948373
Mask of Weakness	57882509

CARD	PASSWORD
Masked Sorcerer	10189126
Mass Driver	34906152
Master Kyonshee	24530661
Mataza the Zapper	22609617
Mausoleum of the Emperor	80921533
Mechanicalchaser	07359741
Mega Ton Magical Cannon	32062913
Megamorph	22046459
Melchid the Four-Faced Beast	86569121
Meltiel, Sage of the Sky	49905576
Mesmeric Control	48642904
Messenger of Peace	44656491
Metal Detector	75646520
Metal Reflect Slime	26905245
Metalmorph	68540058
Metalzoa	50705071
Meteor Black Dragon	90660762
Meteor Dragon	64271667
Michizure	37580756
Micro Ray	18190572
Millennium Shield	32012841
Milus Radiant	07489323
Mind Control	37520316
Mind Crush	15800838
Miracle Dig	63434080
Miracle Kids	55985014
Miracle Restoring	68334074
Mirror Force	44095762
Mispolymerization	58392024
Mist body	47529357
Moisture Creature	75285069
Mokey Mokey	27288416
Mokey Mokey King	13803864
Mokey Mokey Smackdown	01965724
Molten Destruction	19384334
Monster Gate	43040603
Monster Recovery	93108433
Monster Reincarnation	74848038
Mooyan Curry	58074572
Morphing Jar	33508719
Morphing Jar #2	79106360
Mother Grizzly	57839750
Mountain	50913601
Muka Muka	46657337
Multiplication of Ants	22493811
Multiply	40703222
Mushroom Man	14181608
My Body as a Shield	69279219
Mysterious Puppeteer	54098121
Mystic Box	25774450
Mystic Horseman	68516705
Mystic Probe	49251811
Mystic Swordsman LV2	47507260
Mystic Swordsman LV4	74591968
Mystic Swordsman LV6	60482781
Mystic Tomato	83011277

CARD	PASSWORD
Mystical Elf	15025844
Mystical Moon	36607978
Mystical Refpanel	35563539
Mystical Sheep #1	30451366
Mystical Space Typhoon	05318639
Narrow Pass	40172183
Necrovalley	47355498
Needle Wall	38299233
Needle Worm	81843628
Negate Attack	14315573
Neo the Magic Swordsman	50930991
Newdoria	04335645
Next to be Lost	07076131
Nightmare Wheel	54704216
Nimble Momonga	22567609
Nitro Unit	23842445
Non Aggression Area	76848240
Non-Fusion Area	27581098
Non-Spellcasting Area	20065549
Numinous Healer	02130625
Nuvia the Wicked	12953226
Obnoxious Celtic Guard	52077741
Ojama Black	79335209
Ojama Delta Hurricane!!	08251996
Ojama Green	12482652
Ojama King	90140980
Ojama Trio	29843091
Ojama Yellow	42941100
Ojamagic	24643836
Ojamuscle	98259197
Ominous Fortunetelling	56995655
Ookazi	19523799
Opti-Camouflage Armor	44762290
Order to Charge	78986941
Order to Smash	39019325
Otohime	39751093
Overpowering Eye	60577362
Panther Warrior	42035044
Paralyzing Potion	50152549
Parasite Paracide	27911549
Parrot Dragon	62762898
Patrician of Darkness	19153634
Pendulum Machine	24433920
Penguin Knight	36039163
Penguin Soldier	93920745
Perfectly Ultimate Great Moth	48579379
Petit Moth	58192742
Pharaoh's Treasure	63571750
Pigeonholing Books of Spell	96677818
Pikeru's Second Sight	58015506
Pinch Hopper	26185991
Pitch-Black Power Stone	34029630
Poison Fangs	76539047
Poison of the Old Man	08842266
Polymerization	35550694
Pot of Avarice	67169062

CARD	PASSWORD
Premature Burial	70828912
Prepare to Strike Back	04483989
Prevent Rat	00549481
Princess of Tsurugi	51371017
Prohibition	43711255
Protector of the Sanctuary	24221739
Pumpking the King of Ghosts	29155212
Queen's Knight	25652259
Rabid Horseman	94905343
Radiant Jeral	84177693
Radiant Mirror Force	21481146
Raigeki Break	04178474
Rapid-Fire Magician	06337436
Ray of Hope	82529174
Ready for Intercepting	31785398
Really Eternal Rest	28121403
Reaper of the Cards	33066139
Reckless Greed	37576645
Recycle	96316857
Red Archery Girl	65570596
Red Medicine	38199696
Red-Eyes B. Chick	36262024
Red-Eyes Black Dragon	74677422
Red-Eyes Black Metal Dragon	64335804
Reflect Bounder	02851070
Reinforcement of the Army	32807846
Reinforcements	17814387
Release Restraint	75417459
Relieve Monster	37507488
Relinquished	64631466
Remove Trap	51482758
Respect Play	08951260
Restructer Revolution	99518961
Reversal Quiz	05990062
Reverse Trap	77622396
Revival Jam	31709826
Right Arm of the Forbidden One	70903634
Right Leg of the Forbidden One	08124921
Rigorous Reaver	39180960
Ring of Magnetism	20436034
Riryoku Field	70344351
Rising Energy	78211862
Rite of Spirit	30450531
Ritual Weapon	54351224
Robbin' Goblin	88279736
Robbin' Zombie	83258273
Robotic Knight	44203504
Rock Bombardment	20781762
Rocket Warrior	30860696
Rod of Silence - Kay'est	95515060
Rogue Doll	91939608
Roll Out!	91597389
Royal Command	33950246
Royal Decree	51452091
Royal Magical Library	70791313
Royal Oppression	93016201

CARD	PASSWORD
Royal Surrender	56058888
Royal Tribute	72405967
Rude Kaiser	26378150
Rush Recklessly	70046172
Ryu Kokki	57281778
Ryu-Kishin	15303296
Ryu-Ran	02964201
Sage's Stone	13604200
Saggi the Dark Clown	66602787
Sakuretsu Armor	56120475
Salamandra	32268901
Salvage	96947648
Sangan	26202165
Sasuke Samurai #3	77379481
Sasuke Samurai #4	64538655
Satellite Cannon	50400231
Second Coin Toss	36562627
Sengenjin	76232340
Serial Spell	49398568
Serpentine Princess	71829750
Seven Tools of the Bandit	03819470
Shadow Ghoul	30778711
Shadow of Eyes	58621589
Share the Pain	56830749
Shield & Sword	52097679
Shield Crush	30683373
Shift	59560625
Shifting Shadows	59237154
Shinato, King of a Higher Plane	86327225
Shinato's Ark	60365591
Shining Abyss	87303357
Shining Angel	95956346
Shooting Star Bow - Ceal	95638658
Shrink	55713623
Silver Bow and Arrow	01557499
Simultaneous Loss	92219931
Skilled Dark Magician	73752131
Skilled White Magician	46363422
Skull Dice	00126218
Skull Servant	32274490
Skull-Mark Ladybug	64306248
Skyscraper	63035430
Slate Warrior	78636495
Slot Machine	03797883
Smashing Ground	97169186
Smoke Grenade of the Thief	63789924
Snake Fang	00596051
Sogen	86318356
Solar Ray	44472639
Solemn Judgment	41420027
Solemn Wishes	35346968
Sorcerer of the Doomed	49218300
Soul Absorption	68073522
Soul Demolition	76297408
Soul Exchange	68005187
Soul of Purity and Light	77527210

CARD	PASSWORD
Soul of the Pure	47852924
Soul Release	05758500
Soul Resurrection	92924317
Soul Reversal	78864369
Soul Taker	81510157
Spark Blaster	97362768
Spatial Collapse	20644748
Special Hurricane	42598242
Spell Absorption	51481927
Spell Reproduction	29228529
Spell Vanishing	29735721
Spellbinding Circle	18807108
Spell-stopping Statute	10069180
Spiral Spear Strike	49328340
Spirit Message "A"	94772232
Spirit Message "I"	31893528
Spirit Message "L"	30170981
Spirit Message "N"	67287533
Spirit of Flames	13522325
Spirit of the Pharaoh	25343280
Spirit's Invitation	92394653
Spiritual Earth Art - Kurogane	70156997
Spiritual Energy Settle Machine	99173029
Spiritual Fire Art - Kurenai	42945701
Spiritual Water Art - Aoi	06540606
Spiritual Wind Art - Miyabi	79333300
Spiritualism	15866454
St. Joan	21175632
Staunch Defender	92854392
Steel Ogre Grotto #2	90908427
Steel Scorpion	13599884
Stim-Pack	83225447
Stone Statue of the Aztecs	31812496
Stop Defense	63102017
Stray Lambs	60764581
Stumbling	34646691
Swamp Battleguard	40453765
Swift Gaia the Fierce Knight	16589042
Sword of Deep-Seated	98495314
Sword of the Soul-Eater	05371656
Swords of Concealing Light	12923641
Swords of Revealing Light	72302403
Swordsman of Landstar	03573512
System Down	07672244
Tailor of the Fickle	43641473
Terraforming	73628505
The A. Forces	00403847
The Agent of Force - Mars	91123920
The Agent of Judgement - Saturn	91345518
The Big March of Animals	01689516
The Bistro Butcher	71107816
The Cheerful Coffin	41142615
The Creator	61505339
The Creator Incarnate	97093037
The Dark Door	30606547
The Earl of Demise	66989694

CARD	PASSWORD
The Fiend Megacyber	66362965
The First Sarcophagus	31076103
The Flute of Summoning Kuriboh	20065322
The Forgiving Maiden	84080938
The Gross Ghost of Fled Dreams	68049471
The Illusory Gentleman	83764996
The Inexperienced Spy	81820689
The Last Warrior from Another Planet	86099788
The Law of the Normal	66926224
The League of Uniform Nomenclature	55008284
The Little Swordsman of Aile	25109950
The Masked Beast	49064413
The Portrait's Secret	32541773
The Regulation of Tribe	00296499
The Reliable Guardian	16430187
The Rock Spirit	76305638
The Sanctuary in the Sky	56433456
The Second Sarcophagus	04081094
The Secret of the Bandit	99351431
The Shallow Grave	43434803
The Snake Hair	29491031
The Spell Absorbing Life	99517131
The Statue of Easter Island	10261698
The Third Sarcophagus	78697395
The Unhappy Girl	27618634
The Unhappy Maiden	51275027
The Warrior Returning Alive	95281259
The Wicked Worm Beast	06285791
Thestalos the Firestorm Monarch	26205777
Thousand Dragon	41462083
Thousand Energy	05703682
Thousand Knives	63391643
Thousand-Eyes Idol	27125110
Threatening Roar	36361633
Three-Headed Geedo	78423643
Thunder Crash	69196160
Thunder Dragon	31786629
Thunder Nyan Nyan	70797118
Time Machine	80987696
Time Wizard	06285791
Token Feastevil	83675475
Toon Alligator	59383041
Toon Cannon Soldier	79875176
Toon Dark Magician Girl	90960358
Toon Defense	43509019
Toon Gemini Elf	42386471
Toon Goblin Attack Force	15270885
Toon Masked Sorcerer	16392422
Toon Mermaid	65458948
Toon Summoned Skull	91842653
Toon Table of Contents	89997728
Toon World	15259703
Tornado	61068510
Tornado Wall	18605135

CARD	PASSWORD
Torpedo Fish	90337190
Tower of Babel	94256039
Tragedy	35686187
Transcendent Wings	25573054
Trap Hole	04206964
Trap Jammer	19252988
Trap Master	46461247
Tremendous Fire	46918794
Triage	30888983
Triangle Ecstasy Spark	12181376
Triangle Power	32298781
Tribute Doll	02903036
Tribute to the Doomed	79759861
Tri-Horned Dragon	39111158
Twin Swords of Flashing Light - Tryce	21900719
Twin-Headed Behemoth	43586926
Twin-Headed Thunder Dragon	54752875
Two-Headed King Rex	94119974
Two-Pronged Attack	83887306
Tyhone	72842870
Type Zero Magic Crusher	35346968
UFO Turtle	60806437
Ultimate Offering	80604091
Ultra Evolution Pill	22431243
Umiiruka	82999629
Union Attack	60399954
United We Stand	56747793
Unity	14731897
Upstart Goblin	70368879
Uraby	01784619
Valkyrion the Magna Warrior	75347539
Versago the Destroyer	50259460
Vile Germs	39774685
Vorse Raider	14898066

CARD	PASSWORD
Waboku	12607053
Wall of Illusion	13945283
Wall of Revealing Light	17078030
Wall Shadow	63162310
Warrior Elimination	90873992
Warrior Lady of the Wasteland	05438492
Wasteland	98239899
Weapon Change	10035717
Weather Report	72053645
Weed Out	28604635
White Magical Hat	15150365
White-Horned Dragon	73891874
Wicked-Breaking Flamberge - Baou	68427465
Widespread Ruin	77754944
Wild Nature's Release	61166988
Winged Dragon, Guardian of the Fortress #1	87796900
Winged Kuriboh	57116033
Winged Kuriboh LV10	98585345
Witch's Apprentice	80741828
Wolf	49417509
Wolf Axwielder	56369281
Woodland Sprite	06979239
World Suppression	12253117
Xing Zhen Hu	76515293
Yamata Dragon	76862289
Yami	59197169
Yellow Luster Shield	04542651
Yu-Jo Friendship	81332143
Zaborg the Thunder Monarch	51945556
Zero Gravity	83133491
Zoa	24311372
Zolga	16268841
Zombie Warrior	31339260

YU-GI-OH! WORLD CHAMPIONSHIP 2007

CARD PASSWORDS

Select Password from the Shop and enter one of the Card Passwords. You must already have that card or have it in a pack list for the password to work. Refer to the Card List for YU-GI-OH! GX TAG FORCE for PSP. All cards may not be available in World Championship 2007.

ZOO KEEPER

GEKIMUZU DIFFICULTY

Earn a high score in all 4 modes.

Here are the high scores needed for each mode:

MODE	SCORE
Zoo keeper	200000
Tokoton 100	800000
Quest mode	10000
Time attack	600000

ZOO TYCOON DS

UNLOCK EVERYTHING

At the Main menu, press Up, Up, Down, Down, Left, Right, Left, Right, Up, Up, Down , Down, Left, Right, Left, Right.

PLAYSTATION® PORTABLE

CONTENTS

ATV OFFROAD FURY: BLAZIN' TRAILS

UNLOCK EVERYTHING EXCEPT THE FURY BIKE

Select Player Profile from Options. Choose Enter Cheat and enter All Access.

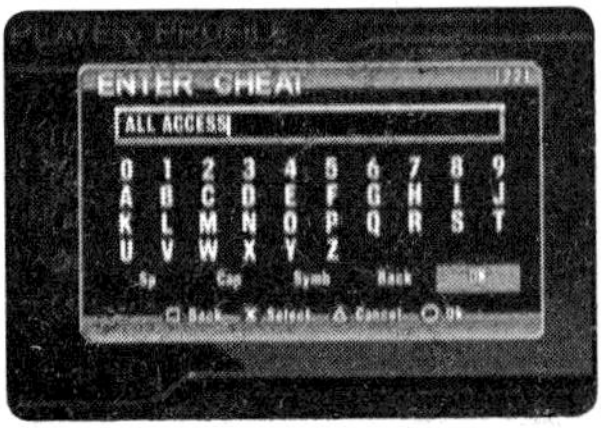

1500 CREDITS

Select Player Profile from Options. Choose Enter Cheat and enter $moneybags$.

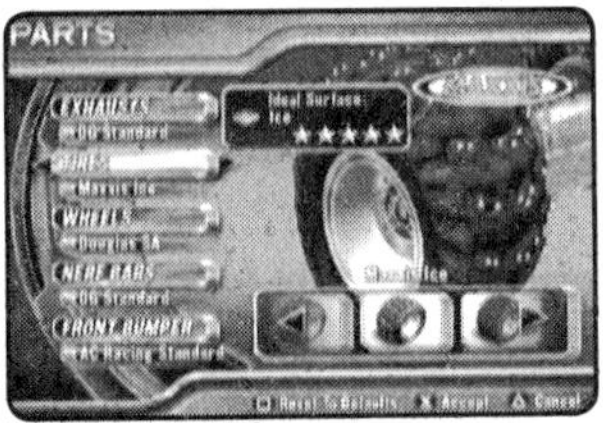

ALL RIDER GEAR

Select Player Profile from Options. Choose Enter Cheat and enter Duds.

MUSIC VIDEOS

Select Player Profile from Options. Choose Enter Cheat and enter Billboards.

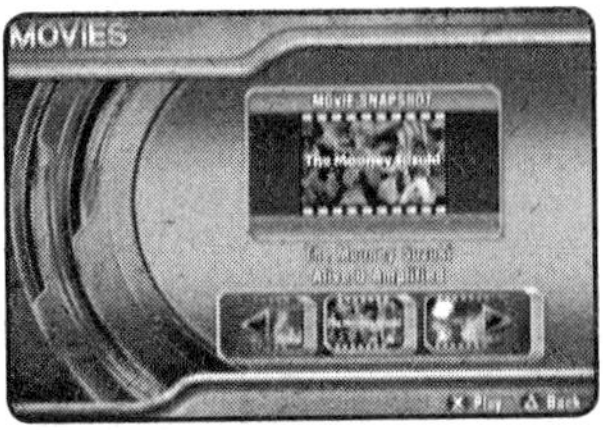

TIRES

Select Player Profile from Options. Choose Enter Cheat and enter Dubs.

BEN 10: ALIEN FORCE THE GAME

LEVEL LORD

Enter Gwen, Kevin, Big Chill, Gwen as a code.

INVINCIBILITY

Enter Kevin, Big Chill, Swampfire, Kevin as a code.

ALL COMBOS

Enter Swampfire, Gwen, Kevin, Ben as a code.

INFINITE ALIENS

Enter Ben, Swampfire, Gwen, Big Chill as a code.

BEN 10: PROTECTOR OF EARTH

INVINCIBILITY

Select a game from the Continue option. Go to the Map Selection screen, press Start and choose Extras. Select Enter Secret Code and enter XLR8, Heatblast, Wildvine, Fourarms.

ALL COMBOS

Select a game from the Continue option. Go to the Map Selection screen, press Start and choose Extras. Select Enter Secret Code and enter Cannonblot, Heatblast, Fourarms, Heatblast.

ALL LOCATIONS

Select a game from the Continue option. Go to the Map Selection screen, press Start and choose Extras. Select Enter Secret Code and enter Heatblast, XLR8, XLR8, Cannonblot.

DNA FORCE SKINS

Select a game from the Continue option. Go to the Map Selection screen, press Start and choose Extras. Select Enter Secret Code and enter Wildvine, Fourarms, Heatblast, Cannonbolt.

DARK HEROES SKINS

Select a game from the Continue option. Go to the Map Selection screen, press Start and choose Extras. Select Enter Secret Code and enter Cannonbolt, Cannonbolt, Fourarms, Heatblast.

ALL ALIEN FORMS

Select a game from the Continue option. Go to the Map Selection screen, press Start and choose Extras. Select Enter Secret Code and enter Wildvine, Fourarms, Heatblast, Wildvine.

MASTER CONTROL

Select a game from the Continue option. Go to the Map Selection screen, press Start and choose Extras. Select Enter Secret Code and enter Cannonbolt, Heatblast, Wildvine, Fourarms.

BURNOUT LEGENDS

COP RACER

Earn a Gold in all Pursuit events.

FIRE TRUCK

Earn a Gold on all Crash Events.

GANGSTER BOSS

Earn Gold in all Race events.

CAPCOM CLASSICS COLLECTION REMIXED

UNLOCK EVERYTHING

At the title screen, press Left on D-pad, Right on D-pad, Left on Analog stick, Right on Analog stick, ■, ●, Up on D-pad, Down on D-pad.

PLAYSTATIO

CAPCOM PUZZLE WORLD

SUPER BUSTER BROS.

LEVEL SELECT IN TOUR MODE

At the Main menu, highlight Tour Mode, hold Down and press ✖.

SUPER PUZZLE FIGHTER

PLAY AS AKUMA

At the character select, highlight Hsien-Ko and press Down.

PLAY AS DAN

At the character select, highlight Donovan and press Down.

PLAY AS DEVILOT

At the character select, highlight Morrigan and press Down.

PLAY AS ANITA

At the character select, hold L + R and choose Donovan.

PLAY AS HSIEN-KO'S TALISMAN

At the character select, hold L + R and choose Hsien-Ko.

PLAY AS MORRIGAN AS A BAT

At the character select, hold L + R and choose Morrigan.

CARS

BONUS SPEEDWAY (REVERSED) IN CUSTOM RACE

At the Main menu hold L and press ✖, ■, ▲, ✖, ▲, ■.

ALL CARS, PAINTJOBS, TRACKS, MOVIE CLIPS AND MODES

At the main menu, hold L and press ▲, ■, ✖, ●, ▲, ✖, ■, ▲, ●, ✖.

UNLIMITED NITROUS

At the main menu, hold L and ✖, ■, ●, ●, ●, ▲, ■, ✖.

CASTLEVANIA: THE DRACULA X CHRONICLES

SYMPHONY OF THE NIGHT

After clearing the game as Alucard, select New Game and enter the following as your name:

PLAY AS ALUCARD, WITH 99 LUCK AND THE LAPIS LAZULI

X-X!V"Q

PLAY AS ALUCARD, WITH THE AXE LORD ARMOR

AXEARMOR

PLAY AS MARIA RENARD

MARIA

PLAY AS RICHTER BELMONT

RICHTER

CRISIS CORE—FINAL FANTASY VII

NEW GAME+

After completing the game, you'll be prompted to make a new save. Loading a game from this new save will begin a New Game+, starting the game over while allowing Zack to retain almost everything he's earned.

The following items transfer to a New Game+:

Level, Experience, SP, Gil, Playtime, Non-Key Items, Materia, and DMW Completion Rate

The following items do not transfer:

Key Items, Materia/Accessory Slot Expansion, Ability to SP Convert, DMW Images, Mission Progress, Mail, and Unlocked Shops

EXIT

SITUATION 8

Complete Situation 1. Then at the Title screen, press L, R, Left, Right, Square, Circle, X, Triangle.

SITUATION 9

Complete Situation 1 and unlock Situation 8. Then at the Title screen, press Triangle, Down, Circle, Left, X, Up, Square, Right.

SITUATION 10

Complete Situation 1 and unlock Situations 8 and 9. Then at the Title screen, press Right, Down, Up, Left, Circle, X, R, L.

FINAL FANTASY TACTICS: THE WAR OF THE LIONS

MUSIC TEST MODE

Enter the main character's name as PolkaPolka at the name entry screen.

FLATOUT: HEAD ON

1 MILLION CREDITS

Select Enter Code from the Extras menu and enter GIVECASH.

ALL CARS AND 1 MILLION CREDITS

Select Enter Code from the Extras menu and enter GIEVEPIX.

BIG RIG

Select Enter Code from the Extras menu and enter ELPUEBLO.

BIG RIG TRUCK

Select Enter Code from the Extras menu and enter RAIDERS.

FLATMOBILE CAR

Select Enter Code from the Extras menu and enter WOTKINS.

MOB CAR

Select Enter Code from the Extras menu and enter BIGTRUCK.

PIMPSTER CAR

Select Enter Code from the Extras menu and enter RUTTO.

ROCKET CAR

Select Enter Code from the Extras menu and enter KALJAKOPPA.

SCHOOL BUS

Select Enter Code from the Extras menu and enter GIEVCARPLZ.

FULL AUTO 2: BATTLELINES

ALL CARS

Select Cheats from the Options and press Up, Up, Up, Up, Left, Down, Up, Right, Down, Down, Down, Down.

ALL EVENTS

Select Cheats from the Options and press Start, Left, Select, Right, Right, Triangle, X, Square, Start, R, Down, Select.

GRADIUS COLLECTION

ALL WEAPONS & POWER-UPS ON EASY DIFFICULTY

Pause the game and press Up, Up, Down, Down, Left, Right, Left, Right, X, Circle.

GRADIUS COLLECTION

ALL WEAPONS & POWER-UPS

Pause the game and press Up, Up, Down, Down, Left, Right, Left, Right, L, R. This code can be used once per level.

HOT BRAIN

119.99 TEMPERATURE IN ALL 5 CATEGORIES

Select New Game and enter Cheat.

HOT SHOTS GOLF 2

UNLOCK EVERYTHING

Enter 2gsh as your name.

IRON MAN

Iron Man's different armor suits are unlocked by completing certain missions.

COMPLETE MISSION	SUIT UNLOCKED
1, Escape	Mark I
2, First Flight	Mark II
3, Fight Back	Mark III
5, Maggia Compound	Gold Tin Can
8, Frozen Ship	Classic
11, Island Meltdown	Stealth
13, Showdown	Titanium Man

PSP MINIGAMES

Minigames can be unlocked by completing the following missions. Access the minigames through the Bonus menu.

COMPLETE MISSION	PSP MINIGAME UNLOCKED
1, Escape	Tin Can Challenge 1 + 2
2, First Flight	DEATH RACE: STARK INDUSTRY
3, Fight Back	BOSS FIGHT: DREADNOUGHT
4, Weapons Transport	DEATH RACE: AFGHAN DESERT BOSS FIGHT: WHIPLASH
5, Maggia Compound	DEATH RACE: MAGGIA MANSION
6, Flying Fortress	SPEED KILL: FLYING FORTRESS SURVIVAL: FLYING FORTRESS
7, Nuclear Winter	DEATH RACE: ARTIC CIRCLE
8, Frozen Ship	SPEED KILL: FROZEN SHIP SURVIVAL: FROZEN SHIP
9, Home Front	BOSS FIGHT: TITANIUM MAN
10, Save Pepper	DEATH RACE: DAM BASSIN
11, Island Meltdown	SPEED KILL: GREEK ISLANDS SURVIVAL: GREEK ISLANDS
12, Battlesuit Factory	SPEED KILL: TINMEN FACTORY SURVIVAL: TINMEN FACTORY
13, Showdown	BOSS FIGHT: IRON MONGER

CONCEPT ART

As you progress through the game and destroy the Weapon Crates, bonuses are unlocked. You can find all of these in the Bonus menu once unlocked.

CONCEPT ART UNLOCKED	NUMBER OF WEAPON CRATES FOUND
Environments Set 1	6
Environments Set 2	12
Iron Man	18
Environments Set 3	24
Enemies	30
Environments Set 4	36
Villains	42
Vehicles	48
Covers	50

JUICED: ELIMINATOR

ALL CARS AND TRACKS IN ARCADE MODE

Select Cheats from the Extras menu and enter PIES.

UNLOCK EVERYTHING

Pause the game, hold L + R and press Down, Left, Up, Right.

INVINCIBLE

Pause the game, hold L + R and press Left, Down, Right, Up, Left, Down, Right, Up.

UNLIMITED ENERGY

Pause the game, hold L + R and press Down, Down, Right, Right, Up, Up, Left, Left.

JUICED 2: HOT IMPORT NIGHTS

LAST MAN STANDING CHALLENGE AND AN ASCARI KZ1

Select Cheats and Challenges from the DNA Lab menu and enter KNOX. Defeat the challenge to earn the Ascari KZ1.

SPECIAL CHALLENGE AND AN AUDI TT 1.8 QUATTRO

Select Cheats and Challenges from the DNA Lab menu and enter YTHZ. Defeat the challenge to earn the Audi TT 1.8 Quattro.

SPECIAL CHALLENGE AND A BMW Z4

Select Cheats and Challenges from the DNA Lab menu and enter GVDL. Defeat the challenge to earn the BMW Z4.

SPECIAL CHALLENGE AND A HOLDEN MONARO

Select Cheats and Challenges from the DNA Lab menu and enter RBSG. Defeat the challenge to earn the Holden Monaro.

SPECIAL CHALLENGE AND A HYUNDAI COUPE 2.7 V6

Select Cheats and Challenges from the DNA Lab menu and enter BSLU. Defeat the challenge to earn the Hyundai Coupe 2.7 V6.

SPECIAL CHALLENGE AND AN INFINITY G35

Select Cheats and Challenges from the DNA Lab menu and enter MRHC. Defeat the challenge to earn the Infinity G35.

SPECIAL CHALLENGE AND AN INFINITY RED G35

Select Cheats and Challenges from the DNA Lab menu and enter MNCH. Defeat the challenge to earn the Infinity G35.

SPECIAL CHALLENGE AND A KOENIGSEGG CCX

Select Cheats and Challenges from the DNA Lab menu and enter KDTR. Defeat the challenge to earn the Koenigsegg CCX.

SPECIAL CHALLENGE AND A MITSUBISHI PROTOTYPE X

Select Cheats and Challenges from the DNA Lab menu and enter DOPX. Defeat the challenge to earn the Mitsubishi Prototype X.

SPECIAL CHALLENGE AND A NISSAN 350Z

Select Cheats and Challenges from the DNA Lab menu and enter PRGN. Defeat the challenge to earn the Nissan 350Z.

SPECIAL CHALLENGE AND A NISSAN SKYLINE R34 GT-R

Select Cheats and Challenges from the DNA Lab menu and enter JWRS. Defeat the challenge to earn the Nissan Skyline R34 GT-R.

SPECIAL CHALLENGE AND A SALEEN S7

Select Cheats and Challenges from the DNA Lab menu and enter WIKF. Defeat the challenge to earn the Saleen S7.

SPECIAL CHALLENGE AND A SEAT LEON CUPRA R

Select Cheats and Challenges from the DNA Lab menu and enter FAMQ. Defeat the challenge to earn the Seat Leon Cupra R.

LEGO BATMAN

BATCAVE CODES

Using the computer in the Batcave, select Enter Code and enter the following codes.

CHARACTERS

CHARACTER	CODE
Alfred	ZAQ637
Batgirl	JKR331
Bruce Wayne	BDJ327
Catwoman (Classic)	M1AAWW
Clown Goon	HJK327
Commissioner Gordon	DDP967
Fishmonger	HGY748
Freeze Girl	XVK541
Joker Goon	UTF782
Joker Henchman	YUN924
Mad Hatter	JCA283
Man-Bat	NYU942
Military Policeman	MKL382
Nightwing	MVY759
Penguin Goon	NKA238
Penguin Henchman	BJH782
Penguin Minion	KJP748
Poison Ivy Goon	GTB899
Police Marksman	HKG984
Police Officer	JRY983
Riddler Goon	CRY928
Riddler Henchman	XEU824
S.W.A.T.	HTF114
Sailor	NAV592
Scientist	JFL786
Security Guard	PLB946
The Joker (Tropical)	CCB199
Yeti	NJL412
Zoo Sweeper	DWR243

VEHICLES

VEHICLE	CODE
Bat-Tank	KNTT4B
Bruce Wayne's Private Jet	LEA664
Catwoman's Motorcycle	HPL826
Garbage Truck	DUS483
Goon Helicopter	GCH328
Harbor Helicopter	CHP735
Harley Quinn's Hammer Truck	RDT637
Mad Hatter's Glider	HS000W
Mad Hatter's Steamboat	M4DM4N
Mr. Freeze's Iceberg	ICYICE
The Joker's Van	JUK657
Mr. Freeze's Kart	BCT229
Penguin Goon Submarine	BTN248
Police Bike	LJP234
Police Boat	PLC999
Police Car	KJL832
Police Helicopter	CWR732
Police Van	MAC788
Police Watercraft	VJD328
Riddler's Jet	HAHAHA
Robin's Submarine	TTF453
Two-Face's Armored Truck	EFE933

CHEATS

CHEAT	CODE
Always Score Multiply	9LRGNB
Fast Batarangs	JRBDCB
Fast Walk	ZOLM6N
Flame Batarang	D8NYWH
Freeze Batarang	XPN4NG
Extra Hearts	ML3KHP
Fast Build	EVG26J
Immune to Freeze	JXUDY6
Invincibility	WYD5CP
Minikit Detector	ZXGH9J
More Batarang Targets	XWP645
Piece Detector	KHJ554
Power Brick Detector	MMN786
Regenerate Hearts	HJH7HJ
Score x2	N4NR3E
Score x4	CX9MAT
Score x6	MLVNF2
Score x8	WCCDB9
Score x10	18HW07

CHARACTERS

Approach the blackboard in the Classsroom and enter the following codes.

CHARACTER	CODE
Bandit	12N68W
Bandit Swordsman	1MK4RT
Barranca	04EM94
Bazooka Trooper (Crusade)	MK83R7
Bazooka Trooper (Raiders)	S93Y5R
Belloq	CHN3YU
Belloq (Jungle)	TDR197
Belloq (Robes)	VE029L
British Commander	B73EUA
British Officer	VJ5TI9
British Soldier	DJ5I2W
Captain Katanga	VJ3TT3
Chatter Lal	ENW936
Chatter Lal (Thuggee)	CNH4RY
Chen	3NK48T
Colonel Dietrich	2K9RKS
Colonel Vogel	8EAL4H
Dancing Girl	C7EJ21
Donovan	3NFTU8
Elsa (Desert)	JSNRT9
Elsa (Officer)	VMJ5US
Enemy Boxer	8246RB
Enemy Butler	VJ48W3
Enemy Guard	VJ7R51
Enemy Guard (Mountains)	YR47WM
Enemy Officer	572E61
Enemy Officer (Desert	2MK450
Enemy Pilot	B84ELP
Enemy Radio Operator	1MF94R
Enemy Soldier (Desert)	4NSU7Q

CHARACTER	CODE
Fedora	V75YSP
First Mate	0GIN24
Grail Knight	NE6THI
Hovitos Tribesman	HOV1SS
Indiana Jones (Desert Disguise)	4J8S4M
Indiana Jones (Officer)	VJ850S
Jungle Guide	24PF34
Kao Kan	WM046L
Kazim	NRH23J
Kazim (Desert)	3M29TJ
Lao Che	2NK479
Maharajah	NFK5N2
Major Toht	13NS01
Masked Bandit	N48SF0
Mola Ram	FJUR31
Monkey Man	3RF6YJ
Pankot Assassin	2NKT72
Pankot Guard	VN28RH
Sherpa Brawler	VJ37WJ
Sherpa Gunner	ND762W
Slave Child	0E3ENW
Thuggee	VM683E
Thuggee Acolyte	T2R3F9
Thuggee Slave Driver	VBS7GW
Village Dignitary	KD48TN
Village Elder	4682E1
Willie (Dinner Suit)	VK93R7
Willie (Pajamas)	MEN4IP
Wu Han	3NSLT8

EXTRAS

Approach the blackboard in the Classsroom and enter the following codes. Some cheats need to be enabled by selecting Extras from the pause menu.

CHEAT	CODE
Artifact Detector	VIKED7
Beep Beep	VNF59Q
Character Treasure	VIES2R
Disarm Enemies	VKRNS9
Disguises	4ID1N6
Fast Build	V83SL0
Fast Dig	378RS6
Fast Fix	FJ59WS
Fertilizer	B1GW1F
Ice Rink	33GM7J
Parcel Detector	VUT673
Poo Treasure	WWQ1SA

CHEAT	CODE
Regenerate Hearts	MDLP69
Secret Characters	3X44AA
Silhouettes	3HE85H
Super Scream	VN3R7S
Super Slap	0P1TA5
Treasure Magnet	H86LA2
Treasure x10	VI3PS8
Treasure x2	VM4TS9
Treasure x4	VLWEN3
Treasure x6	V84RYS
Treasure x8	A72E1M

LEGO STAR WARS II: THE ORIGINAL TRILOGY

BEACH TROOPER

At Mos Eisley Canteena, select Enter Code and enter UCK868. You still need to select Characters and purchase this character for 20,000 studs.

BEN KENOBI (GHOST)

At Mos Eisley Canteena, select Enter Code and enter BEN917. You still need to select Characters and purchase this character for 1,100,000 studs.

BESPIN GUARD

At Mos Eisley Canteena, select Enter Code and enter VHY832. You still need to select Characters and purchase this character for 15,000 studs.

BIB FORTUNA

At Mos Eisley Canteena, select Enter Code and enter WTY721. You still need to select Characters and purchase this character for 16,000 studs.

BOBA FETT

At Mos Eisley Canteena, select Enter Code and enter HLP221. You still need to select Characters and purchase this character for 175,000 studs.

DEATH STAR TROOPER

At Mos Eisley Canteena, select Enter Code and enter BNC332. You still need to select Characters and purchase this character for 19,000 studs.

EWOK

At Mos Eisley Canteena, select Enter Code and enter TTT289. You still need to select Characters and purchase this character for 34,000 studs.

GAMORREAN GUARD

At Mos Eisley Canteena, select Enter Code and enter YZF999. You still need to select Characters and purchase this character for 40,000 studs.

GONK DROID

At Mos Eisley Canteena, select Enter Code and enter NFX582. You still need to select Characters and purchase this character for 1,550 studs.

GRAND MOFF TARKIN

At Mos Eisley Canteena, select Enter Code and enter SMG219. You still need to select Characters and purchase this character for 38,000 studs.

GREEDO

At Mos Eisley Canteena, select Enter Code and enter NAH118. You still need to select Characters and purchase this character for 60,000 studs.

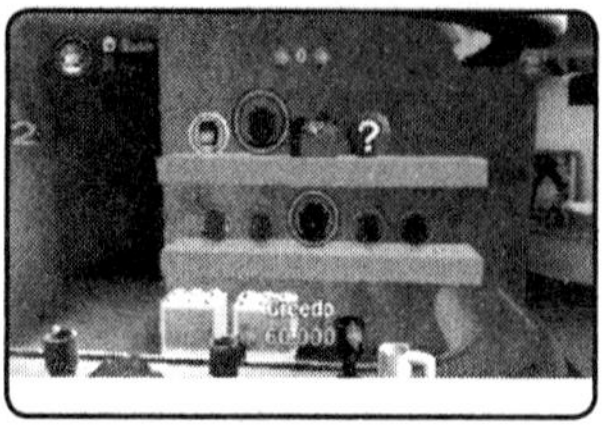

HAN SOLO (HOOD)

At Mos Eisley Canteena, select Enter Code and enter YWM840. You still need to select Characters and purchase this character for 20,000 studs.

IG-88

At Mos Eisley Canteena, select Enter Code and enter NXL973. You still need to select Characters and purchase this character for 30,000 studs.

IMPERIAL GUARD

At Mos Eisley Canteena, select Enter Code and enter MMM111. You still need to select Characters and purchase this character for 45,000 studs.

IMPERIAL OFFICER

At Mos Eisley Canteena, select Enter Code and enter BBV889. You still need to select Characters and purchase this character for 28,000 studs.

IMPERIAL SHUTTLE PILOT

At Mos Eisley Canteena, select Enter Code and enter VAP664. You still need to select Characters and purchase this character for 29,000 studs.

IMPERIAL SPY

At Mos Eisley Canteena, select Enter Code and enter CVT125. You still need to select Characters and purchase this character for 13,500 studs.

JAWA

At Mos Eisley Canteena, select Enter Code and enter JAW499. You still need to select Characters and purchase this character for 24,000 studs.

LOBOT

At Mos Eisley Canteena, select Enter Code and enter UUB319. You still need to select Characters and purchase this character for 11,000 studs.

PALACE GUARD

At Mos Eisley Canteena, select Enter Code and enter SGE549. You still need to select Characters and purchase this character for 14,000 studs.

REBEL PILOT

At Mos Eisley Canteena, select Enter Code and enter CYG336. You still need to select Characters and purchase this character for 15,000 studs.

REBEL TROOPER (HOTH)

At Mos Eisley Canteena, select Enter Code and enter EKU849. You still need to select Characters and purchase this character for 16,000 studs.

SANDTROOPER

At Mos Eisley Canteena, select Enter Code and enter YDV451. You still need to select Characters and purchase this character for 14,000 studs.

SKIFF GUARD

At Mos Eisley Canteena, select Enter Code and enter GBU888. You still need to select Characters and purchase this character for 12,000 studs.

SNOWTROOPER

At Mos Eisley Canteena, select Enter Code and enter NYU989. You still need to select Characters and purchase this character for 16,000 studs.

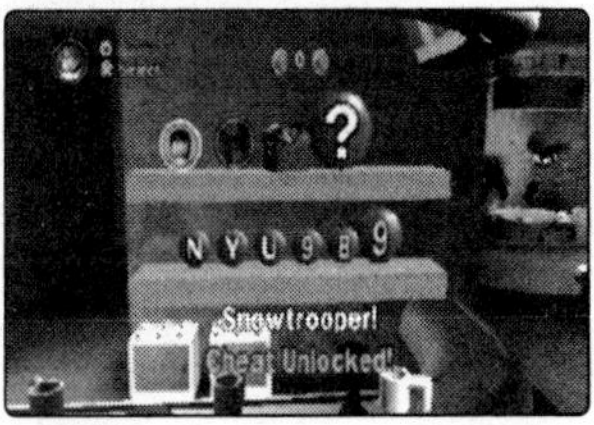

STROMTROOPER

At Mos Eisley Canteena, select Enter Code and enter PTR345. You still need to select Characters and purchase this character for 10,000 studs.

THE EMPEROR

At Mos Eisley Canteena, select Enter Code and enter HHY382. You still need to select Characters and purchase this character for 275,000 studs.

TIE FIGHTER

At Mos Eisley Canteena, select Enter Code and enter HDY739. You still need to select Characters and purchase this character for 60,000 studs.

TIE FIGHTER PILOT

At Mos Eisley Canteena, select Enter Code and enter NNZ316. You still need to select Characters and purchase this character for 21,000 studs.

TIE INTERCEPTOR

At Mos Eisley Canteena, select Enter Code and enter QYA828. You still need to select Characters and purchase this character for 40,000 studs.

TUSKEN RAIDER

At Mos Eisley Canteena, select Enter Code and enter PEJ821. You still need to select Characters and purchase this character for 23,000 studs.

UGNAUGHT

At Mos Eisley Canteena, select Enter Code and enter UGN694. You still need to select Characters and purchase this character for 36,000 studs.

MAJOR LEAGUE BASEBALL 2K7

MICKEY MANTLE ON THE FREE AGENTS LIST

Select Enter Cheat Code from the My 2K7 menu and enter themick.

MICKEY PINCH HITS

Select Enter Cheat Code from the My 2K7 menu and enter phmantle.

UNLOCK EVERYTHING

Select Enter Cheat Code from the My 2K7 menu and enter Derek Jeter. This does not unlock the Topps cheats.

ALL CHEATS

Select Enter Cheat Code from the My 2K7 menu and enter Black Sox.

ALL EXTRAS
Select Enter Cheat Code from the My 2K7 menu and enter Game On.

MIGHTY MICK CHEAT
Select Enter Cheat Code from the My 2K7 menu and enter mightymick.

TRIPLE CROWN CHEAT
Select Enter Cheat Code from the My 2K7 menu and enter triplecrown.

BIG BLAST CHEAT
Select Enter Cheat Code from the My 2K7 menu and enter m4murder.

MARVEL ULTIMATE ALLIANCE

UNLOCK ALL SKINS
At the Team menu, press Up, Down, Left, Right, Left, Right, Start.

UNLOCKS ALL HERO POWERS
At the Team menu, press Left, Right, Up, Down, Up, Down, Start.

ALL HEROES TO LEVEL 99
At the Team menu, press Up, Left, Up, Left, Down, Right, Down, Right, Start.

UNLOCK ALL HEROES
At the Team menu, press Up, Up, Down, Down, Left, Left, Left, Start.

UNLOCK DAREDEVIL
At the Team menu, press Left, Left, Right, Right, Up, Down, Up, Down, Start.

UNLOCK SILVER SURFER
At the Team menu, press Down, Left, Left, Up, Right, Up, Down, Left, Start.

GOD MODE
During gameplay, press Up, Down, Up, Down, Up, Left, Down, Right, Start.

TOUCH OF DEATH
During gameplay, press Left, Right, Down, Down, Right, Left, Start.

SUPER SPEED
During gameplay, press Up, Left, Up, Right, Down, Right, Start.

FILL MOMENTUM
During gameplay, press Left, Right, Right, Left, Up, Down, Down, Up, Start.

UNLOCK ALL COMICS
At the Review menu, press Left, Right, Right, Left, Up, Up, Right, Start.

UNLOCK ALL CONCEPT ART
At the Review menu, press Down, Down, Down, Right, Right, Left, Down, Start.

UNLOCK ALL CINEMATICS
At the Review menu, press Up, Left, Left, Up, Right, Right, Up, Start.

UNLOCK ALL LOAD SCREENS
At the Review menu, press Up, Down, Right, Left, Up, Up Down, Start.

UNLOCK ALL COURSES
At the Comic Missions menu, press Up, Right, Left, Down, Up, Right, Left, Down, Start.

METAL GEAR SOLID: PORTABLE OPS PLUS

SOLDIER PASSWORDS

Enter the following as a password.

SOLDIER	PASSWORD
Alabama	BB6K768KM9
Alaska	XL5SW5NH9S
Arizona	ZHEFPVV947
Arkansas	VNRE7JNQ8WE
Black Genome	WYNGG3JBP3YS
Blue Genome	9GNPHGFFLH
California	6MSJQYWNCJ8
Colorado	W6TAH498DJ
Connecticut	2N2AB3JV2WA
Delaware	AJRL6E7TT9
Female Scientist 1	3W8WVRGB2LNN
Female Scientist 2	FUC72C463KZ
Female Scientist 3	UCAWYTMXB5V
Female Soldier 1	UZZQYRPXM86
Female Soldier 2	QRQQ7GWKHJ
Female Soldier 3	MVNDAZAP8DWE
Florida	A44STZ3BHY5
Fox Soldier 1	FMXT79TPV4U8
Fox Soldier 2	HGMK3WCYURM
Fox Soldier 3	6ZY5NYW4TGK
Georgia	VD5H53JJCRH
Green Genome	TGQ6F5TUHD
GRU Soldier	9V8S7DVYFTR
Gurlukovich's Soldier	6VWM6A22FSS8
Hawaii	TW7ZMZHCBL
Hideochan Soldier	RU8XRCLPUUT
High Official	ADPS2SE5UC8
High Rank Officer 1	DVB2UDTQ5Z
High Rank Officer 2	84ZEC4X5PJ6
High Ranking Officer 3	DTAZ3QRQQDU
High-Tech Soldier	M4MSJ6R87XPP
Idaho	XAFGETZGXHGA
Illinois	QYUVCNDFUPZJ
Indiana	L68JVXVBL8RN
Iowa	B8MW36ZU56S
Kansas	TYPEVDEE24YT
Kentucky	LCD7WGS5X5
KGB Soldier	MNBVYRZP4QH
Louisiana	EHR5VVMHUSG
Maine	T5GYHQABGAC3
Maintenance Crew Member 1	T8EBSRK6F38
Maintenance Crew Member 2	YHQU74J6LLQ
Maintenance Crew Member 3	MFAJMUXZHHKJ
Male Scientist 1	ZFKHJKDEA2
Male Scientist 2	QQ4N3TPCL8PF
Male Scientist 3	CXFCXF4FP9R6
Maryland	L2W9G5N76MH7
Massachusetts	ZLU2S3ULDEVF

SOLDIER	PASSWORD
Michigan	HGDRBUB5P3SA
Minnesota	EEBBM888ZRA
Mississippi	TBF7H9G6TJH7
Missouri	WJND6M9N738
Montana	9FYUFV29B2Y
Nebraska	MCNB5S5K47H
Nevada	Z9D4UGG8T4U6
New Hampshire	7NQYDQ9Y4KMP
New Jersey	LGHTBU9ZTGR
New Mexico	RGJCMHNLSX
New York	6PV39FKG6X
Normal Soldier Long Sleeve	QK3CMV373Y
Normal Soldier Long Sleeve Magazine Vest	D8RV32E9774
Normal Soldier Short Sleeve	N524ZHU9N4Z
Normal Soldier Short Sleeve Magazine Vest	6WXZA7PTT9Z
North Carolina	JGVT2XV47UZ
North Dakota	T5LSAVMPWZCY
Ocelot Female A	9FS7QYSHZ56N
Ocelot Female B	F94XDZSQSGJ8
Ocelot Female C	CRF8PZGXR28
Ocelot Unit	GE6MU3DXL3X
Ohio	AUWGAXWCA3D
Oklahoma	ZQT75NUJH8A3
Oregon	HKSD3PJ5E5
Pennsylvania	PL8GVVUM4HD
Pink Genome	7WRG3N2MRY2
Red Genome	9CM4SY23C7X8
Rhode Island	MMYC99T3QG
Seal	X56YCKZP2V
South Carolina	ZR4465MD8LK
South Dakota	RY3NUDDPMU3
Tengu Soldier	PHHB4TY4J2D
Tennessee	TD2732GCX43U
Texas	QM84UPP6F3
Tsuhan soldier	A9KK7WYWVCV
USSR Female Soldier A	2VXUZQVH9R
USSR Female Soldier B	HPMRFSBXDJ3Y
USSR Female Soldier C	QXQVW9R3PZ
USSR Female Soldier D	GMC3M3LTPVW7
USSR Female Soldier E	5MXVX6UFPMZ5
USSR Female Soldier F	76AWS7WDAV
Utah	V7VRAYZ78GW
Vermont	L7T66LFZ63C8
Virginia	DRTCS77F5N
Washington	G3S4N42WWKTV
Washington DC	Y5YCFYHVZZW
West Virginia	72M8XR99B6

SOLDIER	PASSWORD
White Genome	QJ4ZTQSLUT8
Wisconsin	K9BUN2BGLMT3

SOLDIER	PASSWORD
Wyoming	C3THQ749RA
Yellow Genome	CE5HHYGTSSB

MLB 07: THE SHOW

SILVER ERA AND GOLD ERA TEAMS

At the Main menu, press Left, Up, Right, Down, Down, Left, Up, Down.

MAX BREAK PITCHES

Pause the game and press Right, Up, Right, Down, Up, Left, Left, Down.

MAX SPEED PITCHES

Pause the game and press Up, Left, Down, Up, Left, Right, Left, Down.

MLB 08: THE SHOW

CLASSIC FREE AGENTS AT THE PLAYER MOVEMENT MENU

At the main menu, press Left, Right, Up, Left, Right, Up, Right, Down.

SILVER ERA AND GOLDEN ERA TEAMS

At the main menu, press Right, Up, Right, Down, Down, Left, Up, Down.

BIG BALL

Pause the game and press Right, Down, Up, Left, Right, Left, Down, Up.

BIG HEAD MODE

Pause the game and press Right, Left, Down, Up, Left, Up, Down, Left.

SMALL HEAD MODE

Pause the game and press Left, Right, Down, Up, Right, Left, Down, Left.

N+

25 EXTRA LEVELS

At the main menu, hold L + R and press ⊗, ◉, ⊗, ◉, ⊗, ⊗, ◉.

NEED FOR SPEED CARBON: OWN THE CITY

UNLOCK EVERYTHING

At the start menu, press X, X, Right, Left, Square, Up, Down.

JET CAR

At the start menu, press Up, Down, Left, R1, L1, Circle, Triangle.

LAMBORGINI MERCIALAGO

At the start menu, press X, X, Up, Down, Left, Right, Circle, Circle.

TRANSFORMERS CAR

At the start menu, press X, X, X, Square, Triangle, Triangle, Up, Down.

NEOPETS PETPET ADVENTURE: THE WAND OF WISHING

START GAME WITH 5 CHOCOLATE TREATS

Enter treat4u as your Petpet's name. You can then rename name your character. The chocolate treats are shaped according to the character you chose.

POCKET POOL

ALL PICTURES AND VIDEOS

At the title screen, press L, R, L, L, R, R, L (x3), R (x3), L (x4), R (x4).

SEGA GENESIS COLLECTION

Before using the following cheats, select the ABC Control option. This sets the controller to the following: ■ is A, ⊗ is B, ● is C.

ALTERED BEAST

OPTIONS MENU

At the title screen, hold ⊗ and press Start.

LEVEL SELECT

After enabling the Options menu, select a level from the menu. At the title screen, hold ■ and press Start.

BEAST SELECT

At the title screen, hold ■+ ⊗ + ● + Down/Left and then press Start

SOUND TEST

At the title screen, hold ■ + ● + Up/Right and press Start.

COMIX ZONE

INVINCIBILITY

At the jukebox screen, press C on the following sounds:

3, 12, 17, 2, 2, 10, 2, 7, 7, 11

LEVEL SELECT

At the jukebox screen, press C on the following sounds:

14, 15, 18, 5, 13, 1, 3, 18, 15, 6

Press C on the desired level.

ECCO THE DOLPHIN

INVINCIBILITY

When the level name appears, hold ■ + Start until the level begins.

DEBUG MENU

Pause the game with Ecco facing the screen and press Right, ⊗,●, ⊗,●, Down,●, Up.

INFINITE AIR

Enter LIFEFISH as a password

PASSWORDS

LEVEL	PASSWORD
The Undercaves	WEFIDNMP
The Vents	BQDPXJDS
The Lagoon	JNSBRIKY
Ridge Water	NTSBZTKB
Open Ocean	YWGTTJNI
Ice Zone	HZIFZBMF
Hard Water	LRFJRQLI
Cold Water	UYNFRQLC
Island Zone	LYTIOQLZ
Deep Water	MNOPOQLR
The Marble	RJNTQQLZ
The Library	RTGXQQLE

LEVEL	PASSWORD
Deep City	DDXPQQLJ
City of Forever	MSDBRQLA
Jurassic Beach	IYCBUNLB
Pteranodon Pond	DMXEUNLI
Origin Beach	EGRIUNLB
Trilobite Circle	IELMUNLB
Dark Water	RKEQUNLN
City of Forever 2	HPQIGPLA
The Tube	JUMFKMLB
The Machine	GXUBKMLF
The Last Fight	TSONLMLU

FLICKY

ROUND SELECT

Begin a new game. Before the first round appears, hold ■ + ● + Up + Start. Press Up or Down to select a Round.

GAIN GROUND

LEVEL SELECT

At the Options screen, press ■, ●, ⊗, ●.

GOLDEN AXE

LEVEL SELECT

Select Arcade Mode. At the character select, hold Down/Left +⊗ and press Start. Press Up or Down to select a level.

RISTAR

Select Passwords from the Options menu and enter the following:

LEVEL SELECT

ILOVEU

BOSS RUSH MODE

MUSEUM

TIME ATTACK MODE

DOFEEL

TOUGHER DIFFICULTY

SUPER

ONCHI MUSIC

MAGURO. Activate this from the Sound Test.

CLEARS PASSWORD

XXXXXX

GAME COPYRIGHT INFO

AGES

SONIC THE HEDGEHOG

LEVEL SELECT

At the title screen, press Up, Down, Left, Right. Hold ■ and press Start.

SONIC THE HEDGEHOG 2

LEVEL SELECT

Select Sound Test from the options. Press C on the following sounds in order: 19, 65, 09, 17. At the title screen, hold ■ and press Start.

VECTORMAN

DEBUG MODE

At the options screen, press □, ✕, ✕, □, Down, □, ✕, ✕, □.

REFILL LIFE

Pause the game and press □, ✕, Right, □, ○, □, Down, □, ✕, Right, □.

VECTORMAN 2

LEVEL SELECT

Pause the game and press Up, Right, □,✕, □, Down, Left, □, Down.

EXTRA LIFE

Pause the game and press Right, Up, ✕, □, Down, Up, ✕, Down, Up, ✕. Repeat for more lives.

FULL ENERGY

Pause the game and press ✕, □, ✕, □, Left, Up, Up.

NEW WEAPON

Pause the game and press ○, □, Left, Left, Down, □, Down. Repeat for more weapons.

SHREK THE THIRD

10,000 BONUS COINS

Press Up, Up, Down, Up, Right, Left at the Gift Shop.

THE SIMPSONS GAME

UNLIMITED POWER FOR ALL CHARACTERS

At the Extras menu, press △, Left, Right, △, □, L.

ALL MOVIES

At the Extras menu, press □, Left, □, Right, △, R.

ALL CLICHÉS

At the Extras menu, press Left, □, Right, △, Right, L.

THE SIMS 2: CASTAWAY

CHEAT GNOME

During a game, press L, R, Up, ✕, R. You can now use this Gnome to get the following during Live mode:

ALL PLANS

During a game, press ✕, R, ✕, R, ✕.

ALL CRAFT AND RESOURCES

During a game, press □, △, R, Down, Down, Up.

MAX FOOD AND RESOURCES

During a game, press □ (x4), L.

THE SIMS 2: PETS

CHEAT GNOME

During a game, press L, L, R, ⊗, ⊗, Up. Now you can enter the following cheats:

ADVANCE TIME 6 HOURS

During a game, press Up, Left, Down, Right, R.

GIVE SIM PET POINTS

During a game, press △, ○, ⊗, □, L, R.

$10,000

During a game, press △, Up, Left, Down, Right.

SPIDER-MAN: FRIEND OR FOE

NEW GOBLIN

At the stage complete screen, hold L + R and press ○, Down, ⊗, Right, □, Up, △, Left.

STAR WARS: THE FORCE UNLEASHED

CHEATS

Once you have accessed the Rogue Shadow, select Enter Code from the Extras menu. Now you can enter the following codes:

CHEAT	CODE
Invincibility	CORTOSIS
Unlimited Force	VERGENCE
1,000,000 Force Points	SPEEDER
All Force Powers	TYRANUS
Max Force Power Level	KATARN
Max Combo Level	COUNTDOOKU
Amplified Lightsaber Damage	LIGHTSABER

COSTUMES

Once you have accessed the Rogue Shadow, select Enter Code from the Extras menu. Now you can enter the following codes:

COSTUME	CODE
All Costumes	GRANDMOFF
501st Legion	LEGION
Aayla Secura	AAYLA
Admiral Ackbar	ITSATWAP
Anakin Skywalker	CHOSENONE
Asajj Ventress	ACOLYTE
Ceremonial Jedi Robes	DANTOOINE
Chop'aa Notimo	NOTIMO
Classic stormtrooper	TK421
Count Dooku	SERENNO
Darth Desolous	PAUAN
Darth Maul	ZABRAK
Darth Phobos	HIDDENFEAR
Darth Vader	SITHLORD
Drexl Roosh	DREXLROOSH

COSTUME	CODE
Emperor Palpatine	PALPATINE
General Rahm Kota	MANDALORE
Han Solo	NERFHERDER
Heavy trooper	SHOCKTROOP
Juno Eclipse	ECLIPSE
Kento's Robe	WOOKIEE
Kleef	KLEEF
Lando Calrissian	SCOUNDREL
Luke Skywalker	T16WOMPRAT
Luke Skywalker (Yavin)	YELLOWJCKT
Mace Windu	JEDIMASTER
Mara Jade	MARAJADE
Maris Brook	MARISBROOD
Navy commando	STORMTROOP
Obi Wan Kenobi	BENKENOBI

COSTUME	CODE
Proxy	HOLOGRAM
Qui Gon Jinn	MAVERICK
Shaak Ti	TOGRUTA
Shadow trooper	INTHEDARK

COSTUME	CODE
Sith Robes	HOLOCRON
Sith Stalker Armor	KORRIBAN
Twi'lek	SECURA

STAR WARS: LETHAL ALLIANCE

ALL LEVELS

Select Create Profile from the Profiles menu and enter HANSOLO.

ALL LEVELS AND REFILL HEALTH WHEN DEPLETED

Select Create Profile from the Profiles menu and enter JD1MSTR.

REFILL HEALTH WHEN DEPLETED

Select Create Profile from the Profiles menu and enter BOBAF3T.

SUPER MONKEY BALL ADVENTURE

ALL CARDS

At the mode select, press ■, ▲, ●, ■, ▲, ●, ■, ▲, ●, ■, ▲, ●.

THRILLVILLE: OFF THE RAILS

$50,000

During a game, press ■, ●, ▲, ■, ●, ▲, ✕. Repeat this code as much as desired.

ALL PARKS

During a game, press ■, ●, ▲, ■, ●, ▲, ■.

ALL RIDES

During a game, press ■, ●, ▲, ■ ●, ▲, ▲. Some rides still need to be researched.

COMPLETE MISSIONS

During a game, press ■, ●, ▲, ■, ●, ▲, ●. Then, at the Missions menu, highlight a mission and press ■ to complete that mission. Some missions have Bronze, Silver, and Gold objectives. For these missions the first press of ■ earns the Bronze, the second earns the Silver, and the third earns the Gold.

TOMB RAIDER: LEGEND

You need to unlock the following cheats before they can be used.

BULLETPROOF

During a game, hold L and press ✕, R, ▲, R, ■, R.

DRAW ENEMY HEALTH

During a game, hold L and press ■, ●, ✕, R, R, ▲.

INFINITE ASSUALT RIFLE AMMO

During a game, hold L and press ✕, 0, ✕, R, ■, ▲.

INFINITE GRENADE LAUNCHER

During a game, hold L and press R, ▲, R, ●, R, ■.

INFINITE SHOTGUN AMMO

During a game, hold L and press R, Circle, Square, R, Square, X.

INFINITE SMG AMMO

During a game, hold L and press Circle, Triangle, R, R, X, Circle.

ONE SHOT KILL

During a game, hold L and press Triangle, X, Triangle, Square, R, Circle.

TEXTURELESS MODE

hold L and press R, X, Circle, X, Triangle, R.

WIELD EXCALIBUR

During a game, hold L and press Triangle, X, Circle, R, Triangle, R.

WALL-E

KILL ALL

Select Cheats and then Secret Codes. Enter BOTOFWAR.

UNDETECTED BY ENEMIES

Select Cheats and then Secret Codes. Enter STEALTHARMOR.

LASERS CHANGE COLORS

Select Cheats and then Secret Codes. Enter RAINBOWLAZER.

CUBES ARE EXPLOSIVE

Select Cheats and then Secret Codes. Enter EXPLOSIVEWORLD.

LIGHTEN DARK AREAS

Select Cheats and then Secret Codes. Enter GLOWINTHEDARK.

GOGGLES

Select Cheats and then Secret Codes. Enter BOTOFMYSTERY.

GOLD TRACKS

Select Cheats and then Secret Codes. Enter GOLDENTRACKS.

WORLD CHAMPIONSHIP POKER 2: FEATURING HOWARD LEDERER

SKIP WEEK AND MONEY CHEATS

At the career world map, hold **R1**. Hold **L1** and release **R1**. Hold Up and release **L1**. Hold **L1** and release Up. Hold **R1** and release **L1**. While still holding **R1**, press Up/Down to skip weeks and Right/Left for money.

WRC: FIA WORLD RALLY CHAMPIONSHIP

UNLOCK EVERYTHING

Create a new profile with the name PADLOCK.

EXTRA AVATARS

Create a new profile with the name UGLYMUGS.

GHOST CAR

Create a new profile with the name SPOOKY.

SUPERCHARGER

Create a new profile with the name MAXPOWER.

TIME TRIAL GHOST CARS

Create a new profile with the name AITRIAL.

BIRD CAMERA

Create a new profile with the name dovecam.

REVERSES CONTROLS

Create a new profile with the name REVERSE.

X-MEN LEGENDS II: RISE OF APOCALYPSE

ALL CHARACTERS

At the Team Management screen, press Right, Left, Left, Right, Up, Up, Up, Start.

LEVEL 99 CHARACTERS

At the Team Management screen, press Up, Down, Up, Down, Left, Up, Left, Right, Start.

ALL SKILLS

At the Team Management screen, press Left, Right, Left, Right, Down, Up, Start.

SUPER SPEED

Pause the game and press Up, Up, Up, Down, Up, Down, Start.

UNLIMITED XTREME POWER

Pause the game and press Left, Down, Right, Down, Up, Up, Down, Up Start.

100,000 TECHBITS

At Forge or Beast's equipment screen, press Up, Up, Up, Down, Right, Right, Start.

ALL CINEMATICS

A the Review menu, press Left, Right, Right, Left, Down, Down, Left, Start.

ALL COMIC BOOKS

At the Review menu, press Right, Left, Left, Right, Up, Up, Right, Start.

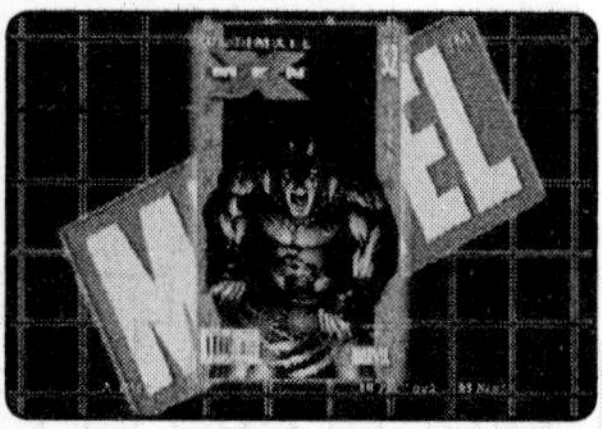

YU-GI-OH! GX TAG FORCE

BOOSTER PACK

At the card shop, press Up, Up, Down, Down, Left, Right, Left, Right, ⊗, ◉.

YU-GI-OH! GX TAG FORCE 2

MIDDDAY CONSTELLATION BOOSTER PACK

When buying booster packs, press Up, Up, Down, Down, Left, Right, Left, Right, ⊗, ◉.

YU-GI-OH! CARD PASSWORDS

Enter the following in the Password Machine to obtain for rental:

PASSWORD	EFFECT
4-Starred Ladybug of Doom	83994646
7 Colored Fish	23771716
A Cat of Ill Omen	24140059
A Deal With Dark Ruler	06850209
A Feather of the Phoenix	49140998
A Feint Plan	68170903
A Hero Emerges	21597117
A Legendary Ocean	00295517
A Man With Wdjat	51351302
A Rival Appears!	05728014
A Wingbeat of Giant Dragon	28596933
A-Team: Trap Disposal Unit	13026402
Abare Ushioni	89718302
Absolute End	27744077
Absorbing Kid From the Sky	49771608
Abyss Soldier	18318842
Abyssal Designator	89801755
Acid Trap Hole	41356845
Acrobat Monkey	47372349
Adhesion Trap Hole	62325062
Adhesive Explosive	53828396

PASSWORD	EFFECT
After the Struggle	25345186
Agido	16135253
Airknight Parshath	18036057
Aitsu	48202661
Alkana Knight Joker	06150044
Alpha the Magnet Warrior	99785935
Altar for Tribute	21070956
Amazon Archer	91869203
Amazoness Archers	67987611
Amazoness Blowpiper	73574678
Amazoness Chain Master	29654737
Amazoness Paladin	47480070
Amazoness Swords Woman	94004268
Amazoness Tiger	10979723
Ambulance Rescueroid	98927491
Ambulanceroid	36378213
Ameba	95174353
Amphibian Beast	67371383
Amphibious Bugroth MK-3	64342551
Amplifier	00303660
An Owl of Luck	23927567

PASSWORD	EFFECT
Ancient Elf	93221206
Ancient Gear	31557782
Ancient Gear Beast	10509340
Ancient Gear Cannon	80045583
Ancient Gear Castle	92001300
Ancient Gear Drill	67829249
Ancient Gear Golem	83104731
Ancient Gear Soldier	56094445
Ancient Lamp	54912977
Ancient Lizard Warrior	43230671
Andro Sphinx	15013468
Anteatereatingant	13250922
Anti-Aircraft Flower	65064143
Anti-Spell	53112492
Apprentice Magician	09156135
Appropriate	48539234
Aqua Madoor	85639257
Aqua Spirit	40916023
Arcane Archer of the Forest	55001420
Archfiend of Gilfer	50287060
Archfiend Soldier	49881766
Archlord Zerato	18378582
Armaill	53153481
Armed Changer	90374791
Armed Dragon LV 3	00980973
Armed Dragon LV 5	46384672
Armed Dragon LV 7	73879377

PASSWORD	EFFECT
Armed Dragon LV10	59464593
Armed Ninja	09076207
Armed Samurai - Ben Kei	84430950
Armor Axe	07180418
Armor Break	79649195
Armored Lizard	15480588
Armored Starfish	17535588
Armored Zombie	20277860
Array of Revealing Light	69296555
Arsenal Bug	42364374
Arsenal Robber	55348096
Arsenal Summoner	85489096
Assault on GHQ	62633180
Astral Barrier	37053871
Asura Priest	02134346
Aswan Apparition	88236094
Atomic Firefly	87340664
Attack and Receive	63689843
Attack Reflector Unit	91989718
Aussa the Earth Charmer	37970940
Autonomous Action Unit	71453557
Avatar of the Pot	99284890
Axe Dragonute	84914462
Axe of Despair	40619825
B. Skull Dragon	11901678
B.E.S. Covered Core	15317640
B.E.S. Crystal Core	22790789

PASSWORD	EFFECT
B.E.S. Tetran	44954628
Baby Dragon	88819587
Back to Square One	47453433
Backfire	82705573
Backup Soldier	36280194
Bad Reaction to Simochi	40633297
Bait Doll	07165085
Ballista of Rampart Smashing	00242146
Banisher of the Light	61528025
Bark of Dark Ruler	41925941
Barrel Dragon	81480460
Basic Insect	89091579
Battery Charger	61181383
Batteryman AA	63142001
Batteryman C	19733961
Batteryman D	55401221
Battle Footballer	48094997
Battle Ox	05053103
Battle-Scarred	94463200
Bazoo The Soul-Eater	40133511
Beast Soul Swap	35149085
Beaver Warrior	32452818
Beckoning Light	16255442
Beelze Frog	49522489
Begone, Knave	20374520
Behemoth the King of All Animals	22996376
Beiige, Vanguard of Dark World	33731070

PASSWORD	EFFECT
Berserk Dragon	85605684
Berserk Gorilla	39168895
Beta the Magnet Warrior	39256679
Bickuribox	25655502
Big Bang Shot	61127349
Big Burn	95472621
Big Core	14148099
Big Koala	42129512
Big Shield Gardna	65240384
Big Wave Small Wave	51562916
Big-Tusked Mammoth	59380081
Bio-Mage	58696829
Birdface	45547649
Black Illusion Ritual	41426869
Black Luster Soldier - Envoy of the Beginning	72989439
Black Pendant	65169794
Black Tyranno	38670435
Blackland Fire Dragon	87564352
Blade Knight	39507162
Blade Rabbit	58268433
Blade Skater	97023549
Bladefly	28470714
Blast Held By a Tribute	89041555
Blast Magician	21051146
Blast with Chain	98239899
Blasting the Ruins	21466326
Blazing Inpachi	05464695

PASSWORD	EFFECT
Blind Destruction	32015116
Blindly Loyal Goblin	35215622
Block Attack	25880422
Blockman	48115277
Blowback Dragon	25551951
Blue-Eyes Shining Dragon	53347303
Blue-Eyes Toon Dragon	53183600
Blue-Eyes Ultimate Dragon	23995346
Blue-Eyes White Dragon	89631139
Blue-Winged Crown	41396436
Bokoichi the Freightening Car	08715625
Bombardment Beetle	57409948
Bonding - H2O	45898858
Boneheimer	98456117
Book of Life	02204140
Book of Moon	14087893
Book of Taiyou	38699854
Boss Rush	66947414
Bottom Dweller	81386177
Bottomless Shifting Sand	76532077
Bottomless Trap Hole	29401950
Bountiful Artemis	32296881
Bowganian	52090844
Bracchio-Raidus	16507828
Brain Control	87910978
Brain Jacker	40267580
Branch!	30548775

PASSWORD	EFFECT
Breaker the Magical Warrior	71413901
Broww, Huntsman of Dark World	79126789
Brron, Mad King of Dark World	06214884
Bubble Blaster	53586134
Bubble Illusion	80075749
Bubble Shuffle	61968753
Bubonic Vermin	06104968
Burning Algae	41859700
Burning Beast	59364406
Burning Land	24294108
Burst Breath	80163754
Burst Return	27191436
Burst Stream of Destruction	17655904
Buster Blader	78193831
Buster Rancher	84740193
Butterfly Dagger - Elma	69243953
Byser Shock	17597059
Call of The Haunted	97077563
Call of the Mummy	04861205
Cannon Soldier	11384280
Cannonball Spear Shellfish	95614612
Card of Safe Return	57953380
Card Shuffle	12183332
Castle of Dark Illusions	00062121
Cat's Ear Tribe	95841282
Catapult Turtle	95727991
Cathedral of Nobles	29762407

PASSWORD	EFFECT
Catnipped Kitty	96501677
Cave Dragon	93220472
Ceasefire	36468556
Celtic Guardian	91152256
Cemetery Bomb	51394546
Centrifugal	01801154
Ceremonial Bell	20228463
Cetus of Dagala	28106077
Chain Burst	48276469
Chain Destruction	01248895
Chain Disappearance	57139487
Chain Energy	79323590
Chain Thrasher	88190453
Chainsaw Insect	77252217
Change of Heart	04031928
Chaos Command Magician	72630549
Chaos Emperor Dragon - Envoy of the End	82301904
Chaos End	61044390
Chaos Greed	97439308
Chaos Necromancer	01434352
Chaos Sorcerer	09596126
Chaosrider Gutaph	47829960
Charcoal Inpachi	13179332
Charm of Shabti	50412166
Charubin the Fire Knight	37421579
Chiron the Mage	16956455
Chopman the Desperate Outlaw	40884383

PASSWORD	EFFECT
Chorus of Sanctuary	81380218
Chthonian Alliance	46910446
Chthonian Blast	18271561
Chthonian Polymer	72287557
Chu-Ske the Mouse Fighter	08508055
Clay Charge	22479888
Cliff the Trap Remover	06967870
Cobra Jar	86801871
Cobraman Sakuzy	75109441
Cold Wave	60682203
Collected Power	07565547
Combination Attack	08964854
Command Knight	10375182
Commander Covington	22666164
Commencement Dance	43417563
Compulsory Evaculation Device	94192409
Confiscation	17375316
Conscription	31000575
Continuous Destruction Punch	68057622
Contract With Exodia	33244944
Contract With the Abyss	69035382
Contract with the Dark Master	96420087
Convulsion of Nature	62966332
Cost Down	23265313
Covering Fire	74458486
Crab Turtle	91782219
Crass Clown	93889755

PASSWORD	EFFECT
Creature Swap	31036355
Creeping Doom Manta	52571838
Crimson Ninja	14618326
Criosphinx	18654201
Cross Counter	37083210
Crush D. Gandra	64681432
Cure Mermaid	85802526
Curse of Aging	41398771
Curse of Anubis	66742250
Curse of Darkness	84970821
Curse of Dragon	28279543
Curse of the Masked Beast	94377247
Curse of Vampire	34294855
Cyber Dragon	70095154
Cyber End Dragon	01546123
Cyber Twin Dragon	74157028
Cyber-Dark Edge	77625948
Cyber-Stein	69015963
Cyberdark Dragon	40418351
Cyberdark Horn	41230939
Cyberdark Keel	03019642
D - Shield	62868900
D - Time	99075257
D. D. Assailant	70074904
D. D. Borderline	60912752
D. D. Crazy Beast	48148828
D. D. Dynamite	08628798

PASSWORD	EFFECT
D. D. M. - Different Dimension Master	82112775
D. D. Trainer	86498013
D. D. Trap Hole	05606466
D. D. Warrior Lady	07572887
Dancing Fairy	90925163
Dangerous Machine TYPE-6	76895648
Dark Artist	72520073
Dark Bat	67049542
Dark Blade	11321183
Dark Blade the Dragon Knight	86805855
Dark Driceratops	65287621
Dark Dust Spirit	89111398
Dark Elf	21417692
Dark Energy	04614116
Dark Factory of Mass Production	90928333
Dark Flare Knight	13722870
Dark Hole	53129443
Dark Magic Attack	02314238
Dark Magic Ritual	76792184
Dark Magician	46986414
Dark Magician Girl	38033121
Dark Magician of Chaos	40737112
Dark Magician's Tome of Black Magic	67227834
Dark Master - Zorc	97642679
Dark Mirror Force	20522190
Dark Paladin	98502113
Dark Room of Nightmare	85562745

PASSWORD	EFFECT
Dark Sage	92377303
Dark Snake Syndrome	47233801
Dark-Piercing Light	45895206
Darkfire Dragon	17881964
Darkfire Soldier #1	05388481
Darkfire Soldier #2	78861134
Darkworld Thorns	43500484
De-Spell	19159413
Deal of Phantom	69122763
Decayed Commander	10209545
Dedication Through Light And Darkness	69542930
Deepsea Shark	28593363
Dekoichi the Battlechanted Locomotive	87621407
Delinquent Duo	44763025
Demotion	72575145
Des Counterblow	39131963
Des Croaking	44883830
Des Dendle	12965761
Des Feral Imp	81985784
Des Frog	84451804
Des Kangaroo	78613627
Des Koala	69579761
Des Lacooda	02326738
Des Wombat	09637706
Desert Sunlight	93747864
Destertapir	13409151
Destiny Board	94212438

PASSWORD	EFFECT
Destiny Hero - Captain Tenacious	77608643
Destiny Hero - Diamond Dude	13093792
Destiny Hero - Doom Lord	41613948
Destiny Hero - Dreadmaster	40591390
Destiny Signal	35464895
Destroyer Golem	73481154
Destruction Ring	21219755
Dian Keto the Cure Master	84257639
Dice Jar	03549275
Dimension Distortion	95194279
Dimensional Warrior	37043180
Disappear	24623598
Disarmament	20727787
Disc Fighter	19612721
Dissolverock	40826495
Divine Dragon Ragnarok	62113340
Divine Wrath	49010598
DNA Surgery	74701381
DNA Transplant	56769674
Doitsu	57062206
Dokurorider	99721536
Dokuroyaiba	30325729
Don Turtle	03493978
Don Zaloog	76922029
Doriado	84916669
Doriado's Blessing	23965037
Dragon Seeker	28563545

PASSWORD	EFFECT
Dragon Treasure	01435851
Dragon Zombie	66672569
Dragon's Mirror	71490127
Dragon's Rage	54178050
Dragoness the Wicked Knight	70681994
Draining Shield	43250041
Dream Clown	13215230
Drillago	99050989
Drillroid	71218746
Dunames Dark Witch	12493482
Dust Tornado	60082867
Earth Chant	59820352
Earthbound Spirit	67105242
Earthquake	82828051
Eatgaboon	42578427
Ebon Magician Curran	46128076
Electro-Whip	37820550
Elegant Egotist	90219263
Element Dragon	30314994
Elemental Burst	61411502
Elemental Hero Avian	21844576
Elemental Hero Bladedge	59793705
Elemental Hero Bubbleman	79979666
Elemental Hero Burstinatrix	58932615
Elemental Hero Clayman	84327329
Elemental Hero Electrum/ Erekshieler	29343734
Elemental Hero Flame Wingman	35809262

PASSWORD	EFFECT
Elemental Hero Mariner	14225239
Elemental Hero Necroid Shaman	81003500
Elemental Hero Neos	89943723
Elemental Hero Phoenix Enforcer	41436536
Elemental Hero Shining Flare Wingman	25366484
Elemental Hero Shining Phoenix Enforcer	88820235
Elemental Hero Sparkman	20721928
Elemental Hero Thunder Giant	61204971
Elemental Mistress Doriado	99414158
Elemental Recharge	36586443
Elf's Light	39897277
Emblem of Dragon Destroyer	06390406
Embodiment of Apophis	28649820
Emergency Provisions	53046408
Emes the Infinity	43580269
Empress Judge	15237615
Empress Mantis	58818411
Enchanted Javelin	96355986
Enchanting Mermaid	75376965
Enemy Controller	98045062
Enraged Battle Ox	76909279
Enraged Muka Muka	91862578
Eradicating Aerosol	94716515
Eternal Draught	56606928
Eternal Rest	95051344
Exhausting Spell	95451366
Exile of the Wicked	26725158

PASSWORD	EFFECT
Exiled Force	74131780
Exodia Necross	12600382
Exodia the Forbidden One	33396948
Fairy Box	21598948
Fairy Dragon	20315854
Fairy King Truesdale	45425051
Fairy Meteor Crush	97687912
Faith Bird	75582395
Fatal Abacus	77910045
Fenrir	00218704
Feral Imp	41392891
Fiber Jar	78706415
Fiend Comedian	81172176
Fiend Scorpion	26566878
Fiend's Hand	52800428
Fiend's Mirror	31890399
Final Countdown	95308449
Final Destiny	18591904
Final Flame	73134081
Final Ritual of the Ancients	60369732
Fire Darts	43061293
Fire Eye	88435542
Fire Kraken	46534755
Fire Princess	64752646
Fire Reaper	53581214
Fire Sorcerer	27132350
Firegrass	53293545

PASSWORD	EFFECT
Firewing Pegasus	27054370
Fireyarou	71407486
Fissure	66788016
Five God Dragon (Five Headed Dragon)	99267150
Flame Cerebrus	60862676
Flame Champion	42599677
Flame Dancer	12883044
Flame Ghost	58528964
Flame Manipulator	34460851
Flame Swordsman	45231177
Flame Viper	02830619
Flash Assailant	96890582
Flower Wolf	95952802
Flying Fish	31987274
Flying Kamakiri #1	84834865
Flying Kamakiri #2	03134241
Follow Wind	98252586
Foolish Burial	81439173
Forest	87430998
Fortress Whale	62337487
Fortress Whale's Oath	77454922
Frenzied Panda	98818516
Frozen Soul	57069605
Fruits of Kozaky's Studies	49998907
Fuh-Rin-Ka-Zan	01781310
Fuhma Shuriken	09373534
Fulfillment of the Contract	48206762

PASSWORD	EFFECT
Fushi No Tori	38538445
Fusion Gate	33550694
Fusion Recovery	18511384
Fusion Sage	26902560
Fusion Weapon	27967615
Fusionist	01641883
Gadget Soldier	86281779
Gagagigo	49003308
Gaia Power	56594520
Gaia the Dragon Champion	66889139
Gaia the Fierce Knight	06368038
Gale Dogra	16229315
Gale Lizard	77491079
Gamble	37313786
Gamma the Magnet Warrior	11549357
Garma Sword	90844184
Garma Sword Oath	78577570
Garoozis	14977074
Garuda the Wind Spirit	12800777
Gatling Dragon	87751584
Gazelle the King of Mythical Beasts	05818798
Gear Golem the Moving Fortress	30190809
Gearfried the Iron Knight	00423705
Gearfried the Swordmaster	57046845
Gemini Elf	69140098
Getsu Fuhma	21887179
Giant Axe Mummy	78266168

PASSWORD	EFFECT
Giant Germ	95178994
Giant Kozaky	58185394
Giant Orc	73698349
Giant Rat	97017120
Giant Red Seasnake	58831685
Giant Soldier of Stone	13039848
Giant Trunade	42703248
Gift of the Mystical Elf	98299011
Giga Gagagigo	43793530
Giga-Tech Wolf	08471389
Gigantes	47606319
Gigobyte	53776525
Gil Garth	38445524
Gilasaurus	45894482
Giltia the D. Knight	51828629
Girochin Kuwagata	84620194
Goblin Attack Force	78658564
Goblin Calligrapher	12057781
Goblin Elite Attack Force	85306040
Goblin Thief	45311864
Goblin's Secret Remedy	11868825
Gogiga Gagagigo	39674352
Golem Sentry	82323207
Good Goblin Housekeeping	09744376
Gora Turtle	80233946
Graceful Charity	79571449
Graceful Dice	74137509

PASSWORD	EFFECT
Gradius	10992251
Gradius' Option	14291024
Granadora	13944422
Grand Tiki Elder	13676474
Granmarg the Rock Monarch	60229110
Gravedigger Ghoul	82542267
Gravekeeper's Cannonholder	99877698
Gravekeeper's Curse	50712728
Gravekeeper's Guard	37101832
Gravekeeper's Servant	16762927
Gravekeeper's Spear Soldier	63695531
Gravekeeper's Spy	24317029
Gravekeeper's Vassal	99690140
Graverobber's Retribution	33737664
Gravity Bind	85742772
Gray Wing	29618570
Great Angus	11813953
Great Long Nose	02356994
Great Mammoth of Goldfine	54622031
Green Gadget	41172955
Gren Maju Da Eiza	36584821
Ground Attacker Bugroth	58314394
Ground Collapse	90502999
Gruesome Goo	65623423
Gryphon Wing	55608151
Gryphon's Feather Duster	34370473
Guardian Angel Joan	68007326

PASSWORD	EFFECT
Guardian of the Labyrinth	89272878
Guardian of the Sea	85448931
Guardian Sphinx	40659562
Guardian Statue	75209824
Gust Fan	55321970
Gyaku-Gire Panda	09817927
Gyroid	18325492
Hade-Hane	28357177
Hamburger Recipe	80811661
Hammer Shot	26412047
Hamon	32491822
Hand of Nephthys	98446407
Hane-Hane	07089711
Hannibal Necromancer	05640330
Hard Armor	20060230
Harpie Girl	34100324
Harpie Lady 1	91932350
Harpie Lady 2	27927359
Harpie Lady 3	54415063
Harpie Lady Sisters	12206212
Harpie's Brother	30532390
Harpies' Hunting Ground	75782277
Hayabusa Knight	21015833
Headless Knight	05434080
Heart of Clear Water	64801562
Heart of the Underdog	35762283
Heavy Mech Support Platform	23265594

PASSWORD	EFFECT
Heavy Storm	19613556
Helios - The Primordial Sun	54493213
Helios Duo Megistus	80887952
Helios Tris Megiste	17286057
Helping Robo for Combat	47025270
Hero Barrier	44676200
HERO Flash!!	00191749
Hero Heart	67951831
Hero Kid	32679370
Hero Ring	26647858
Hero Signal	22020907
Hidden Book of Spell	21840375
Hidden Soldier	02047519
Hieracosphinx	82260502
Hieroglyph Lithograph	10248192
High Tide Gyojin	54579801
Hiita the Fire Charmer	00759393
Hino-Kagu-Tsuchi	75745607
Hinotama Soul	96851799
Hiro's Shadow Scout	81863068
Hitotsu-Me Giant	76184692
Holy Knight Ishzark	57902462
Homunculus the Alchemic Being	40410110
Horn of Heaven	98069388
Horn of Light	38552107
Horn of the Unicorn	64047146
Horus The Black Flame Dragon LV4	75830094

PASSWORD	EFFECT
Horus The Black Flame Dragon LV6	11224103
Horus The Black Flame Dragon LV8	48229808
Hoshiningen	67629977
House of Adhesive Tape	15083728
Howling Insect	93107608
Huge Revolution	65396880
Human-Wave Tactics	30353551
Humanoid Slime	46821314
Humanoid Worm Drake	05600127
Hungry Burger	30243636
Hydrogeddon	22587018
Hyena	22873798
Hyozanryu	62397231
Hyper Hammerhead	02671330
Hysteric Fairy	21297224
Icarus Attack	53567095
Illusionist Faceless Mage	28546905
Impenetrable Formation	96631852
Imperial Order	61740673
Inaba White Rabbit	77084837
Incandescent Ordeal	33031674
Indomitable Fighter Lei Lei	84173492
Infernal Flame Emperor	19847532
Infernal Queen Archfiend	08581705
Inferno	74823665
Inferno Fire Blast	52684508
Inferno Hammer	17185260

PASSWORD	EFFECT
Inferno Reckless Summon	12247206
Inferno Tempest	14391920
Infinite Cards	94163677
Infinite Dismissal	54109233
Injection Fairy Lily	79575620
Inpachi	97923414
Insect Armor with Laser Cannon	03492538
Insect Barrier	23615409
Insect Imitation	96965364
Insect Knight	35052053
Insect Princess	37957847
Insect Queen	91512835
Insect Soldiers of the Sky	07019529
Inspection	16227556
Interdimensional Matter Transporter	36261276
Invader From Another Dimension	28450915
Invader of Darkness	56647086
Invader of the Throne	03056267
Invasion of Flames	26082229
Invigoration	98374133
Iron Blacksmith Kotetsu	73431236
Island Turtle	04042268
Jack's Knight	90876561
Jade Insect Whistle	95214051
Jam Breeding Machine	21770260
Jam Defender	21558682
Jar of Greed	83968380

PASSWORD	EFFECT
Jar Robber	33784505
Javelin Beetle	26932788
Javelin Beetle Pact	41182875
Jellyfish	14851496
Jerry Beans Man	23635815
Jetroid	43697559
Jinzo	77585513
Jinzo #7	32809211
Jirai Gumo	94773007
Jowgen the Spiritualist	41855169
Jowls of Dark Demise	05257687
Judge Man	30113682
Judgment of Anubis	55256016
Just Desserts	24068492
KA-2 Des Scissors	52768103
Kabazauls	51934376
Kagemusha of the Blue Flame	15401633
Kaibaman	34627841
Kaiser Dragon	94566432
Kaiser Glider	52824910
Kaiser Sea Horse	17444133
Kaminari Attack	09653271
Kaminote Blow	97570038
Kamionwizard	41544074
Kangaroo Champ	95789089
Karate Man	23289281
Karbonala Warrior	54541900

PASSWORD	EFFECT
Karma Cut	71587526
Kelbek	54878498
Keldo	80441106
Killer Needle	88979991
Kinetic Soldier	79853073
King Dragun	13756293
King Fog	84686841
King of the Skull Servants	36021814
King of the Swamp	79109599
King of Yamimakai	69455834
King Tiger Wanghu	83986578
King's Knight	64788463
Kiryu	84814897
Kiseitai	04266839
Kishido Spirit	60519422
Knight's Title	87210505
Koitsu	69456283
Kojikocy	01184620
Kotodama	19406822
Kozaky	99171160
Kozaky's Self-Destruct Button	21908319
Kryuel	82642348
Kumootoko	56283725
Kurama	85705804
Kuriboh	40640057
Kuwagata Alpha	60802233
Kwagar Hercules	95144193

PASSWORD	EFFECT
Kycoo The Ghost Destroyer	88240808
La Jinn The Mystical Genie of The Lamp	97590747
Labyrinth of Nightmare	66526672
Labyrinth Tank	99551425
Lady Assailant of Flames	90147755
Lady Ninja Yae	82005435
Lady of Faith	17358176
Larvas	94675535
Laser Cannon Armor	77007920
Last Day of Witch	90330453
Last Turn	28566710
Launcher Spider	87322377
Lava Battleguard	20394040
Lava Golem	00102380
Layard the Liberator	67468948
Left Arm of the Forbidden One	07902349
Left Leg of the Forbidden One	44519536
Legendary Black Belt	96438440
Legendary Flame Lord	60258960
Legendary Jujitsu Master	25773409
Legendary Sword	61854111
Leghul	12472242
Lekunga	62543393
Lesser Dragon	55444629
Lesser Fiend	16475472
Level Conversion Lab	84397023
Level Limit - Area A	54976796

PASSWORD	EFFECT
Level Limit - Area B	03136426
Level Modulation	61850482
Level Up!	25290459
Levia-Dragon	37721209
Light of Intervention	62867251
Light of Judgment	44595286
Lighten the Load	37231841
Lightforce Sword	49587034
Lightning Blade	55226821
Lightning Conger	27671321
Lightning Vortex	69162969
Limiter Removal	23171610
Liquid Beast	93108297
Little Chimera	68658728
Little-Winguard	90790253
Lizard Soldier	20831168
Lord of D.	17985575
Lord of the Lamp	99510761
Lost Guardian	45871897
Luminous Soldier	57282479
Luminous Spark	81777047
Luster Dragon	11091375
Luster Dragon #2	17658803
M-Warrior #1	56342351
M-Warrior #2	92731455
Machine Conversion Factory	25769732
Machine Duplication	63995093

PASSWORD	EFFECT
Machine King	46700124
Machine King Prototype	89222931
Machiners Defender	96384007
Machiners Force	58054262
Machiners Sniper	23782705
Machiners Soldier	60999392
Mad Dog of Darkness	79182538
Mad Lobster	97240270
Mad Sword Beast	79870141
Mage Power	83746708
Magic Drain	59344077
Magic Jammer	77414722
Magical Cylinder	62279055
Magical Dimension	28553439
Magical Explosion	32723153
Magical Hats	81210420
Magical Labyrinth	64389297
Magical Marionette	08034697
Magical Merchant	32362575
Magical Plant Mandragola	07802006
Magical Scientist	34206604
Magical Thorn	53119267
Magician of Black Chaos	30208479
Magician of Faith	31560081
Magician's Circle	00050755
Magician's Unite	36045450
Magician's Valkyrie	80304126

PASSWORD	EFFECT
Magnet Circle	94940436
Maha Vailo	93013676
Maharaghi	40695128
Maiden of the Aqua	17214465
Maji-Gire Panda	60102563
Maju Garzett	08794435
Makiu	27827272
Makyura the Destructor	21593977
Malevolent Nuzzler	99597615
Malfunction	06137095
Malice Ascendant	14255590
Malice Dispersion	13626450
Mammoth Graveyard	40374923
Man Eater	93553943
Man-Eater Bug	54652250
Man-Eating Black Shark	80727036
Man-Eating Treasure Chest	13723605
Man-Thro' Tro'	43714890
Manga Ryu-Ran	38369349
Manju of the Ten Thousand Hands	95492061
Manticore of Darkness	77121851
Marauding Captain	02460565
Marie the Fallen One	57579381
Marine Beast	29929832
Marshmallon	31305911
Marshmallon Glasses	66865880
Maryokutai	71466592

PASSWORD	EFFECT
Masaki the Legendary Swordsman	44287299
Mask of Brutality	82432018
Mask of Darkness	28933734
Mask of Restrict	29549364
Mask of Weakness	57882509
Masked Dragon	39191307
Masked of the Accursed	56948373
Masked Sorcerer	10189126
Mass Driver	34906152
Master Kyonshee	24530661
Master Monk	49814180
Master of Dragon Knight	62873545
Master of Oz	27134689
Mataza the Zapper	22609617
Mavelus	59036972
Maximum Six	30707994
Mazera DeVille	06133894
Mech Mole Zombie	63545455
Mecha-Dog Marron	94667532
Mechanical Hound	22512237
Mechanical Snail	34442949
Mechanical Spider	45688586
Mechanicalchaser	07359741
Meda Bat	76211194
Medusa Worm	02694423
Mefist the Infernal General	46820049
Mega Thunderball	21817254

PASSWORD	EFFECT
Mega Ton Magical Cannon	32062913
Megamorph	22046459
Megarock Dragon	71544954
Melchid the Four-Face Beast	86569121
Memory Crusher	48700891
Mermaid Knight	24435369
Messenger of Peace	44656491
Metal Armored Bug	65957473
Metal Dragon	09293977
Metallizing Parasite	07369217
Metalmorph	68540058
Metalzoa	50705071
Metamorphosis	46411259
Meteor B. Dragon	90660762
Meteor Dragon	64271667
Meteor of Destruction	33767325
Meteorain	64274292
Michizure	37580756
Micro-Ray	18190572
Mid Shield Gardna	75487237
Mighty Guard	62327910
Mikazukinoyaiba	38277918
Millennium Golem	47986555
Millennium Scorpion	82482194
Millennium Shield	32012841
Milus Radiant	07489323
Minar	32539892

PASSWORD	EFFECT
Mind Control	37520316
Mind Haxorz	75392615
Mind on Air	66690411
Mind Wipe	52718046
Mine Golem	76321376
Minefield Eruption	85519211
Minor Goblin Official	01918087
Miracle Dig	06343408
Miracle Fusion	45906428
Miracle Kid	55985014
Miracle Restoring	68334074
Mirage Dragon	15960641
Mirage Knight	49217579
Mirage of Nightmare	41482598
Mirror Force	44095762
Mirror Wall	22359980
Misfortune	01036974
Mispolymerization	58392024
Mistobody	47529357
Moai Interceptor Cannons	45159319
Mobius the Frost Monarch	04929256
Moisture Creature	75285069
Mokey Mokey	27288416
Mokey Mokey King	13803864
Mokey Mokey Smackdown	01965724
Molten Behemoth	17192817
Molten Destruction	19384334

PASSWORD	EFFECT
Molten Zombie	04732017
Monk Fighter	03810071
Monster Egg	36121917
Monster Eye	84133008
Monster Gate	43040603
Monster Reborn	83764718
Monster Recovery	93108433
Monster Reincarnation	74848038
Mooyan Curry	58074572
Morale Boost	93671934
Morphing Jar	33508719
Morphing Jar #2	79106360
Mother Grizzly	57839750
Mountain	50913601
Mr. Volcano	31477025
Mudora	82108372
Muka Muka	46657337
Multiplication of Ants	22493811
Multiply	40703222
Musician King	56907389
Mustering of the Dark Scorpions	68191243
Mysterious Puppeteer	54098121
Mystic Horseman	68516705
Mystic Lamp	98049915
Mystic Plasma Zone	18161786
Mystic Swordsman LV 2	47507260
Mystic Swordsman LV 4	74591968

PASSWORD	EFFECT
Mystic Swordsman LV 6	60482781
Mystic Tomato	83011277
Mystic Wok	80161395
Mystical Beast Serket	89194033
Mystical Elf	15025844
Mystical Knight of Jackal	98745000
Mystical Moon	36607978
Mystical Sand	32751480
Mystical Sheep #2	30451366
Mystical Shine Ball	39552864
Mystical Space Typhoon	05318639
Mystik Wok	80161395
Mythical Beast Cerberus	55424270
Nanobreaker	70948327
Necklace of Command	48576971
Necrovalley	47355498
Needle Ball	94230224
Needle Burrower	98162242
Needle Ceiling	38411870
Needle Wall	38299233
Needle Worm	81843628
Negate Attack	14315573
Nemuriko	90963488
Neo Aqua Madoor	49563947
Neo Bug	16587243
Neo the Magic Swordsman	50930991
Neo-Space	40215635

PASSWORD	EFFECT
Neo-Spacian Aqua Dolphin	17955766
Newdoria	04335645
Next to be Lost	07076131
Night Assailant	16226786
Nightmare Horse	59290628
Nightmare Penguin	81306586
Nightmare Wheel	54704216
Nightmare's Steelcage	58775978
Nimble Momonga	22567609
Nin-Ken Dog	11987744
Ninja Grandmaster Sasuke	04041838
Ninjitsu Art of Decoy	89628781
Ninjitsu Art of Transformation	70861343
Nitro Unit	23842445
Niwatori	07805359
Nobleman of Crossout	71044499
Nobleman of Extermination	17449108
Nobleman-Eater Bug	65878864
Non Aggression Area	76848240
Non-Fusion Area	27581098
Non-Spellcasting Area	20065549
Novox's Prayer	43694075
Nubian Guard	51616747
Numinous Healer	02130625
Nutrient Z	29389368
Nuvia the Wicked	12953226
0 - Oversoul	63703130

PASSWORD	EFFECT
Obnoxious Celtic Guardian	52077741
Ocubeam	86088138
Offerings to the Doomed	19230407
Ojama Black	79335209
Ojama Delta Hurricane	08251996
Ojama Green	12482652
Ojama King	90140980
Ojama Trio	29843091
Ojama Yellow	42941100
Ojamagic	24643836
Ojamuscle	98259197
Old Vindictive Magician	45141844
Ominous Fortunetelling	56995655
Oni Tank T-34	66927994
Opti-Camaflauge Armor	44762290
Opticlops	14531242
Option Hunter	33248692
Orca Mega-Fortress of Darkness	63120904
Ordeal of a Traveler	39537362
Order to Charge	78986941
Order to Smash	39019325
Otohime	39751093
Outstanding Dog Marron	11548522
Overdrive	02311603
Oxygeddon	58071123
Painful Choice	74191942
Paladin of White Dragon	73398797

PASSWORD	EFFECT
Pale Beast	21263083
Pandemonium	94585852
Pandemonium Watchbear	75375465
Parasite Paracide	27911549
Parasitic Ticky	87978805
Patrician of Darkness	19153634
Patroid	71930383
Penguin Knight	36039163
Penumbral Soldier Lady	64751286
People Running About	12143771
Perfect Machine King	18891691
Performance of Sword	04849037
Petit Angel	38142739
Petit Dragon	75356564
Petit Moth	58192742
Phantasmal Martyrs	93224848
Phantom Beast Cross-Wing	71181155
Phantom Beast Thunder-Pegasus	34961968
Phantom Beast Wild-Horn	07576264
Pharaoh's Servant	52550973
Pharonic Protector	89959682
Phoenix Wing Wind Blast	63356631
Photon Generator Unit	66607691
Pikeru's Circle of Enchantment	74270067
Pikeru's Second Sight	58015506
Pinch Hopper	26185991
Pineapple Blast	90669991

PASSWORD	EFFECT
Piranha Army	50823978
Pitch-Black Power Stone	34029630
Pitch-Black Warwolf	88975532
Pitch-Dark Dragon	47415292
Poison Draw Frog	56840658
Poison Fangs	76539047
Poison Mummy	43716289
Poison of the Old Man	08842266
Polymerization	24094653
Possessed Dark Soul	52860176
Pot of Avarice	67169062
Pot of Generosity	70278545
Pot of Greed	55144522
Power Bond	37630732
Power Capsule	54289683
Precious Card from Beyond	68304813
Premature Burial	70828912
Prepare to Strike Back	04483989
Prevent Rat	00549481
Prickle Fairy	91559748
Primal Seed	23701465
Princess Curran	02316186
Princess of Tsurugi	51371017
Princess Pikeru	75917088
Protective Soul Ailin	11678191
Protector of the Sanctuary	24221739
Protector of the Throne	10071456

PASSWORD	EFFECT
Proto-Cyber Dragon	26439287
Pumpking the King of Ghosts	29155212
Punished Eagle	74703140
Pyramid of Light	53569894
Pyramid Turtle	77044671
Queen's Knight	25652259
Rabid Horseman	94905343
Rafflesia Seduction	31440542
Raging Flame Sprite	90810762
Raigeki	12580477
Raigeki Break	04178474
Rain Of Mercy	66719324
Rainbow Flower	21347810
Rallis the Star Bird	41382147
Rancer Dragonute	11125718
Rapid-Fire Magician	06337436
Rare Metalmorph	12503902
Raregold Armor	07625614
Raviel, Lord of Phantasms	69890967
Ray & Temperature	85309439
Ray of Hope	82529174
Re-Fusion	74694807
Ready For Intercepting	31785398
Really Eternal Rest	28121403
Reaper of the Cards	33066139
Reaper of the Nightmare	85684223
Reasoning	58577036

PASSWORD	EFFECT
Reborn Zombie	23421244
Reckless Greed	37576645
Recycle	96316857
Red Archery Girl	65570596
Red Gadget	86445415
Red Medicine	38199696
Red Moon Baby	56387350
Red-Eyes B. Chick	36262024
Red-Eyes B. Dragon	74677422
Red-Eyes Black Metal Dragon	64335804
Red-Eyes Darkness Dragon	96561011
Reflect Bounder	02851070
Regenerating Mummy	70821187
Reinforcement of the Army	32807846
Release Restraint	75417459
Relinquished	64631466
Reload	22589918
Remove Trap	51482758
Rescue Cat	14878871
Rescueroid	24311595
Reshef the Dark Being	62420419
Respect Play	08951260
Return from the Different Dimension	27174286
Return of the Doomed	19827717
Reversal of Graves	17484499
Reversal Quiz	05990062
Revival Jam	31709826

PASSWORD	EFFECT
Right Arm of the Forbidden One	70903634
Right Leg of the Forbidden One	08124921
Ring of Defense	58641905
Ring of Destruction	83555666
Ring of Magnetism	20436034
Riryoku Field	70344351
Rising Air Current	45778932
Rising Energy	78211862
Rite of Spirit	30450531
Ritual Weapon	54351224
Robbin' Goblin	88279736
Robbin' Zombie	83258273
Robolady	92421852
Robotic Knight	44203504
Roboyarou	38916461
Rock Bombardment	20781762
Rock Ogre Grotto	68846917
Rocket Jumper	53890795
Rocket Warrior	30860696
Rod of the Mind's Eye	94793422
Roll Out!	91597389
Root Water	39004808
Rope of Life	93382620
Rope of Spirit	37383714
Roulette Barrel	46303688
Royal Command	33950246
Royal Decree	51452091

PASSWORD	EFFECT
Royal Keeper	16509093
Royal Knight	68280530
Royal Magical Library	70791313
Royal Surrender	56058888
Royal Tribute	72405967
Ruin, Queen of Oblivion	46427957
Rush Recklessly	70046172
Ryu Kokki	57281778
Ryu Senshi	49868263
Ryu-Kishin Clown	42647539
Ryu-Kishin Powered	24611934
Saber Beetle	49645921
Sacred Crane	30914564
Sacred Phoenix of Nephthys	61441708
Saggi the Dark Clown	66602787
Sakuretsu Armor	56120475
Salamandra	32268901
Salvage	96947648
Samsara	44182827
Sand Gambler	50593156
Sand Moth	73648243
Sangan	26202165
Sanwitch	53539634
Sasuke Samurai	16222645
Sasuke Samurai #2	11760174
Sasuke Samurai #3	77379481
Sasuke Samurai #4	64538655

PASSWORD	EFFECT
Satellite Cannon	50400231
Scapegoat	73915051
Scarr, Scout of Dark World	05498296
Science Soldier	67532912
Scroll of Bewitchment	10352095
Scyscraper	63035430
Sea Serpent Warrior of Darkness	42071342
Sealmaster Meisei	02468169
Second Coin Toss	36562627
Second Goblin	19086954
Secret Barrel	27053506
Self-Destruct Button	57585212
Senri Eye	60391791
Serial Spell	49398568
Serpent Night Dragon	66516792
Serpentine Princess	71829750
Servant of Catabolism	02792265
Seven Tools of the Bandit	03819470
Shadow Ghoul	30778711
Shadow Of Eyes	58621589
Shadow Tamer	37620434
Shadowknight Archfiend	09603356
Shadowslayer	20939559
Share the Pain	56830749
Shield & Sword	52097679
Shield Crash	30683373
Shien's Spy	07672244
Shift	59560625

PASSWORD	EFFECT
Shifting Shadows	59237154
Shinato's Ark	60365591
Shinato, King of a Higher Plane	86327225
Shining Abyss	87303357
Shining Angel	95956346
Shooting Star Bow - Ceal	95638658
Silent Insect	40867519
Silent Magician Lv4	73665146
Silent Magician Lv8	72443568
Silent Swordsman LV3	01995985
Silent Swordsman LV5	74388798
Silent Swordsman LV7	37267041
Sillva, Warlord of Dark World	32619583
Silpheed	73001017
Silver Fang	90357090
Simorgh, Bird of Divinity	14989021
Simultaneous Loss	92219931
Sinister Serpent	08131171
Sixth Sense	03280747
Skill Drain	82732705
Skilled Dark Magician	73752131
Skilled White Magician	46363422
Skull Archfiend of Lightning	61370518
Skull Descovery Knight	78700060
Skull Dog Marron	86652646
Skull Invitation	98139712
Skull Lair	06733059
Skull Mariner	05265750

PASSWORD	EFFECT
Skull Red Bird	10202894
Skull Servant	32274490
Skull Zoma	79852326
Skull-Mark Ladybug	64306248
Skyscraper	63035430
Slate Warrior	78636495
Smashing Ground	97169186
Smoke Grenade of the Thief	63789924
Snatch Steal	45986603
Sogen	86318356
Soitsu	60246171
Solar Flare Dragon	45985838
Solar Ray	44472639
Solemn Judgment	41420027
Solemn Wishes	35346968
Solomon's Lawbook	23471572
Sonic Duck	84696266
Sonic Jammer	84550200
Sorcerer of Dark Magic	88619463
Soul Absorption	68073522
Soul Exchange	68005187
Soul of Purity and Light	77527210
Soul Release	05758500
Soul Resurrection	92924317
Soul Reversal	78864369
Soul Tiger	15734813
Soul-Absorbing Bone Tower	63012333

PASSWORD	EFFECT
Souleater	31242786
Souls Of The Forgotten	04920010
Space Mambo	36119641
Spark Blaster	97362768
Sparks	76103675
Spatial Collapse	20644748
Spear Cretin	58551308
Spear Dragon	31553716
Spell Canceller	84636823
Spell Economics	04259068
Spell Purification	01669772
Spell Reproduction	29228529
Spell Shield Type-8	38275183
Spell Vanishing	29735721
Spell-Stopping Statute	10069180
Spellbinding Circle	18807108
Spherous Lady	52121290
Sphinx Teleia	51402177
Spiral Spear Strike	49328340
Spirit Barrier	53239672
Spirit Caller	48659020
Spirit Message A	94772232
Spirit Message I	31893528
Spirit Message L	30170981
Spirit Message N	67287533
Spirit of Flames	13522325
Spirit of the Breeze	53530069

PASSWORD	EFFECT
Spirit of the Harp	80770678
Spirit of the Pharaoh	25343280
Spirit Reaper	23205979
Spirit Ryu	67957315
Spiritual Earth Art - Kurogane	70156997
Spiritual Energy Settle Machine	99173029
Spiritual Fire Art - Kurenai	42945701
Spiritual Water Art - Aoi	06540606
Spiritual Wind Art - Miyabi	79333300
Spiritualism	15866454
St. Joan	21175632
Stamping Destruction	81385346
Star Boy	08201910
Statue of the Wicked	65810489
Staunch Defender	92854392
Stealth Bird	03510565
Steam Gyroid	05368615
Steamroid	44729197
Steel Ogre Grotto #1	29172562
Steel Ogre Grotto #2	90908427
Stim-Pack	83225447
Stop Defense	63102017
Storming Wynn	29013526
Stray Lambs	60764581
Strike Ninja	41006930
Stronghold	13955608
Stumbling	34646691

PASSWORD	EFFECT
Success Probability 0%	06859683
Summon Priest	00423585
Summoned Skull	70781052
Summoner of Illusions	14644902
Super Conductor Tyranno	85520851
Super Rejuvenation	27770341
Super Robolady	75923050
Super Roboyarou	01412158
Supply	44072894
Susa Soldier	40473581
Swarm of Locusts	41872150
Swarm of Scarabs	15383415
Swift Gaia the Fierce Knight	16589042
Sword Hunter	51345461
Sword of Deep-Seated	98495314
Sword of Dragon's Soul	61405855
Sword of the Soul Eater	05371656
Swords of Concealing Light	12923641
Swords of Revealing Light	72302403
Swordsman of Landstar	03573512
Symbol of Heritage	45305419
System Down	18895832
T.A.D.P.O.L.E.	10456559
Tactical Espionage Expert	89698120
Tailor of the Fickle	43641473
Taunt	90740329
Tenkabito Shien	41589166

PASSWORD	EFFECT
Terra the Terrible	63308047
Terraforming	73628505
Terrorking Archfiend	35975813
Terrorking Salmon	78060096
Teva	16469012
The Agent of Creation - Venus	64734921
The Agent of Force - Mars	91123920
The Agent of Judgment - Saturn	91345518
The Agent of Wisdom - Mercury	38730226
The All-Seeing White Tiger	32269855
The Big March of Animals	01689516
The Bistro Butcher	71107816
The Cheerful Coffin	41142615
The Creator	61505339
The Creator Incarnate	97093037
The Dark - Hex Sealed Fusion	52101615
The Dark Door	30606547
The Dragon Dwelling in the Cave	93346024
The Dragon's Bead	92408984
The Earl of Demise	66989694
The Earth - Hex Sealed Fusion	88696724
The Emperor's Holiday	68400115
The End of Anubis	65403020
The Eye Of Truth	34694160
The Fiend Megacyber	66362965
The Flute of Summoning Dragon	43973174
The Flute of Summoning Kuriboh	20065322

PASSWORD	EFFECT
The Forceful Sentry	42829885
The Forces of Darkness	29826127
The Forgiving Maiden	84080938
The Furious Sea King	18710707
The Graveyard in the Fourth Dimension	88089103
The Gross Ghost of Fled Dreams	68049471
The Hunter With 7 Weapons	01525329
The Illusionary Gentleman	83764996
The Immortal of Thunder	84926738
The Kick Man	90407382
The Last Warrior From Another Planet	86099788
The Law of the Normal	66926224
The League of Uniform Nomenclature	55008284
The Legendary Fisherman	03643300
The Light - Hex Sealed Fusion	15717011
The Little Swordsman of Aile	25109950
The Masked Beast	49064413
The Portrait's Secret	32541773
The Regulation of Tribe	00296499
The Reliable Guardian	16430187
The Rock Spirit	76305638
The Sanctuary in the Sky	56433456
The Second Sarcophagus	04081094
The Secret of the Bandit	99351431
The Shallow Grave	43434803
The Spell Absorbing Life	99517131

PASSWORD	EFFECT
The Thing in the Crater	78243409
The Third Sarcophagus	78697395
The Trojan Horse	38479725
The Unhappy Girl	27618634
The Unhappy Maiden	51275027
The Warrior Returning Alive	95281259
Theban Nightmare	51838385
Theinen the Great Sphinx	87997872
Thestalos the Firestorm Monarch	26205777
Thousand Dragon	41462083
Thousand Energy	05703682
Thousand Needles	33977496
Thousand-Eyes Idol	27125110
Thousand-Eyes Restrict	63519819
Threatening Roar	36361633
Three-Headed Geedo	78423643
Throwstone Unit	76075810
Thunder Crash	69196160
Thunder Dragon	31786629
Thunder Nyan Nyan	70797118
Thunder of Ruler	91781589
Time Seal	35316708
Time Wizard	71625222
Timeater	44913552
Timidity	40350910
Token Festevil	83675475
Token Thanksgiving	57182235

PASSWORD	EFFECT
Tongyo	69572024
Toon Cannon Soldier	79875176
Toon Dark Magician Girl	90960358
Toon Defense	43509019
Toon Gemini Elf	42386471
Toon Goblin Attack Force	15270885
Toon Masked Sorcerer	16392422
Toon Mermaid	65458948
Toon Summoned Skull	91842653
Toon Table of Contents	89997728
Toon World	15259703
Tornado Bird	71283180
Tornado Wall	18605135
Torpedo Fish	90337190
Torrential Tribute	53582587
Total Defense Shogun	75372290
Tower of Babel	94256039
Tradgedy	35686187
Transcendent Wings	25573054
Trap Dustshoot	64697231
Trap Hole	04206964
Trap Jammer	19252988
Treeborn Frog	12538374
Tremendous Fire	46918794
Tri-Horned Dragon	39111158
Triage	30888983
Trial of Nightmare	77827521

PASSWORD	EFFECT
Trial of the Princesses	72709014
Triangle Ecstasy Spark	12181376
Triangle Power	32298781
Tribe-Infecting Virus	33184167
Tribute Doll	02903036
Tribute to The Doomed	79759861
Tripwire Beast	45042329
Troop Dragon	55013285
Tsukuyomi	34853266
Turtle Oath	76806714
Turtle Tiger	37313348
Twin Swords of Flashing Light	21900719
Twin-Headed Beast	82035781
Twin-Headed Behemoth	43586926
Twin-Headed Fire Dragon	78984772
Twin-Headed Thunder Dragon	54752875
Twin-Headed Wolf	88132637
Two Thousand Needles	83228073
Two-Man Cell Battle	25578802
Two-Mouth Darkruler	57305373
Two-Pronged Attack	83887306
Tyhone	72842870
Type Zero Magic Crusher	21237481
Tyranno Infinity	83235263
Tyrant Dragon	94568601
UFOroid	07602840
UFOroid Fighter	32752319
Ultimate Insect LV1	49441499

PASSWORD	EFFECT
Ultimate Insect LV3	34088136
Ultimate Insect LV5	34830502
Ultimate Insect LV7	19877898
Ultimate Obedient Fiend	32240937
Ultimate Tyranno	15894048
Ultra Evolution Pill	22431243
Umi	22702055
Umiiruka	82999629
Union Attack	60399954
United Resistance	85936485
United We Stand	56747793
Unity	14731897
Unshaven Angler	92084010
Upstart Goblin	70368879
Uraby	01784619
Uria, Lord of Sealing Flames	06007213
V-Tiger Jet	51638941
Valkyrion the Magna Warrior	75347539
Vampire Genesis	22056710
Vampire Lord	53839837
Vampire Orchis	46571052
Vengeful Bog Spirit	95220856
Victory D	44910027
Vilepawn Archfiend	73219648
VW-Tiger Catapult	58859575
VWXYZ-Dragon Catapult Cannon	84243274
W-Wing Catapult	96300057
Waboku	12607053

PASSWORD	EFFECT
Wall of Revealing Light	17078030
Wandering Mummy	42994702
Warrior Dai Grepher	75953262
Warrior of Zera	66073051
Wasteland	23424603
Water Dragon	85066822
Water Omotics	02483611
Wave Motion Cannon	38992735
Weed Out	28604635
Whiptail Crow	91996584
Whirlwind Prodigy	15090429
White Dragon Ritual	09786492
White Horn Dragon	73891874
White Magical Hat	15150365
White Magician Pikeru	81383947
White Ninja	01571945
Wicked-Breaking Flameberge-Baou	68427465
Wild Nature's Release	61166988
Winged Dragon, Guardian of the Fortress #1	87796900
Winged Kuriboh	57116033
Winged Kuriboh LV10	98585345
Winged Minion	89258225
Winged Sage Falcos	87523462
Wingweaver	31447217
Witch Doctor of Chaos	75946257
Witch of the Black Forest	78010363
Witch's Apprentice	80741828
Witty Phantom	36304921

PASSWORD	EFFECT
Wolf Axwielder	56369281
Woodborg Inpachi	35322812
Woodland Sprite	06979239
Worm Drake	73216412
Wroughtweiler	06480253
Wynn the Wind Charmer	37744402
X-Head Cannon	62651957
Xing Zhen Hu	76515293
XY-Dragon Cannon	02111707
XYZ-Dragon Cannon	91998119
XZ-Tank Cannon	99724761
Y-Dragon Head	65622692
Yamata Dragon	76862289
Yami	59197169
Yata-Garasu	03078576
Yellow Gadget	13839120
Yellow Luster Shield	04542651
Yomi Ship	51534754
YZ-Tank Dragon	25119460
Z-Metal Tank	64500000
Zaborg the Thunder Monarch	51945556
Zero Gravity	83133491
Zoa	24311372
Zolga	16268841
Zombie Tiger	47693640
Zombyra the Dark	88472456
Zure, Knight of Dark World	07459013

GAME BOY® ADVANCE

TABLE OF CONTENTS

BANJO PILOT

GRUNTY

Defeat Grunty in the Broomstick battle race. Then, you can purchase Grunty from Cheato.

HUMBA WUMBA

Defeat Humba Wumba in the Jiggu battle race. Then, you can purchase Humba Wumba from Cheato.

JOLLY

Defeat Jolly in the Pumpkin battle race. Then, you can purchase Jolly from Cheato.

KLUNGO

Defeat Klungo in the Skull battle race. Then, you can purchase Klungo from Cheato.

BARBIE AS THE PRINCESS AND THE PAUPER

PASSWORDS

LEVEL	PASSWORD
1-2	Preminger, Wolfie, Erika, Serafina
1-3	Wolfie, Preminger, Serafina, Preminger
1-4	Preminger, Wolfie, Serfania, Wolfie
Boss 1	Serafina, Woflia. Erika, Preminger
2-1	Princess Anneliese, Preminger, Wolfie, Erika
2-2	Preminger, Princess Anneliese, Wolfie, Erika
2-3	Preminger, Serafina, Preminger, Erika
2-4	Serafina, Erika, Preminger, Wolfie
Boss 2	Preminger, Erika, Serafina, Wolfie

LEVEL	PASSWORD
3-1	Wolfie, Preminger, Wolfie, Erika
3-2	Serafina, Preminger, Erika, Serafina
3-3	Erika, Wolfie, Serafina, Princess Anneliese
3-4	Erika, Serafina, Erika, Preminger
Boss 3	Preminger, Serafina, Princess Anneliese, Serafina
4-1	Wolfie, Serafina, Preminger, Serafina
4-2	Preminger, Serafina, Princess Anneliese, Preminger
4-3	Wolfie, Serafina, Erika, Serafina
Boss 4	Erika, Serafina, Princess Anneliese, Wolfie
Final Boss	Erika, Princess Anneliese, Princess Anneliese, Man
Arcade Level	Princess Anneliese, Serafina, Erika, Wolfie

CASTLEVANIA: ARIA OF SORROW

NO ITEMS

Start a new game with the name NOUSE to use no items in the game.

NO SOULS

Start a new game with the name NOSOUL to use no souls in the game.

DK: KING OF SWING

ATTACK BATTLE 3

At the Title screen, press Up + L + A + B to bring up a password screen. Enter 65942922.

CLIMBING RACE 5

At the Title screen, press Up + L + A + B to bring up a password screen. Enter 55860327.

OBSTACLE RACE 4

At the Title screen, press Up + L + A + B to bring up a password screen. Enter 35805225.

UNLOCK TIME ATTACK

Complete the game as DK.

UNLOCK DIDDY MODE

Collect 24 medals as DK.

UNLOCK BUBBLES

Complete Diddy Mode with 24 Medals.

UNLOCK KREMLING

Collect 6 gold medals in Jungle Jam.

UNLOCK KING K. ROOL

Collect 12 gold medals in Jungle Jam.

DONKEY KONG COUNTRY 2: DIDDY KONG'S QUEST

ALL LEVELS

Select Cheats from the Options and enter freedom.

START WITH 15 LIVES
Select Cheats from the Options and enter helpme.

START WITH 55 LIVES
Select Cheats from the Options and enter weakling.

START WITH 10 BANANA COINS
Select Cheats from the Options and enter richman.

START WITH 50 BANANA COINS
Select Cheats from the Options and enter wellrich.

NO DK OR HALF WAY BARRELS
Select Cheats from the Options and enter rockard.

MUSIC PLAYER
Select Cheats from the Options and enter onetime.

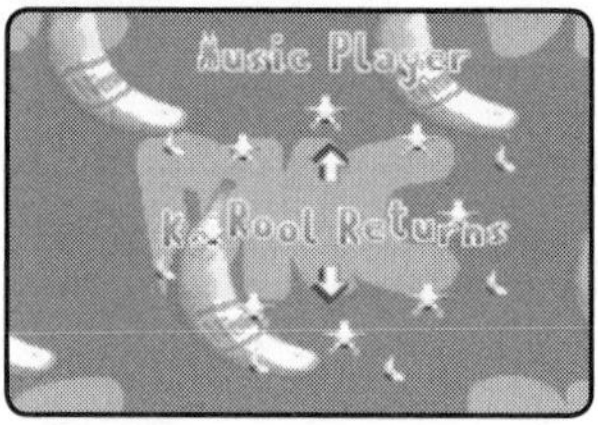

CREDITS
Select Cheats from the Options and enter kredits.

FINAL FANTASY I & II: DAWN OF SOULS

FF I TILE GAME
During a game of Final Fantasy I and after you get the ship, hold A and press B about 55 times.

FF II CONCENTRATION GAME
Once you obtain the Snowcraft, hold B and press A about 20 times.

MONSTER FORCE

RESTART LEVEL
Pause the game, hold L + R and press A.

FINISH LEVEL
During a game, hold L + R + A and press Up.

PLAY AS MINA OR DREW
At the Character Select screen, hold L + R + B and press Right.

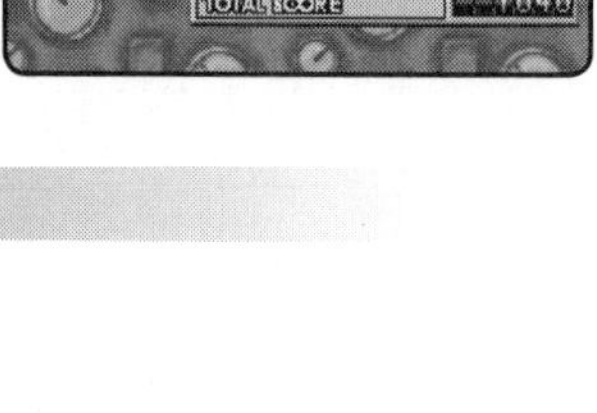

RATATOUILLE

INVINCIBILITY
Enter X4V!3RJ as a password.

ALL CHAPTERS
Enter H3L!X3! as a password. Press L or R at the Chapter Select screen.

ALL MINI-GAMES
Enter JV4ND1Z as a password.

ALL BONUS PICTURES
Enter 3R1CQRR as a password.

RIVER CITY RANSOM EX

Select the status menu and change your name to the following:

MAX STATS
DAMAX

$999999.99
PLAYA

CUSTOM CHAR
XTRA0

CUSTOM SELF
XTRA1

CUSTOM MOVE
XTRA2

CLEAR SAVE
ERAZE

TECHNIQUES 1
FUZZY. This group includes Mach Punch, Dragon Kick, Acro Circus, Grand Slam, Javelin Man, Slick Trick, Nitro Port, Twin Kick, Deadly Shot, Top Spin, Helicopter, Torpedo.

TECHNIQUES 2
WUZZY. This group includes Slap Happy, Pulper, Headbutt, Kickstand, Big Bang, Wheel Throw, Glide Chop, Head Bomb, Chain Chump, Jet Kick, Shuriken, Flip Throw.

TECHNIQUES 3
WAZZA. This group includes Boomerang, Charge It, Bat Fang, Flying Kick, Speed Drop, Bomb Blow, Killer Kick, Bike Kick, Slam Punk, Dragon Knee, God Fist, Hyperguard.

TECHNIQUES 4
BEAR*. This group includes PhoenixWing, Inlines, Springlines, Rocketeers, Air Merc's Narcishoes, Magic Pants, Pandora Box, Skaterz, Custom Fit.

STREET FIGHTER ALPHA 3

ALL FIGHTERS
At the Title screen, press Left, Right, Down, Right, L, L, A, L, L, B, R, A, Up.

ALL MODES
At the Title screen, press A, Up, A, L, R, Right, L, Right, A, Down, Right. Now press L, Right, A, R, Up,L, Right, B, A, Up, Right, Down, Right.

PLAY AS SUPER BISON
At the Character Select screen, hold Start and select Bison.

PLAY AS SHIN AKUMA
At the Character Select screen, hold Start and select Akuma.

ALTERNATE COSTUMES
At the Character Select screen, press L or R.

FINAL BATTLE
At the Speed Select option, hold A + B.

THAT'S SO RAVEN 2: SUPERNATURAL STYLE

COSTUME MODE
At the Title screen, press Left, Right, Up, Down, B, B, B, Up, Down.

UNLIMITED ENERGY MODE
At the Title screen, press B, B, L, R, Up, Down, Up, Left, Right.

TRON 2.0: KILLER APP

ALL MINIGAMES

At the Title screen, press Left, Left, Left, Left, Up, Right, Down, Down, Select.

YOSHI TOPSY-TURVY

CHALLENGE MODE AND CHALLENGE 1

Defeat Bowser for the second time in Story Mode.

CHALLENGES 2, 3, 4

Complete the Egg Gallery in Story Mode.

FINAL CHALLENGE

Earn all Golds in Story Mode.

YU-GI-OH! 7 TRIALS TO GLORY: WORLD CHAMPIONSHIP TOURNAMENT 2005

PURPLE TITLE SCREEN

Completing the game changes the Title screen from blue to purple. To switch it back, press Up, Up, Down, Down, Left, Right, Left, Right, B, A at the Title screen.

CREDITS

Defeat the game, then press Up, Up, Down, Down, Left, Right, Left, Right, B, A.

CARD PASSWORDS

At the password machine, press R and enter a password.

Refer to the Card List for YU-GI-OH! GX TAG FORCE for PSP. All cards are not available in World Championship Tournament 2005.

YU-GI-OH! ULTIMATE MASTERS: WORLD CHAMPIONSHIP TOURNAMENT 2006

CARD PASSWORDS

Enter the 8-digit codes at the Password screen to unlock that card for purchase.

Refer to the Card List for YU-GI-OH! GX TAG FORCE for PSP. All cards may not be available in World Championship Tournament 2006.

ONLINE GAMING FOR KIDS: A PARENT'S GUIDE

There are plenty of great games for kids on the web, but which ones are best for your child, and how can you ensure they don't visit a site that's inappropriate? Well, we've compiled a list of the most impressive and trusted gaming spots for kids, then categorized them by age. Visit these sites and determine which ones your family likes most. Once you've determined your favorites, you can then make accessing them safe and easy for your child in just three easy steps:

SAFE ONLINE GAMING FOR KIDS IS AS EASY AS 1-2-3

Here's how you can create an **Internet Games Page**—a clickable document that allows your child to safely and easily visit your family's favorite online gaming sites for kids:

1. Open a new document in Microsoft Word.
2. Type in the URLs (web site addresses) listed in this section that best suit your child's age and interests. After each URL, press ENTER to automatically create a Hyperlink. The address will then appear in blue, underlined text. That means you can now immediately go directly to that web site. Just simultaneously press CTRL and click on the blue text. See our note below for an even slicker way of doing this.
3. When your list of Hyperlinks is complete, save the file as "[Your Child's Name]'s Games" on your computer's desktop.

USER FRIENDLY LINKS

If you think your child might find it difficult to visit his or her favorite gaming sites by selecting from a list of long and sometimes unwieldy internet addresses, then customize the lists on your Internet Games Page by renaming them with something more easily recognizable. It's easy. Simply type the name you wish to use (LEGO, for example) and highlight the word with your mouse. Next, right-click on the highlighted word and select Hyperlink from the window that pops up. Another window appears with your cursor blinking in the empty Address field. Type in the proper URL here (in the case of LEGO, you would type *http://play.lego.com/en-US/games/default.aspx* into this field), then click OK. The word you highlighted on your Internet Games Page is now a Hyperlink. Using our example, that means your child can simply click on (left-click + CTRL) the word "LEGO" to visit the LEGO games site!

You can even dress up this document with colorful backgrounds and clip art to make it even more personal and appealing. You now have a resource that provides a quick and easy path for your child to access safe and entertaining gaming sites that you have seen and trust.

BEST ONLINE GAMING SITES FOR KIDS

AGES 6–7

Children in this age group may not be as computer savvy and certainly won't have as strong reading skills as older kids. So, you may need to get your child started until he or she is comfortable navigating these sites and properly understands the rules to the games.

Slime Slinger Online Game

http://www.scholastic.com/goosebumps/slimeslinger/game.asp

A fun game based on the popular Goosebumps series of books.

Highlights Kids Hidden Pictures

http://www.highlightskids.com/GamesandGiggles/HiddenPics/HIddenPixFlashObjects/h8hpiArchive.asp

More than just games, these puzzle-oriented offerings really work kids' brains.

CBeebies at BBC

http://www.bbc.co.uk/cbeebies/fun/

Lots of cute games for younger kids.

Yahooligans Games

http://kids.yahoo.com/games

Loads of fun for all ages here with a wide variety of games—puzzles, arcade, sports, and more!

Pauly's Playhouse Online Games

http://www.paulysplayhouse.com/paulys_playhouse/game_page/game.html

Wow! This site has loads of games! All pretty simple and most will have your child smiling from ear to ear.

Nick.com Games Online

http://www.nick.com/games/

Lots of good stuff here, all associated with Nick programming your child likely already enjoys.

Lego Club Games

http://play.lego.com/en-US/games/default.aspx

Great interactive fun that provides exciting scenarios that simulate playing with LEGO toys.

Barbie.com Games Online

http://barbie.everythinggirl.com/activities/fun_games/

Let's face it, most girls like Barbie as much as just about anything. The games your daughter plays on this site will not disappoint her.

EDUCATIONAL FUN!

Chicken Stacker

http://pbskids.org/lions/games/stacker.html

You can never go wrong with PBS when it comes to kids, and Between the Lions is one of many great programs. This game based on the show helps kids build their word power.

Play Kids Games.com

http://www.playkidsgames.com/

Everything from simple math to word and memory games. Plenty here for the next age group, too.

AGES 8–9

Scholastic Games

http://www.scholastic.com/kids/games.htm

Solve mysteries, answer trivia, collect rare items, and more! The fun here is all based on popular books with this age group.

Monkeybar TV

http://www.hasbro.com/monkeybartv/default.cfm?page=Entertainment/OnlineGames/GameHome

This site is operated by Hasbro, so the characters and toys associated with the games are all classics known and loved by kids and adults—including Transformers, Littlest Pet Shop, Monopoly, GI Joe, Star Wars, and others!

Cartoon Network Games Online

http://www.cartoonnetwork.com/games/index.html

Kids can't read and be active all the time, and cartoons nicely fill that need to laugh and take it easy. This is the place for hilarious games from hilarious toons.

I Spy Games Online

http://www.scholastic.com/ispy/play/

Another Scholastic gem that allows kids to use their powers of observation online!

Disney Channel Games Online

http://tv.disney.go.com/disneychannel/games/index.html

Have you ever met a fourth grader who isn't into Disney? Hannah Montana, Kim Possible, Zack & Cody… what's not to like? This site has plenty of familiar faces and fun stuff.

Kidnetics Active Online Games

http://www.kidnetic.com/

Fitness focused games and projects for kids.

EDUCATIONAL FUN!

Multiplication.com

http://www.multiplication.com/interactive_games.htm

Cute and entertaining games that help make multiplication tables a breeze.

Big Brainz

http://www.bigbrainz.com/index.php

Download a free version of Timez Attack, a great looking action video game that boosts multiplication skills!

AGE 10 & UP

If you're 10 years old, there's no reason you still can't have fun playing the games we've listed in the previous two age groups, but these will definitely appeal to the big kids.

ESPN Arcade

http://arcade.espn.go.com/

ESPN offers a great online gaming site for kids who are into sports.

Zeeks Board & Card Games

http://games.zeeks.com/games.php

Tons of free games. Not just entertaining, but a little edgy, too!

Battleship

http://www.creativecalendar.com/kids/Games/games_battleship.html

Everyone loves this game. Just as much fun online!

OTHER ONLINE GAMES

We've put these games in a separate category because they're not free. They either require a subscription or the purchase of a toy to play. However, you may consider these investments worthwhile, as they do provide some intriguing gameplay and learning opportunities. Plus, if your kids are into gaming or have friends who are, they're bound to mention these sites to you sooner or later, so you may want to see what they're all about for yourself.

Webkinz

http://www.webkinz.com/

Requires you to buy a toy before "adopting" one online, but the game experience is pretty cool. Webkinz allows kids to care for their pet, including improving and furnishing its home. Earn Kinz cash by answering trivia and doing other fun activities.

Club Penguin

http://www.clubpenguin.com/

This subscription-based online game is operated by Disney. It provides a kid-friendly virtual world where children can play games, have fun, and interact with each other...but it's not free.